Study and Solutions Guide

for

UNDERSTANDABLE STATISTICS

Fifth Edition
Brase/Brase

Elizabeth Farber
Bucks County Community College

D.C. Heath and Company
Lexington, Massachusetts   Toronto

Please address editorial correspondence to:

D.C. Heath and Company
Mathematics Editorial
125 Spring Street
Lexington, MA 02173

Published simultaneously in Canada.

Printed in the United States of America.

International Standard Book Number: 0-669-39479-3

10 9 8 7 6 5 4 3 2

Preface

This *Study and Solutions Guide* is designed to be used as a supplement to *Understandable Statistics*, Fifth Edition by Brase and Brase. The guide is correlated section-by-section with the text, and each section of the guide is developed around the following five elements:

Review
 Outlines a review of all new concepts and important information discussed within the corresponding section of the text.

Problem Solving Warm-Up
Presents sample problems in a format designed so that the student has an opportunity to provide intermediate steps in the solution process. Detailed solutions are included.

Thinking About Statistics
Poses questions which prompt students to think critically about the statistical concepts and methods being discussed.

Selected Solutions
Provides complete annotated solutions to every other odd problem from the text. Included in this section are warnings about common errors that students make.

Answers to Thinking About Statistics
Offers answers to the guide's critical thinking questions.

To the Student:

This supplement has been written with *you* in mind. Many students feel intimidated by the language, symbols and concepts of statistics. Hopefully, this guide will help you pass smoothly over those barriers.

When using this guide it is important that you do it as an active participant with a pencil, a calculator and the Brase and Brase text on hand. After you have read the appropriate material in your text, read the corresponding *Review* section highlighting the important points of the lesson. Next try to work the problems presented in the *Problem Solving Warm-Up* by filling in the blank spaces provided. Compare your answers with the detailed solutions that have been provided. Write out your answers to the *Thinking About Statistics* questions. These will help you express your understanding and make meaningful connections among ideas before moving on to the text section problems. After working the problems from the textbook, check your solutions with those in this guide. Remember that there is no real substitute for making the effort to solve these problems on your own. Finally, compare your responses to the thinking questions with those provided in *Answers to Thinking About Statistics*.

Good luck in your study of statistics! I would appreciate hearing from you if you have any corrections or suggestions for improving this guide. You may also contact the editorial offices of D.C. Heath and Company. Their address appears on the copyright page of this guide.

I would like to thank Philip Lanza of D.C. Heath for his invaluable help in revising this *Study and Solutions Guide* for the fifth edition of the Brase and Brase text. I would especially like to thank my husband, Richard and sons Douglas and Michael for their encouragement.

Elizabeth Farber
Professor of Mathematics
Bucks County Community College
Newtown, Pennsylvania 18940

Table of Contents

Chapter 1

GETTING STARTED

Section 1.1
What is Statistics?

Review

I. Statistics is the study of how to collect, organize and interpret numerical information. It is an indispensable tool used to help make intelligent decisions in all aspects of life, even when there may be incomplete information available.

    A. Professionally, a businessperson makes recommendations about marketing strategies based on Statistics, a psychologist uses Statistics to evaluate her patients and a civil engineer uses Statistics to decide what type of bridge to build.

    B. Our daily lives are affected when the program manager for a local television station makes decisions on which shows to broadcast based on statistical "ratings."

    C. In sports, the head coach of a football team relies on statistics to decide which players to use in a given situation.

II. Statistical decisions are made on the basis of a particular set of measurements, counts or observations.

    A. A **population** is the set of *all* possible measurements, counts or observations that are of interest.

    B. It is usually impossible, impractical or even in terms of time or money, to obtain every possible response, so we must usually rely on information available on subset of the population called a **sample**.

    C. A central theme, which will be repeated throughout the study of Statistics, *is that of using information obtained from a **sample** to make decisions or inferences concerning an entire **population*** from which the sample has been drawn. Techniques, which we will later study will enable us to do this with a high level of reliability.

1

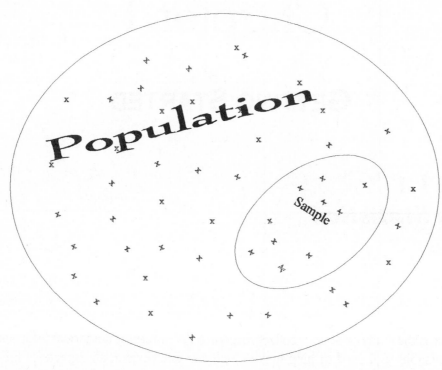

III.   Methods of Acquiring Data
   A.   **Sampling:** Measuring a subset of the population.
   B.   **Experimenting:** Imposing a treatment and observing its effects.
   C.   **Simulating:** Artificially producing outcomes when its impractical to do real life experiments. Simulations are often performed on computers.
   D.   **Taking a Census:** Measuring the entire population of interest.

IV.   Levels of Measurement: When we collect data it is important to know its level of measurement so we can determine which types of computation are appropriate. Calculations appropriate for each level can be used at any *higher* level but should not be used for any lower level. Levels are listed from lowest to highest.
   A.   **Nominal Data** (can be put into categories)
        1.   Consists of names, categories, qualities or labels. Example: Type of car you drive.
        2.   Can put data into categories but we are unable to determine if one piece of data is *better* or *higher* than another.
        3.   When numbers are used as labels, such as on a football uniform they are classified as nominal data. (It is not meaningful to average the numbers on the uniforms for the Philadelphia Eagles.)
   B.   **Ordinal Data** (can be placed in rank order and be put into categories)

1. Designations or numerical rankings which can be arranged in ascending or descending order. Example: T.V. ratings for #1 show, #2 show, etc.
2. We can compare rankings as to which is higher, however it does not make sense to subtract one rank value from another. *Differences* in rankings are not meaningful computations. Example: you interview 3 candidates for a job and rank them in order of preference 1, 2 and 3. You can tell which candidate is ahead of the others but only in terms of *order* of preference, not in terms of magnitude or degree of preference.

C. **Interval Data** (can be subtracted to find the difference between two values, put in order and put into categories)
1. Data is numerical; 0 can be used to indicate a *position* in time or space however, however, the zero at this level does not correspond to "none" of the specific variable being measured. Example: the year you graduate from high school. The "year 0" has no meaning.
2. Differences between data values are meaningful but it does not make sense to compare one data value as being twice (or any multiple of) another.

D. **Ratio Data** (values can be divided, subtracted, put in order and put into categories)
1. The highest level of measurement. Example: the number of gallons of gas you put in your car today.
2. There is a zero on this scale which is interpreted as "none" of the variable in question.(i.e. you can put 0 gallons of gas in your car today.)
3. It is meaningful to say one measure is two times or three times as much as another.

FROM LOWEST LEVEL OF MEASUREMENT TO HIGHEST

Nominal ➜ Ordinal ➜ Interval ➜ Ratio

Problem Solving Warm-Up

Throughout this manual, practice exercises will be included for each text section. Cover the right hand column and fill in the blanks on the left. Then compare your answers with those given.

1. A Roper poll asked 938 adults in the United States if they thought feeling financially secure was an important aspect of having money.

    a) The population is

    a) The set of responses from <u>all</u> adults in the U.S.

    _____

b)   The sample is

_____

b)   The 938 responses which were recorded in the poll.

2.   (i) Respond to each of the following questions with a realistic answer.
(ii) State the highest level of measurement which you used.

a)   What is your favorite brand of jeans?

(i)_____
(ii)_____

a)   (i) Example: Levi
(ii) <u>Nominal</u> data. Your answer is a label or a name.

b)   How many credits have you earned before this semester?
(i)_____
(ii)_____

b)   (i) Example: 15.
(ii) <u>Ratio</u> data. Differences in numbers of credits are meaningful computations.   Zero would be a meaningful answer for a first term freshman. Additionally, one person could have twice as many credits as another.

c)   What year were you born?
(i)_____
(ii)_____

c)   (i) Example: 1978.
(ii) <u>Interval</u> data; An answer of 0, meaning the beginning of time, is impossible.

d)   What is your academic major?
(i)_____
(ii)_____

d)   (i) Example: Psychology.
(ii) <u>Nominal</u> data. The data is a label. One answer can not be compared numerically with another.

e)   What is your evaluation of your professor on a scale of 1 to 5 with 1 being the best?
(i)_____
(ii)_____

e)   (i) Example: 4.
(ii) <u>Ordinal</u> data. Differences in rankings are not numerically significant.

f)   What is your telephone
     number?
     (i)_____
     (ii)_____

f)   (i) Example: 555-1995
     (ii) <u>Nominal</u> data. The numbers are
     used as an identifying label. (We
     would not add or subtract numbers
     used this way.)

Thinking About Statistics

1.   In order to determine the television viewing preferences of college students, a survey was
     done at a local shopping mall, asking every tenth person who entered if they would prefer
     to watch a) *Seinfeld* b) *Home Improvement* or c) *Murphy Brown*. What is wrong with this
     survey from a statistical viewpoint?

2.   Consumer Reports ranked the top rated CD players as follows:

Rank	Model
1	Technics SL-PD927
2	Philips CDC935
3	Sony CDP-C79ES
4	Carver SD/A-350
5	JVC XL-F207TN
6	Yamaha CDC-735
7	Denon DCM-520
8	Onkyo DX-C606

Can we say that the Philips CD which is in second place is twice as good as the Carver which is in
fourth? Explain.

Selected Solutions Section 1.1

In this text the symbol of ♦ marks the end of each answer or solution.

1.   The implied population is the number of times each adult in the U.S. ate in fast-food
     restaurants each week. The sample consists of the numerical responses of the 1261 adults
     who participated in the survey. Note that in statistics, the *population* consists of the entire
     set of ALL measurements, counts or observations which are of interest. The *sample* is the
     set of measurements, counts or observations that are actually recorded. ♦

5. The population is the set of measures of time intervals between the arrival of a payment and the clearing of the check for *all* insurance checks in the given 5-state region. The sample consists of the set of 32 recorded time intervals. ♦

7   a. Ratio. It could of course take zero minutes to finish the test. (Since all answers would be blank, you would not want to brag about your score!)♦

    b. Interval. The time difference between two -o'clock and four-o'clock is meaningful but there is not a zero on the measurement scale that indicates "no time". *Six o'clock is not twice as late as three o'clock!* ♦

    c. Ordinal. These categories can be arranged in order. A junior is at a higher level than a sophomore. ♦

    d. Ordinal A rating of "good" is better than that of "acceptable", but we can not measure by how much.♦

    e. Ratio. A zero is a meaningful (although embarrassing) score. A score of 90 indicates twice as many points as a score of 45♦

    f. Ratio. A 20 year old is twice as old as a 10 year old. *Do not be fooled by the fact that no one is zero years old.*♦

9. a. Census. The ages for all members of each group are used. The ages constitute the entire population. ♦

    b. Experimental. Treatment was given to a part of the population and effects observed. ♦

    c. Simulation. Actual running was not done. ♦

    d. Sampling. Only a portion of the population was questioned. ♦

Answers to Thinking About Statistics

1. The implied population is the set of responses from all college students. By questioning those at a mall, it is likely that many of the respondents would not_be college students and that their viewing habits would be different form those of college students. Such a study would give biased results about opinions of college students since we are not questioning a subset of *that* population. In addition, responses are made voluntarily-another fact likely to bias the responses.

2. In ordinal data such as the ranking of C.D.'s it is meaningless to say one model is twice as good as another. The distances between consecutive ranks may be uneven. It's possible that the ratings for Technics and Philips (the top two brands) are very close with Sony (the third place brand) following at a great distance.

Chapter 2

ORGANIZING DATA

Section 2.1
Random Samples

Review

I.   Types of Random Samples

    A.   **Simple Random Sample**

        1.   Every member of the population has an equal chance of belonging to a simple random sample.

        2.   It insures we have an *unbiased representation* of the population.

        3.   The Table of Random Numbers in Appendix II is one method by which members of a population can be selected to be in such a sample.

            a.   The table consists of rows of digits (symbols 0,1,2...9) which are separated into groups of five for ease in reading.

            b.   Each member of the population should be labeled with a number. Separate the digits in the Random Number Table into blocks which have the same number of digits as the largest number assigned.

            c.   Decide on the number of measures to be used in the sample. We call this "n" **(n = sample size)**.

            d.   Randomly select a starting point and read the digits in blocks, listing only those numbers that are in the population.

            e.   The simple random sample consists of the *measures, counts or responses* that correspond to the selected members of the population.

B. **Stratified Random Sample**

    1.   Members of the population are separated into subgroups and a random sample is drawn from each subgroup.

    2.   This insures that each subgroup will be represented and that no group will be omitted from the sample.

C. **Systematic Sample**

    1.   To select a sample of 10 from a population of 529, divide 529/10 $\approx$52. Select a random number from 1 to 52-the measure or response for this number will be the first member of your sample.

    2.   Once the first member is selected, select every 52nd number for the sample. Ex. If the random value selected is 23, the sample will consist of measures or responses from population members number 23, 75, 127, 179, 231, 283, 335, 387, 439, and 491.

    3.   Once the first member is selected, the others are automatically selected. This method of sampling can be used when there is no danger of cyclical phenomena. (For example: choose every 10th member of the population, but do not choose every 4th season or every 7th day.)

D. **Cluster Sample**

    1.   The unit for sampling is not an individual but a naturally occurring subgroup.

    2.   One or more of the subgroups is randomly selected.

    3.   The sample is then taken from the selected subgroup(s). (Some subgroups will be omitted completely.)

E. **Convenience sample**

    1.   The sample consists only of the members of the population that are readily available.

    2.   This method of sampling may produce misleading or biased results.

Problem Solving Warm-Up

1.   There are 529 students enrolled in a statistics course for the semester at your school. You are asked to interview a sample of ten of these students for a research project. What steps would you take to select a simple random sample?

    Answer: First assign a number to each student in the population. College I.D. numbers could be used, however it is probably easier to get the class lists and assign numbers 1 to 529. Select a starting point on your random number table (Appendix I) For example, your random digit sequence might look like the following:

```
26907 52180 05538 56277 54190 10910 97564 11278 03772
83834 57300 21769 78972 05007 19561 91610 00432 08299
63480 04119
```

Draw a vertical line at intervals of every 3 digits to separate the digits into sets of 3 (since 529 is a 3 digit number). The first groups are 269, 075 and 218. Select the first ten three-digit numbers which that are less than 530. The digits would group as follows:

269 |075 |218 |005 |538 |562 |775 |419 |010 |910 |975 |641
|127 |803 772 |838 |345 |730 |021 |969 |789 |720 | 500

The random sample consists of the responses from the students who were assigned the following numbers: 269, 75, 218, 5, 419, 10, 127, 345, 21, and 500. (Note that 75 is expressed as a three digit number 075 in the random number table. A one digit number like 5 is expressed 005.)

Thinking About Statistics

Suppose, from the problem above, you decided to question the first ten students who came to a Statistics Club meeting. What problems might this present for your study?

Selected Solutions Section 2.1

1. Answers will vary. Random numbers are those which are formed from digits generated by a computer into which a mathematical formula has been programmed such that every digit has an equal chance of appearing. A series of random digits has been reproduced in a table in the back of your text. We could generate a random digit table ourselves by marking ten equal sized pieces of paper, 0,1,2...9, placing them in a hat, mixing them up, drawing one piece of paper and recording the number on it. Replace the paper you drew out and draw another. Repeat this process until you have enough digits. Random samples are those samples in which every member of the population has an equal chance of being included. They are important because they insure that a study (with unbiased questions) will be unbiased. ♦

5. Since 500 has 3 digits, separate your random digits into groups of three. Choose your starting place in the random number table. List the first seven three digit numbers which are less than 500. Your sample will consist of the measures or responses from the seven elements (could be people or products) corresponding to the numbers that appear. ♦

9.   This time separate the digits into blocks of two (since 42 is a two digit number). Select the first 6 two-digit numbers that are less than 43. ♦

13.   Read one digit at a time and record the first 20 digits included in the set {1,2,3,4,5,6}. (Ignore 0,7,8 and 9.) ♦

17.   Read one digit at a time and record the first 10 digits included in the set {1,2,3,4,5}. ♦

19.   a)   Simple random: Responses from every business have equal chances of being represented. ♦

        b)   Cluster sample: The zip codes represent different subgroups. Only businesses in these the 10 zip code areas will be represented. There will be zip code areas which are not represented in the sample.♦

        c)   Convenience sample: Only businesses in downtown Honolulu will be represented. This will probably bias the study.♦

        d)   Systematic sampling: Every 50th business will be selected. Once the first is selected, the others will be automatically selected. ♦

        e)   Stratified sample: The population has been divided into subgroups. Random samples will then be drawn from each of these subgroups. Each group will be represented by 10 businesses. Note that this method differs from cluster sampling since in cluster sampling some groups will not be represented.♦

Answers to Thinking About Statistics

Using a convenience sample of the first ten students would probably cause a bias in the responses. Belonging to a Statistics Club might be characteristic of a certain type of individual. In addition, anyone who arrived late would not have an opportunity to be in the sample.

Section 2.2
Graphs

Review

This section explores several types of graphs which can be used to produce a visual description or pictorial representation of the data.

I.   **Bar Graphs**
   A.   Bars can represent data categories from any of the four levels of measurement (nominal, ordinal, interval or ratio). Thus each bar can represent a label, a response or a class of numerical measurements.
   B.   The height of each bar must correspond to some interval or ratio measure. We can compute differences in heights of bars.
   C.   Bars are of uniform width.
   D.   There is equal spacing between the bars.

II.   **Pareto Chart**
   A.   Bar graphs-the height of the bar represents frequency of type of problem or defect.
   B.   The bars are arranged left to right from tallest to shortest.
   C.   Used in Quality Control to detect which problems occur most commonly.

III.   **Pictograms**
   A.   A symbol or picture is used to represent a specified quantity of something. Example: An ear of corn representing 1000 bushels produced.
   B.   Pictures should be of equal size.

IV.   **Circle Graphs** (Pie Graphs)
   A.   Used when a total quantity (such as a budget) is apportioned into several non-overlapping categories.
   B.   A full circle contains 360°, half a circle contains 180°, etc.. We determine the number of degrees in a sector (slice of the pie) by multiplying the percentage of the pie it occupies by 360°. For example: if a category occupies 35% of the total, it should be represented by $(.35)(360) = 126°$ of the circle.

V.   **Time Plots**
   A.   The horizontal axis marks regularly spaced time intervals.
   B.   The vertical axis shows measurements of the same quantity taken at regular time intervals.
   C.   Points are plotted and connected to form a line graph which is useful in detecting trends.

Problem Solving Warm-Up

1.   There were 1,859 single people or married couples filing separately for the 1994 Federal Income Tax for with a large accounting firm . The percentage of these individuals within five specific income brackets is shown as follows:

	earnings	%
A.	less than $20,000	64%
B.	$20,001 to $35,000	24%
C.	$35,001 to $40,000	8%
D.	$40,001 to $75,000	3%
E.	$75,001 or more	1%

a)   Make a circle graph to display this information.

Fill in: First compute the number of degrees for each sector.

A. _____
B. _____
C. _____
D. _____
E. _____

A.   (.64)(360) =   230.4°
B.   (.24)(360) =   86.4°
C.   (.08)(360) =   28.8°
D.   (.03)(360) =   10.8°
E.   (.01)(360) =   3.6°

        TOTAL =   360.0°

Use a protractor to separate the circle into 5 sectors, each having the corresponding number of degrees as computed above.

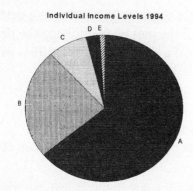

Individual Income Levels 1994

b) Construct a bar graph

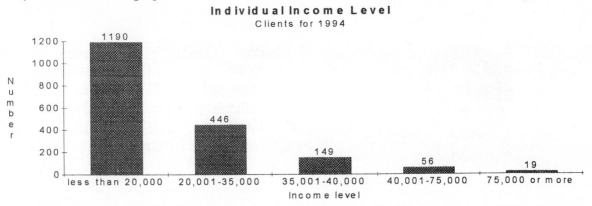

To form the bar graph, construct the horizontal axis so that it describes the earnings variable categories. The vertical axis is used to compare the number of clients in each category.

Thinking About Statistics

Enrollment figure for Studymore University revealed in 1992 the enrollment was 9053 students, in 1993 it was 10,273 and for 1994 it was 11,047.
a)   Which types of graphs would be appropriate to describe this data?
b)   Which types of graphs would not be suitable to describe this data?
c)   Construct a graph describing this data.

Selected Solutions Section 2.2

1.   Categories represent ordinal data. The bar graph indicates an upward trend in income.

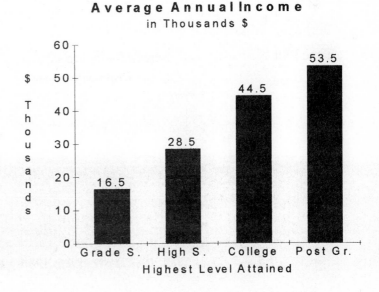

Where Do we Hide the Mess?

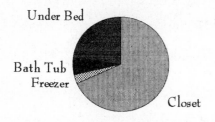

Under Bed

Bath Tub
Freezer

Closet

5. <u>Location</u>   <u>(%)(360)=° size of sector</u>
    closet   (.68)(360)= 244.8°
    under bed   (.23)(360)= 82.8°
    bath tub   (.06)(360)= 21.6°
    freezer   <u>(.03)(360)= 10.8°</u>
total percent = 100%   total degrees = 360°.

9. Nominal data. Height of bar represents percentage of households that own gadget. Since a household might have more than one gadget, it is not appropriate to use a circle graph.

Percentage of Households Owning Gadgets

98% 98% 90% 61% 24%

Percent
100
80
60
40
20
0

TV   Radio   Audio System   VCR   Answering Machine

Gadget

13.   Time Plot

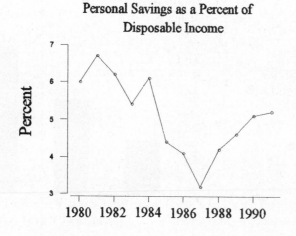

Personal Savings as a Percent of Disposable Income

Percent

7

6

5

4

3

1980 1982 1984 1986 1988 1990

Year

Answers to Thinking About Statistics

The most appropriate type of graph is a bar graph. Also suitable would be a pictogram, with a symbol (such as a diploma) representing 1000 students. How could a change in scale make it appear as if there was a large increase in enrollment?

It would not be possible to construct a circle graph depicting this information since a circle graph describes how parts of a whole are apportioned.

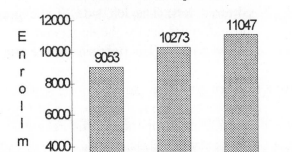

Section 2.3
Histograms and Frequency Distributions

Review

I.   A **histogram** is a form of bar graph in which:

  A.   The width of a bar is designated by an interval or ratio data value and thus has numerical significance.
  B.   The height of a bar corresponds to the number of times the data values fall in that *class*. (Called the frequency and symbolized with f.)
  C.   The bars touch.

II.   **Frequency Polygon** (line graph)
  A.   Line segments connect the top midpoints of the bars of a histogram.
  B.   They can be drawn with or without showing the histogram. (Just connect the appropriate points.)

III.   Shapes of distributions
    A.   **Symmetric:** The right half the histogram is the mirror image of the left.
    B.   **Uniform:** All bars are equal in height. (Appearance is rectangular in shape.)
    C.   **Skewed left:** The left side of the graph has a longer "tail," leaving a greater proportion of data at the upper end.
    D.   **Skewed right:** The right side of the graph has a longer "tail."

IV. **Relative frequency histogram**
    A.   Horizontal scale is the same as a histogram.
    B.   Vertical scale measures the relative frequency of a class.

$$Relative\ frequency = \frac{class\ frequency}{total\ frequency}$$

V.   **Ogive**
    C.   Describes the cumulative frequency of a class
    D.   Cumulative frequency is a count of the number of measures less than or equal to the upper class limit.
    E.   Drawn as a line graph.

VI.   In order to construct a histogram, it is necessary to determine the following significant numbers:
    A.   **Number of Classes (bars)**
        1.   Too few tends to "lump" the data together whereas too many will "chop it up" too finely.
        2.   This number may be determined by convenience, but is usually between 5 and 15.
    B.   **Range**
        1.   Determine the highest data value.
        2.   Determine the lowest data value.
        3.   Find the difference between the highest and lowest data values. **Range = High - Low** (High value minus low value.)
    C.   **Class Width**
        1.   Divide the range by the number of classes.
        2.   Round this number *up* to the next convenient value. (Rounding *up* insures that all data values will fit inside the designated classes.)

VII.   A **frequency distribution table** will consist of the following:

    A.   **Class Limits**
        1.   Lower class limit (lowest data value in a class).
        2.   Upper class limit (highest data value in a class).
    B.   **Class Boundaries**
        1.   Lower class boundary (Subtract ½ the distance between class limits from the

lower class limit).

    2.   Upper class boundary (Add ½ the distance between the class limits to the upper class limit).

C.   **Class Midpoints** Average of lower class limit and upper class limit. (Also average of class boundaries.)

D.   **Frequencies** The number of times the data values fall in each class. (Determines the heights of the corresponding bars.)

E.   **Relative Frequencies** The frequency of the class divided by the total frequency. This value is always between 0 and 1. When multiplied by 100 this gives the percent of the data that falls in each class. The total will always be equal to 100%=1, but round offs may cause a slight variation.

VIII.   Steps in constructing a frequency distribution table:

A.   Let the lower class limit for the first class be the lowest data value. To obtain the lower class limit for the second class, add the class width. Continue adding the class width to produce subsequent lower class limits. List in a vertical column.

B.   Enter the corresponding upper class limits. The upper class limit for the first class is found by subtracting 1 from the lower class limit of the second class. The rest of the upper class limits can be found by adding the class width to each upper class limit value.

C.   Place a tally mark in the appropriate class corresponding to each data value. Form a vertical column labeled "f" (frequency) to numerically represent the tally count for each class.

D.   Form a vertical column for class boundaries. Note that the addition and subtraction of ½ guarantees that the bars will touch. i.e. the upper class boundary for the first class = the lower class boundary for the second class.

IX.   Construct the graphs

A.   If the horizontal axis does not begin with zero, place a ⌇ symbol at the corner.

B.   Label the horizontal axis with either the class boundaries or the class midpoints spaced at equal intervals. Identify the variable represented in words and the identify the units used.

C.   Mark the vertical axis with "f". Be sure you have enough space on both axes to include all the data.

D.   Construct rectangular bars
        a.   width of bar = class width
        b.   height of each bar = frequency of data values in that class.

E.   Connect the midpoints of the tops of each rectangle to form a frequency polygon.

Problem Solving Warm-Up

1.   A random sample of 30 department stores was selected and the price of Bache PX-200 CD players was checked at each store. The results to the nearest dollar were:

95	122	108	86	103	82	77	75	112	118	87	1 0 2
104	116	85	122	87	100	104	97	107	69	78	125
109	99	105	99	101	85						

Using five classes, make a frequency distribution table. Construct a histogram, a frequency polygon, a relative frequency histogram and an ogive.

For the frequency distribution table, Fill in the blanks.

Cover these answers while you are working. then check your own results.

a)   number of classes

_____

a)   5 classes

b)   range

_____

b)   Highest number = 125
Lowest = 69.
Range = 125 - 69 = 56.

c)   class width

_____

c)   To determine the class width, divide $56 \div 5 = 11.2$. Round up to 12.

d)   lower class limits

_____

d)   We will start with the lowest number which is 69. This will be the lower limit for the first class. We can now compute all the lower limits by adding the class width, 12. The lower limit in the second class is $69 + 12 = 81$. The lower limit in the third class is 81 (previous lower limit) + 12 (class width) = 93. Continue in this way until we have the lower limits for each of the five classes. The lower limits will be 69, 81, 93, 105 and 117. Place the lower class limits in column I.

e)   Upper class limits

_____

e)   The upper limit in the first class is one less than the lower limit for the second class. Therefore, since the lower limit for the second class is 81, we know the upper limit in the first class is 80. We can continue to fill in the upper limits by adding 12 (class width). The upper limits for the 5 classes are 80, 92, 104, 116 and 128. Also place the upper class limits in Column I.

f)   Class boundaries

_____

f)   We compute the class boundaries most easily by subtracting ½ from the lower limit and adding ½ to the upper limit of each class. The class boundaries for the first class are 68.5 to 89.5. For each remaining class, the class boundaries could also be determined by adding 12 to the lower and upper class boundaries in the previous class. Thus for the second class the lower boundary is 68.5 +12 = 80.5 and the upper class boundary is 80.5 + 12 = 92.5. Note that the bars will now touch since adjacent boundaries are equal. Place the class boundaries in column II.

g)   Class midpoints

_____

g)   Compute the midpoints of each class. Add the lower class limit to the upper class limit and divide by two. Place these midpoints in column III.

h)   Determine the frequencies in each class.

h)   In this problem, start with 95, the first data entry, and determine that it is in the 3rd class. Place a tally mark | to represent this. Continue until you

19

have all 30 entries tallied. The number of tally marks in a class is the frequency.

i)   Determine the relative frequency for each class.

i)   Divide each class frequency by the total frequency.

j)   Determine the cumulative frequency for each class.

j)   Start with 4 for the first row. Then add 6 to get a cumulative frequency of 10 for the 2nd class. Proceed by adding the frequency of each row to the ones above it. The cumulative frequency in the last class is 30.

Frequency distribution table

I	II	III	IV	V	VI
class limits	class boundaries	midpoints	frequency	relative frequency	cumulative frequency
69-80	68.5-80.5	74.5	4	0.13	4
81-92	80.5-92.5	86.5	6	0.20	10
93-104	92.5-104.5	98.5	10	0.33	20
105-116	104.5-116.5	110.5	6	0.20	26
117-128	116.5-128.5	122.5	4	0.13	30
		Sum	30.00	1.00	

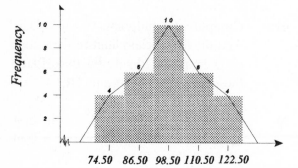

Price of Bache PX-200 CD Players

For the histogram, mark the horizontal axis with midpoint values spaced at equal intervals. Draw a bar centered at this value with a height equal to the frequency of the class. Be sure that adjacent bars touch. *The histogram for this data is __symmetric__ in shape.*

For the frequency polygon, locate a point over the midpoint of each class at the center of the top line of the bar. Connect these points. Extend the polygon down to the horizontal axis on either side.

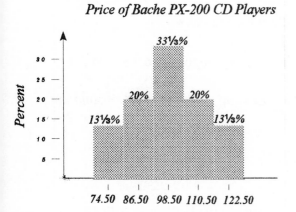

Price of Bache PX-200 CD Players

For the relative frequency histogram, mark equal spaces representing the midpoints for each class on the horizontal axis. The vertical axis marks the percent of the total frequency that each graph represents. Like the corresponding histogram, this graph is symmetric in shape.

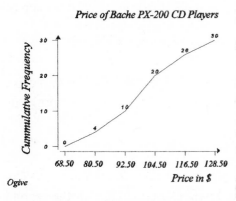

Price of Bache PX-200 CD Players

Ogive

To construct the ojive, mark the horizontal axis with the boundary values for each class. Start y value at zero for the first boundary. Each subsequent y value will correspond to the cumulative frequency for that class from the frequency distribution table.

Thinking About Statistics

1.   Suppose the upper and lower *class limits* for a frequency distribution with 5 classes are computed as:

class 1	class 2	class 3	class 4	class 5
.05-.10	.11-.16	.17-.22	.23-.28	.29-.34

Compute the corresponding *class boundaries* for each of the five classes.

2.   Suppose the lower and upper *class limits* for a frequency distribution with four classes are:

class 1	class 2	class 3	class 4
17.2-17.6	17.7-18.1	18.2-18.6	18.7-19.6

Compute the corresponding *class boundaries*.

21

Selected Solutions Section 2.3

1.   a) The number of classes (bars) is five. This is stated in the problem. ♦

   b) The highest value is 258 and the lowest is 14. Therefore the range is 258-14 = 244. ♦

   c) Divide the range 244 by the number of classes 5 and round up. 244/48= 48.8. Round up to 49 for the class width. ♦

<u>SET UP A FREQUENCY DISTRIBUTION TABLE AS FOLLOWS:</u>

Lower Limits
Since the lowest value is 14, start with 14 as the lower limit for the first class. Add 49 (the class width) to get the next lower limit until you have computed the lower limit for each of the 5 classes.

Upper Limits
Note that since the lower limit for the *second* class is 63, the upper limit for the *first* class must be 62. Proceed to determine the remaining upper limits by adding 49 to each previous upper limit.

Lower and Upper Boundaries
Subtract ½ from the lower limit and add ½ to the upper limit to get the class boundaries. The upper boundary for the first class must be equal to the lower class boundary of the second class so the bars will touch.

Class Midpoints
Compute the class midpoints by adding the lower limit to the upper limit and dividing by two. After the midpoint of the first class has been computed, the others can be determined by adding the class width (49) to the previous midpoint.

Frequencies and Relative Frequencies
Tally the entries in each class and compute the frequencies. Compute the relative frequencies by dividing each class frequency by the total of the frequencies for this problem its 44).

Cumulative Frequencies
To compute the cumulative frequency, total the current line's frequency with that of those above it. For the first class, start with the frequency of that class. Then for the second, add the first class frequency to that of the second. Continue until the cumulative frequency in the last class is equal to the total frequency of the data.

	I	II	III	IV	V	VI
	class limits	class boundaries	class midpoints	f	rel. f	cum. freq.
	14-62	13.5-62.5	38	5	.11	5
	63-111	62.5-111.5	87	14	.32	19
	112-160	111.5-160.5	136	18	.40	37
	161-209	160.5-209.5	185	5	.11	42
	210-258	209.5-258.5	234	2	.05	44

Speed of Dot Matrix Printer

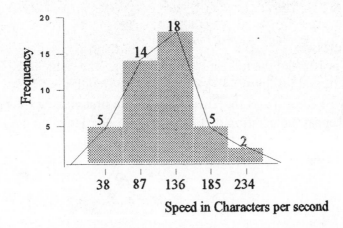

Note that the histogram and the frequency histogram are the same shape and are skewed right. (The longer tail is to the right.)

Speed of Dot Matrix Printers

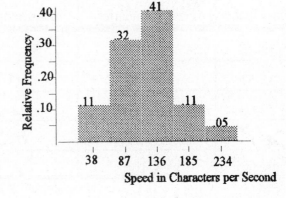

23

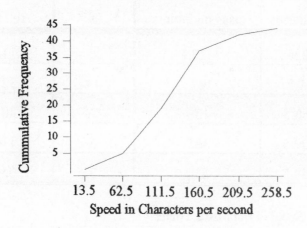

Speed of Dot Matrix Printers

5.   a)   There are 5 classes.
The highest value is 102 and the lowest is 18. Therefore, the range is 102-18 =84.
The class width is the round-up of 84÷5=16.8. The class width is 17.
Start with the lowest score 18 as the lower limit in the first class. Add 17 to compute the next lower limit. Repeat the addition of 17 until all 5 lower limits are determined.

I	II	III	IV	V	VI
class limits	class boundaries	class midpoint	f	rel f	cum. freq.
18-34	17.5-34.5	26	1	0.029	1
35-51	34.5-51.5	43	2	0.057	3
52-68	51.5-68.5	60	5	0.143	8
69-85	68.5-85.5	77	15	0.429	23
86-102	85.5-102.5	94	12	0.343	35

The distribution shape is skewed left.

c)   Connect the center points at the top of each bar to construct the frequency polygon.

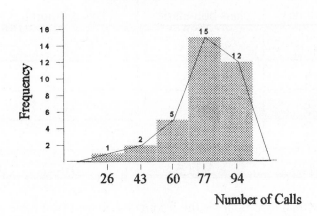

Number of Room Calls at Nurses' Station

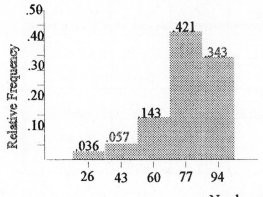

Number of Room Calls at Nurses' Station

Relative frequency histogram on the left.

Ogive on the right.

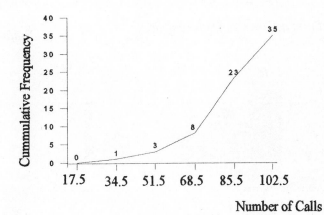

Number of Room Calls at Nurses' Station

9. For the food companies the frequency distribution table is:

I	II	III	IV		V
class limits	class boundaries	class midpoint	f	rel f	cum. freq.
-3-(-1)	-3.5-(-.5)	-2	2	0.051	2
0-2	-.5-2.5	1	16	0.41	18
3-5	2.5-5.5	4	10	0.256	28
6-8	5.5-8.5	7	9	0.231	37
9-11	8.5-11.5	10	2	0.051	39

For the electronic companies the frequency distribution table is:

I	II	III	IV		V
class limits	class boundaries	class midpoint	f	rel. f	cum. freq.
-6-(-2)	-6.5-(-1.5)	-4	3	0.07	3
-1-3	-1.5-3.5	1	13	0.30	16
4-8	3.5-8.5	6	20	0.45	36
9-13	8.5-13.5	11	7	0.16	43
14-18	13.5-18.5	16	1	0.02	44

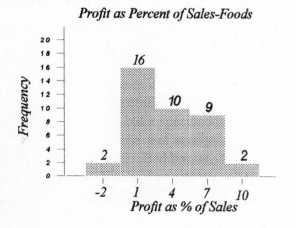

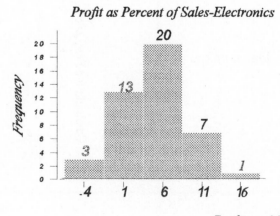

The two distributions are difficult to compare in this format since the sizes of the samples are different (39 for foods and 44 for electronics). Furthermore, the widths of the classes in the foods distribution are different than those in the electronics. The electronic industry percents are more spread out (wider range) than those of the food industry. Perhaps a better comparison could be made by constructing a frequency polygon for each on the same graph as shown. From the frequency polygons, it

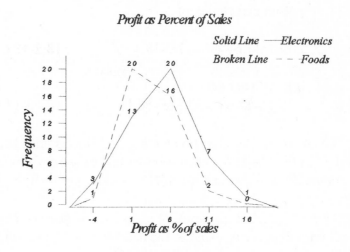

appears that profit as a percent of sales in the electronics industry (solid line) leads that of the foods industry (broken line). A relative frequency for the two data sets would give a more accurate comparison.

13. Test version 1 is skewed left. Many more grades in the A and B range than in the D and F range.
Test version 2 shows a uniform distribution. Grades are equally distributed (equal numbers of A's, B's, C's D's and F's).
Test version 3 is symmetric. The bulk of the grades are in the middle (C range) with few A's and few F's.
Test version 4 is bimodal. (Two peaks).
Test version 5 is skewed right. Many more grades are in the D and F range than are in the A and B range. As a student, you probably would like version 1 since you would have the greatest chance of getting an A with that version. Conversely, you probably would not like version 5.

Answers to Thinking About Statistics

1.   With class limits of :

   .05-.10   .11-.16   .17-.22   .23-.28   .29-.34

Use class boundaries:

   .055-.105   .105-.165   .165-.225   .225-.285   .285-.345

2.   With class limits of

17.2-17.6   17.7-18.1   18.2-18.6   18.7-19.6

Use class boundaries:
17.15-17.65   17.65-18.15   18.15-18.65   18.65-19.65

When computing class boundaries, find the distance between consecutive classes and compute half of that distance. Then subtract that quantity from each lower limit to get each lower boundary and add that quantity to each upper limit to get each upper boundary.

Thus if your data is expressed in integers, add and subtract .5.
If your data is expressed to the nearest .1, add and subtract .05 and if your data is expressed to the nearest .01, add and subtract .005.

Section 2.4
Stem and Leaf Displays

Review

I.   **All** data values are displayed in a stem and leaf display. This provides an advantage over a histogram in which the data is "lumped" together into classes.

II.   The digits in each number in the data are divided into two groups.

F.   The digit that is the left most significant digit is the **leaf.** The digits to its right represent the **stem.**

G.   There is no hard and fast rule for separating the digits. However, the leaves usually consist of the significant digit furthest to the right in each number. Data may be rounded off so that the digits o the right are all zeros. In the case use the first place value in which all digits are not zero. For data such as 52**3**,000, 65**6**,000 and 89**0**,000... the leaf unit should be 1000 and the first three leafs would be 3, 6 and 0.

III.   You can put all numbers that have the same stem on one line, two lines or five lines.

A.   When two lines per stem are used, the first line of a stem will have leaves of 0,1,2,3 and 4 (the first five digits) and the second line will have 5,6,7,8 and 9.

B.   If we turn a stem and leaf display on the side, we can classify the shape of the distribution in the same ways as we did a histogram (symmetric, uniform, skewed etc.).

C.   Sometimes the leaves are placed in numerical order, but this is not necessary. In fact, the leaves may be written in any order.

D.   A stem and leaf display should include a key to the units used. This is so that others who read it will be able to interpret the information displayed.

Problem Solving Warm-up

In the following sets of numbers, decide where to separate the stem from the leaf. Include a key or explanation of your units.

1.   23   4 65 36 28 54 8 22 36
       43 51   5 42 29
       Leaf unit _____
       Key:_____

2.   235 153 137   95 158 148 89
       164 175 214 186
       Leaf unit _____
       Key:_____

3.   13,400 15,800 21,000 16,700
       14,300 12,400 9,500
       Leaf unit _____
       Key:_____

1.   Answer: Treat each data entry as a two digit number. The leaf unit = 1. Use the tens place as the stem. The stems will range from 0 to 6. (Key 2|3 means 23.)

2.   Answer: Consider each data entry as a three digit number. The leaf unit = 1. Use the digits in the hundreds and tens place for the stem. The stems will range from 08 to 23. (Key 23|5 means 235.)

3.   Answer: Each data entry ends in two zeros and it appears that numbers have been rounded to the closest hundred. The leaf = 100 with the stem being the thousands digit and above. *We can ignore the zeros in the tens and units places in our display as long as a key is provided. (ex. 13|4 means 13,400.)*

Thinking About Statistics

When constructing your stem and leaf displays be sure the leaves have equal spacing between them. The order in which the leaves are written does not matter, however it is probably easier to read if they are placed in ascending numerical order.   Meaningful stem-and-leaf displays can be done with 1 line per stem, 2 lines per stem or 5 lines per stem since those numbers divide evenly into 10 (the number of digits).

Selected Solutions Section 2.4

1. Stem-and-leaf of Prices of walking shoes:
   Leaf Unit is $1.
   Key 5|9 means 59 dollars

```
 4 |06
 5 |025558899
 6 |00025599
 7 |0068
 8 |
 9 |
10 |9
11 |0
```

It is reasonable to let the leaves represent the ones place for the values. Then the stems will range from 4 (representing values in the $40 range) to 11 (representing values from 110 to 119). The prices are skewed right meaning most of the shoes are in the lower end of the scale. There is a gap in the $80 and $90 price range.

5. Stem-and-leaf of Pills
   Leaf Unit = 1 pill
   Key: 1|3 mean 13 pills

```
0 |*112223334444
0 | 55666777788888899999
1 |*00011222222234
1 | 555
```

The leaf unit is one pill. Using two lines per stem, the stems will be 0 and 1. Values from 0 to 4 will be on the first line with a stem of 0 and values of 5 to 9 will be on the second line. The distribution is slightly skewed to the right and there are no gaps.

9. Stem-and-leaf of per capita energy use by state
in millions of BTUs.

Leaf Unit = 10 million BTUs.
Key 9|9 means 990 million BTU's

```
2| 02233344567789
3| 000001111222333345555556899
4| 02257
5|
6|
7| 89
8|
9| 9
```

The distribution is skewed right. The entry of 9|9, representing 990 million BTU's is an unusual value (an outlier). Checking back to the data it's not surprising that the unusually high energy consumption is in the state of Alaska.

Chapter 3

AVERAGES AND VARIATION

Section 3.1
Mode, Median and Mean

Review

I   There are several ways of defining the *average* for a set of data. Each has its own characteristics.

     A.   **Mean**

         1.   The sum of all the data values divided by the number of data values. In symbols the *sample* mean (denoted as x̄) is:

$$\bar{x} = \frac{\sum x}{n}$$

             a. $\sum x$ means add all the x values.

             b.   n = the number of values in the sample.

         2.   In most cases, we will be computing a sample mean, x̄.

         3.   However, we use μ, the Greek letter mu to indicate the mean of a *population*.

             a.   N = the number of values in the population.

$$\mu = \frac{\sum x}{N}$$

         4.   An extreme value can greatly affect the mean.

         5.   It is the most commonly used "average."

         6.   It can only be computed when the data is at the interval or the ratio level.

     B.   **Median**

         1.   The point that separates the top half of the data from the bottom half. i.e. Half the data values fall above the median and half fall below.

2. To determine the median all data values must be ranked in either ascending or in descending order. The ranks will be numbered 1,2,3...n.

3. The *rank* of the median is computed by (n+1) ÷ 2. Add 1 to the number of data entries and divide by 2. The median is the value which is in this rank.

    a. If n represents an odd number (there are an odd number of data entries) the median will be the value which is in the middle once the data has been written in order. Example: if n=27 then the rank of the median will be (27+1)÷2 = 28÷2 = 14.

    b. If n is even, the median is the average of the two middle values. Example: if n=16, the rank of the median is (16+1)÷2 = 17÷2 = 8.5. We can interpret a rank of 8.5 as the average (mean) of the 8th and the 9th ranked data values.

    c. The median is **more resistant** than the mean. This means it is more stable since it is not affected greatly by extreme values.

    d. It can be determined with ordinal, interval or ratio data.

C. **Mode**

1. If it exists, the mode is the value or response that occurs most frequently.

2. It is the easiest average to determine.

3. It can be determined with data at all four levels of measurement (nominal, ordinal, interval or ratio).

D. **Trimmed Mean**

1. Place the data in ranked order.

2. For the 5% trimmed mean, determine the closest value to 5% of the data frequency.

3. Eliminate this number of data entries from the lowest end of the data and also from the highest end of the data. Then compute the mean of the remaining 90% of the middle values.

4. When there are no extreme values, the mean and the trimmed mean will be close. When there are extreme values, they may differ significantly.

Problem Solving Warm-Up

1. An instructor of statistics was interested in the average number of absences for her students over a semester. By random numbers she selected a sample of 9 students from those who were enrolled and recorded the number of times each was absent. The data were:

2 3 2 0 40 2 4 3 7

Compute the sample mean, $\bar{x}$, the median and the mode for this data. Which do you think best represents a "typical" student?

1.   *Solution:* For the sample mean, $\sum x = 63$, n = 9 so $\bar{x} = 63 \div 9 = 7$ ♦

To compute the median, *place the values in rank order.*

rank	1	2	3	4	5	6	7	8	9
value	0	2	2	2	**3***	3	4	7	40

The median **rank** is computed by $(9+1) \div 2 = 5$. There are four values above and four below this rank.
The value corresponding to this rank is 3. Thus the **median** is 3. ♦

The mode is 2. ♦ It has a frequency of three.

2.   Suppose we discovered the student from problem 1 with 40 absences, had to withdraw from the class after he studied "averages". If his absence count is removed from our sample, what are the three averages for the remaining 8 values?

2.   *Solution:* For the sample mean: $\sum x = 23$, n = 8 $\bar{x} = 23 \div 8 = 2.75$ ♦

The median rank will be $(8+1) \div 2 = 4.5$. This indicates that the median will be the mean of the 4th and the 5th data values (when they are ranked in order.) There are four values below and four above this rank.
The median is $(2+3) \div 2 = 2.5$ ♦

rank	1	2	3	4	5	6	7	8
value	0	2	2	2	3	3	4	7

The mode is 2. ♦

Thinking About Statistics

In each problem below, a question or situation is described with a set of possible responses. Which averages would be appropriate for the set of responses?

1.   What color is your car?
        Data: red, blue, black, red, grey, blue, red.

2.   Sam Quick is a member of the track team at his college. The following data represent which place he finished in for last year's races.
Data: 1, 5 , 3, 2, 2, 3, 2, 1, 2.

3.   What was your grade on your last statistics test?
Data: 87, 82, 75, 61, 95, 54, 81.

4.   Five-day high temperatures in Fahrenheit degrees were recorded during the month of September in Newtown, Pa. They were
Data: 85, 72, 92, 81, 78, 73.

Selected Solutions Section 3.1

1.   The sample mean $\bar{x}$: $\sum x = 1876$ and n = 12; so $\bar{x} = 1876 \div 12 = 156.33$ ♦

To compute the median, rank the data.

rank	1	2	3	4	5	**6**	**7**	8	9	10	11	12
value	144	148	152	153	156	**157**	**157**	157	161	161	162	168

The median rank is $(12+1) \div 2 = 6.5$. The median is the mean of the data values in ranks 6 and 7. The median is $(157+157) \div 2 = 157$. ♦

The mode is 157 since this value occurs 3 times which is the highest frequency. ♦

The gardener could say that the mean number of frost free days in this region is 156.33. Half the time there were fewer than 157 frost free days and half the time there were more than 157 frost free days. The most commonly recorded number of frost free days was 157.♦

5. $\sum x = 404$, n = 26 $\bar{x} = 404 \div 26 = 15.54$ ♦

Rank	1	2	3	4	5	6	7	8	9	10	11	12	**13**	**14**
Value	1	3	4	4	4	5	7	9	10	10	12	13	**16**	**17**

Rank	15	16	17	18	19	20	21	22	23	24	25	26
Value	17	17	18	19	19	21	21	22	25	29	36	45

The median rank is $(26+1) \div 2 = 13.5$. There are 13 values below and 13 values above this rank. Compute the mean of the data values in positions ranked 13 and 14. $(16 + 17) / 2 = 16.5$. ♦

There is no mode. The distribution is bimodal with 4 and 19 having the highest frequency♦

b) There were 12 point margins below the mean of 15.58 but 13 below the median (16.5).♦

c) For the 5% trimmed mean compute 5% of $26 = 1.3$. Rounding this result off to 1, eliminate the highest value of 45 and the lowest of 1 from the data. Summing the remaining 24 values, we get 358. And $358/24 = 14.92$. ♦Note that he trimmed mean will be is more resistant than the mean.

9.   a)   The mean is $102 \div 7 = 14.57$ ♦

Rank	1	2	3	4	5	6	7
Value	10	12	15	15	15	17	18

The median rank is $(7+1) \div 2 = 4$. The median value is 15. ♦

The mode is 15. ♦

b)   The mean is $221 \div 9 = 24.56$ ♦

Rank	1	2	3	4	5	6	7	8	9
Value	10	12	15	15	15	17	18	57	62

The median rank is $(9+1) \div 2 = 5$. The median value is 15. ♦

The mode is 15. ♦

c)   The mean was affected significantly after the last two night's data were included. However the median and the mode remained the same. ♦

13.   a)   Nominal data. The only meaningful average is the mode.(Which offered the most) ♦
       b)   Ratio data. All three averages would be appropriate.♦
       c)   Interval data. Only the mode and median would be appropriate.♦

Answers to Thinking About Statistics

1. The only meaningful average for this nominal data is the mode. You would be interested in this if you were in a management position of an automobile corporation.

2. This is ordinal data. The median and the mode are meaningful. It makes no sense to discuss the mean of the positions.

3. In ratio data, all three averages are meaningful. This data has no mode.

4. In interval data all three averages may be determined. The mode does not exist in this set of data.

Section 3.2
Measures of Variation

Review

I.   Measures of variation: In order to give a more complete description of the population or the sample, it is necessary to measure the dispersion or the "spread " of the data.

    A.   **Range**
        1.   Easy to compute.
        2.   Highest data value minus the lowest data value.
        3.   Greatly affected by an extreme data value.

    B.   **Sample variance**
        1.   Sample variance is denoted s^2
        2.   Write the data values in vertical column I, labeled x.

$$s^2 = \frac{\sum (x-\bar{x})^2}{n-1}$$

        3.   Compute the sample mean $= \bar{x}$.
        4.   Subtract the mean from each data value. The quantity $(x-\bar{x})$ is called the *deviation* and it may be positive, negative or zero. *The algebraic sum of the deviations is always zero.* Place the deviations in vertical column II.
        5.   To eliminate the negative numbers, square the deviations. Place these squares in a vertical column labeled $(x-\bar{x})^2$.

6.   Add the squares of the deviations. This is called the "sum of squares of x" and is also denoted SS_x.

$$SS_x = \sum(x-\bar{x})^2$$

7.   Divide the sum of squares by (n-1)

C.   For a **population variance,** denoted σ^2
1.   Find the population mean μ.
2.   Find the deviation (x-μ) for each value x.
3.   Square each deviation.
4.   Divide by N the size of the population.

$$\sigma^2 = \frac{\sum(x-\mu)^2}{N}$$

D.   **Sample standard deviation,** denoted s

$$s = \sqrt{s^2} = \sqrt{\frac{\sum(x-\bar{x})^2}{(n-1)}}$$

The square root of the sample variance.

E.   A **population standard deviation** denoted σ (lower case Greek letter sigma).

The square root of the population variance. $\sigma = \sqrt{\sigma^2} = \sqrt{\dfrac{\sum(x-\mu)^2}{N}}$

Thus to find a standard deviation, compute the variance and take the square root.

The standard deviation will be in the same units as the original data. (The variance is in units "squared" which usually has no meaning.)

With a calculator, the computation is simpler if you work across the horizontal rows, computing the values for each column heading. If you store the last column (deviations squared) in your calculator memory and use the "sum to memory" function you will be able to compute the sum of squares SS_x easily. After you recall this sum from the calculator memory, divide by (n-1) if you are working with sample data or divide by N if you are using population data. To find the standard deviation, take the square root.

It can be shown that SS_x can also be computed by: $SS_x = \sum x^2 - \dfrac{(\sum x)^2}{n}$

Both formulas for SS_x give the same result but the
latter one is sometimes easier to compute. $\sum x^2$ means square each value of x and find the sum of these squared numbers. $(\sum x)^2$ means add all the x values and *then* square the result.

F.   The **Coefficient of Variation** CV
1.   Measures the standard deviation relative to the mean.

2.   It has no units, so we can compare the variability of two populations (or two samples) that are measured in different units.
3.   To compute, divide the standard deviation by the mean and multiply by 100.
    a.   For a sample use: $CV = \frac{s}{\overline{x}} \cdot 100$

    b.   For a population use: $CV = \frac{\sigma}{\mu} \cdot 100$

II.   What can be learned from measures of dispersion?
    A.   Smaller measures of dispersion indicate a group is more homogeneous.
    B.   **Chebyshev's Theorem** tells us what proportion of the data values will be within 2, 3, 4 etc. standard deviations on either side of the mean.

    The proportion is given by: $1 - \frac{1}{k^2}$ *where* $k > 1$

    Thus if k=**2**, Chebyshev's
    Theorem guarantees that 1-(½)² = 1 - ¼ = ¾ = 75% of the data will fall between the values which are **two** standard deviations below the mean and **two** standard deviations above the mean.
    In actual practice, this number may by higher than 75%. In fact this percentage will be much higher when the distributions are symmetrically mound shaped.

Problem Solving Warm-Up

As a stock broker, you wish to examine the record of two stocks in which your client has expressed an interest.

1.   Ten days during the last year were selected at random and the selling price for Albion, Inc. brand stock on each of those days was recorded as:

                26 26 27 28 31 33 33 37 37 37

    a.   Compute the mean of the sample = $\overline{x}$.
    b.   Compute the median.
    c.   Compute the mode.
    d.   Compute the range.
    e.   Compute the standard deviation for the sample.
    f.   Compute the coefficient of variation.

2.   During those ten days the selling price for X-Tech brand stock was also recorded. The data

for X-Tech is :

3 12 18 22 27 37 37 47 52 60

Repeat the questions a to f in problem 1 for the X-Tech stock prices.

Solutions:

1.   a)   The mean is 31.5 ♦
     b)   The median is 32 (average of the fifth and sixth ranked values.) ♦
     c)   The mode is 37 ♦
     d)   The range is 11 (37-26) ♦
     e)   To calculate the standard deviation of the sample, construct a table.

             Place the data for Albion, Inc. stock prices in vertical columns labeled
             x, x-x̄, and (x-x̄)² .

             From part a we know the sample mean is 31.5.

     (1)   Enter each of the 10 values in column I, labeled x.

     (2)   Starting with row 1, enter 26 into your calculator, then subtract the mean (31.5) from
             26 and enter this result in column II. This result is a negative number since 26 is less
             than the mean of 31.5.

     (3)   Working across to column III, square the result from column II. Note that -5.5 is
             already in your calculator display. You will now have to send 30.25 into your
             calculator memory.

     (4)   Next go to row 2 and repeat the three steps above, sending the number in the last
             column to your memory.

     (5)   Repeat these steps until you have reached the last data entry. Your table should
             appear as follows:

I	II	III
x	x-x̄	(x-x̄)²
26	-5.50	30.25
26	-5.50	30.25
27	-4.50	20.25
28	-3.50	12.25
31	-0.50	0.25
33	1.50	2.25
33	1.50	2.25
37	5.50	30.25
37	5.50	30.25
37	5.50	30.25
315.00	**0.00**	**188.50**

(6)   The entry is the last line of the last column is the sum of squares= 188.50.

(7)   While 188.50 is in your calculator display, divide it by (10-1) = 9. The result, 20.9444 (rounded to 4 places), is the sample variance.

(8)   To get the sample standard deviation s, find
the square root of the sample variance. $s = \sqrt{20.9944} \approx 4.58$

f)

$$CV = \frac{4.58}{31.5} (100) = 14.54$$

Since calculators vary in their memory functions and in the squaring and square root functions, be sure to familiarize yourself with the particular calculator you own. It is a good idea to use the same kind of calculator throughout the course, especially when you are taking a test!

2.   a)   The mean is 31.5 ♦
      b)   The median is 32 ♦
      c)   The mode is 37 ♦
            (If these numbers look strangely familiar, you've been paying attention! Each of the three measures of central tendency for the X-Tech stock are the same as the corresponding averages for the Albion, Inc. stock in problem 1.)

d)   The range is 57. (60-3) ◆

e)   To compute the sample standard deviation, construct a table as shown below. Fill in the missing entries to the table on the left. Check your entries with those in the right hand table.

I	II	III
x	x-x̄	(x-x̄)²
3		812.25
12		
18	-13.50	
22		90.25
27		
37	5.50	
37		
47		
52	20.50	
60		812.25

I	II	III
x	x-x̄	(x-x̄)²
3.00	-28.50	812.25
12.00	-19.50	380.25
18.00	-13.50	182.25
22.00	-9.50	90.25
27.00	-4.50	20.25
37	5.50	30.25
37.00	5.50	30.25
47.00	15.50	240.25
52.00	20.50	420.25
60.00	28.50	812.25
315.00	0.00	3,018.50

The sum of squares is 3018.5. Divide by 9 (*why*??) to get 335.3889 which is the sample variance.

$$s = \sqrt{335.3889} = 18.31 ◆$$

f) $CV = \dfrac{18.31}{31.5} (100) = 58.13$

Thinking About Statistics

1. Compare the two stocks from the Problem Solving Warm-Up section using measures of central tendency (averages) and measures of variation. What would you tell your client?

2. Find the number of standard deviations (k) that are necessary to guarantee (according to Chebychev's Theorem) that 99% of the population of values will fall within k standard deviations.

Selected Solutions Section 3.2

1. a)   The range = Maximum value - minimum value = 58 - 4 = 54 deer/km^2♦
    b) $\sum x = 251$ n = 12 sample mean = $251 \div 12 = 20.92$ deer/km^2♦

    c)   For the sample variance and sample standard deviation, construct a table as below:

I	II	III
x	x - $\bar{x}$	(x - $\bar{x}$)^2
30	9.08	82.4464
20	-0.92	0.8464
20	-0.92	0.8464
18	-2.92	8.5264
5	-15.92	253.4464
4	-16.92	286.2864
29	8.08	65.2864
29	8.08	65.2864
58	37.08	1,374.9264
22	1.08	1.1664
7	-13.92	193.7664
9	-11.92	142.0864
251	-0.04	2,474.9168

note that the sum of the deviations is -.04 which is close to 0. The error is due to round-offs.

For the sample variance, divide 2474.9168 by 11 (in a sample variance you divide by (n-1)) to get 224.9924. ♦

For the sample standard deviation, find the square root of the variance: $s = \sqrt{224.9924} = 15$

The sample standard deviation is 15 deer per square kilometer. ♦

$$CV = \frac{15}{20.92} \cdot 100 = 71.70$$

b) 71.70 is the standard deviation as a percent of the mean. It seems there was a considerable variation in the distribution of deer in different sections of the park.♦

5.   a)   range = 63.1 - 19.8 = 43.3 ♦
       b) $\sum x$ = 282.20   n = 7   μ = 282.20 ÷ 7 ≈ 40.31 ♦

For the *population* standard deviation, construct a table as below.

	I	II	III
	x	$x-\bar{x}$	$(x-\bar{x})^2$
	19.8	-20.51	420.66
	43.8	3.49	12.18
	36.1	-4.21	17.72
	52.4	12.09	146.17
	63.1	22.79	519.38
	20.7	-19.61	384.55
	46.3	5.99	35.88
	282.20	**0.03**	**1,536.54**

note that the sum of the deviations is .03 which is close to 0. The error is due to round-offs.

To compute the *population* standard deviation, divide 1536.54 by 7 (the number of data entries). 1536.54/7 = 219.5057. This is the population variance.

To compute the population standard deviation, take the square root of the population variance.

σ≈$\sqrt{219.5057}$≈14.82 ♦

Please note that because of the different ways calculators round off, your answers may differ slightly. Do not be concerned!

9.   a) $\bar{x} = 7.83$ $s = 2.32$ CV = 29.62   range = 4.8 ♦

	I	II	III
	x	x-$\bar{x}$	(x-$\bar{x}$)^2
	10.1	2.27	5.1529
	6.2	-1.63	2.6569
	9.8	1.97	3.8809
	5.3	-2.53	6.4009
	9.9	2.07	4.2849
	5.7	-2.13	4.5369
	47.000	**0.02**	**26.9134**

Divide 26.91 by 5 and take the square root. $s = \sqrt{5.382} \approx 2.32$♦

To calculate the coefficient of variation, divide the standard deviation by the mean and multiply the result by 100. Thus CV = (2.32÷7.83) · 100 = 29.62 ♦

     b) $\bar{x} = 9.95$ s= .29   CV= 2.9   range =.7 ♦

	I	II	III
	x	x-$\bar{x}$	(x-$\bar{x}$)^2
	10.2	0.25	0.0625
	9.7	-0.25	0.0625
	9.8	-0.15	0.0225
	10.3	0.35	0.1225
	9.6	-0.35	0.1225
	10.1	0.15	0.0225
	59.700	**0.00**	**0.4150**

.4150/5 = .083   The sample standard deviation is: $s = \sqrt{.083} \approx .29$

$$CV = (.29 \div 9.95) \cdot 100 = .029 \cdot 100 = 2.9 \quad \blacklozenge$$

The second spool had a much more *consistent* performance since the standard deviation, coefficient of variation and the range for this spool were smaller.

13.

	DJIA	Sears	Delta	AT&T	Kodak	McDonald's
$\bar{x}$	3576.63	52.31	51.48	62.15	57.23	52.35
s	30.37	1.80	1.32	2.03	3.97	1.96
CV	0.85	3.44	2.56	3.27	6.94	3.74

With a CV of 6.94, Kodak' was the highest. McDonald's, Sears, AT&T and Delta followed in the given order. The CV for the DJIA (0.85) was the smallest.

Whereas an individual stock may show a great deal of variability, the average of 30 stocks will not be as variable. (This is one reason many people choose to invest in mutual funds instead of individual stocks.). $\blacklozenge$

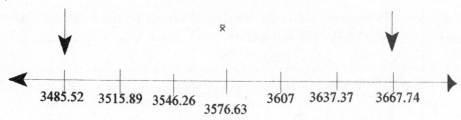

$$1 - \frac{1}{3^2} - 1 - \frac{1}{9} - \frac{8}{9} - 88.9\%$$

c) Construct a number line as shown. Locate the sample mean 35.76.63. Mark the line in standard deviation units of 30.37. Chebyshev's Theorem guarantees that for any distribution of values, 88.9% of the values will fall within 3 standard deviations of the mean. To compute the endpoints for the interval for the DJIA go back 3 standard deviations units from the mean and then go forward 3 standard deviations from the mean:

$$\bar{x} - 3s = 3576.63 - 3(30.37) = 3576.63 - 91.11 = 3485.52$$

$$\bar{x} + 3s = 3576.63 + 3(30.37) = 3576.63 + 91.11 = 3667.74$$

Thus at least 88.9% of the time, the DJIA will fall between 3485.52 and 3667.74. In stock broker terminology, 3485.52 could be thought of as a support and 3667.74 as a resistance at the 88.9% level. The closing value of 3652.09 for August 25, 1993 was close to the resistance value. The following decline was a normal adjustment. ♦

c) Subtract from and then add 3 standard deviations to the mean to compute the ends of the interval. For Delta stock we compute the 88.9% interval from 51.48 -3(1.32) = 47.52 to 51.48 +3(1.32) = 55.44. So $47.52 could be considered a support value and $55.44. a resistance value. The August 25, 1993 closing value of $55.50 is above the resistance value so the stock would be expected to decline. Of course the stock could go below the support or above the resistance since Chebyshev's theorem does not guarantee *all* the values to be within the computed range, only 88.9% of the values.♦

d)The intervals between which Chebyshev's Theorem guarantees 88.9% of the values will fall are computed as follows:
For Sears:52.31 -3(1.80) = 46.91   and 52.31 +3(1.80) = 57.71 ♦
For AT&T 62.15 - 3(2.03) = 56.06   and 62.15 + 3(2.03)= 64.24 ♦
For Kodak 57.23 - 3(3.97) = 45.32   and 57.23 + 3(3.97)= 69.14 ♦
For McDonald's 52.35 -3(1.96) = 46.47   and 52.35 +3(1.96) = 58.23♦

Answers to Thinking About Statistics

1. The mean, the median and the mode of Albion, Inc. stock were the same as the mean the median and the mode for X-Tech stock. The range of X-Tech was far greater than that of Albion, Inc.. But remember, the range only uses two values in its calculation so if the high value for Albion, Inc. were the only number changed, the range of Albion, Inc. would be affected greatly. The standard deviation, which takes every value in the sample into account is a better indicator of the variability of the stocks. The stock Albion, Inc. has a much more consistent daily price, while the stock X-Tech has much more variability, thus Albion, Inc. would be a better stock for a client who did not want to take too many risks. Comparing the coefficient of variation of the two stocks, the CV for Albion = 14.54 is lower than that of X-Tech = 58.13. Relative to its mean, Albion has a smaller amount of variation.

2. Use some elementary algebra to solve the equation in Chebychev's Theorem for the value of k.
No matter how unusually shaped a distribution may be, we are guaranteed at least 99% of its values will fall within 10 standard deviations of the mean.

$$We\ know:\ 1-\frac{1}{k^2} = \frac{99}{100}.$$
$$\frac{1}{100} = \frac{1}{k^2}$$
$$k^2 = 100\ so\ k = 10$$

Section 3.3
Mean and Standard Deviation of Grouped Data

Review

I.   The formulas introduced earlier for the mean and standard deviation can be extremely tedious when working with large data sets.

    A.   One solution is to group the data into classes and make a frequency distribution table in the same way we did to construct a histogram.

    B.   When a class consists of an interval of numbers, for example 7-16, treat each data entry in that class as if it were equal to the midpoint (in this case, 11).

    C.   The midpoint for each class is designated as the **class mark** and is used as the replacement for x in the formulas.

II.   Computation of the mean and standard deviation for grouped data.

    A.   **Sample mean of grouped data**

        1.   Note that $\Sigma\ f = n$. The sum of the frequencies is equal to the sample size.

$$\overline{x} = \frac{\sum x \cdot f}{\sum f} = \frac{\sum x \cdot f}{n}$$

        2.   Form a frequency distribution table

            a.   Column I = x the class mark (midpoint)

            b.   Column II = f (frequency) or number of data entries in each class.

            c.   Column III = x · f the product of I and II.
            (Multiply each class mark by its corresponding frequency).

        3.   Add the products in column III.

        4.   Add the frequencies in column II.

        5.   The mean will be the sum of column III (the product of x·f) divided by the total frequency, (the sum of column II).

    B.   **Population mean of grouped data**

        1.   The population mean is designated μ, the Greek letter which is pronounced mu.

$$\mu = \frac{\sum x \cdot f}{\sum f} = \frac{\sum x \cdot f}{N}$$

        2.   It is computed in the same manner as the sample mean.

        3.   In most cases we will be computing the sample mean.

C.   The **sample standard deviation for grouped data**

$$s = \sqrt{\frac{\sum (x-\bar{x})^2 \cdot f}{(n-1)}}$$

     a.   First compute the mean $\bar{x}$.

     b.   Use vertical columns I and II from your computation of the mean for x and f.

     c.   Form vertical column IV to compute the deviations $x-\bar{x}$ for each class mark. To compute σ you will not need column III, but it will be part of the table from your computation of the mean.

     d.   Square each of the deviations from column IV to form column V,

     e. $(x-\bar{x})^2$. This is done to eliminate the negative numbers.

     f.   Multiply the squares of the deviations in column V by their respective frequencies in column II and place the product in the last column VI.

1.   Add the entries in column VI. This is the sum of squares $SS_x = \Sigma(x-\bar{x})^2$

2.   Divide the sum of squares by (n-1) which is one less than the total of column II. The result will be the variance.

3.   Finally, take the square root of the variance.

D.   **Population standard deviation for grouped data**
(It is denoted by σ, the lower case Greek letter sigma.)

$$\sigma = \sqrt{\frac{\sum (x-\mu)^2 \cdot f}{N}}$$

1.   Follow steps 1-6 above except that you will be computing μ as the population mean.

2.   Divide the sum of squares by N the size of the population (the sum of column II.)

3.   Take the square root.

III.   Other situations where grouped data formulas are useful.

    A.   Data with repeated values.

1.   Often data sets consist of many entries of the same values. The previous formulas should be used. The class mark x will be the data value itself. (If there is only one number in a class, the midpoint will be at that number.)

2.   For example if the data set is:

2, 2, 2, 2, 2, 2, 2, 2, 2, 2, 2, 2, 2, 2, 2, 2, 2, 2, 2, 2, 9, 9, 9

it is possible to use the individual entry formulas where each number is entered separately. Therefore, to compute the mean we would add all entries and get a sum of 69. We would then divide 69 by the number of entries which is 24 and get 2.875.

3.   It is much easier to set up a table as described above and compute 2(21) + 9(3) = 69 and then divide by 24, to get a mean 2.875.

4.   Use the formula

$$\bar{x} = \frac{\sum x \cdot f}{\sum f}$$

5.   Note, it would be a mistake to add (2+9), the only two numbers in your data set and divide by 2. If this were done, you would of course get 5.5 which is

incorrect.

6. Similarly the standard deviations can be computed using the grouped data formula. Remember to divide by n-1 if you are working with a sample (most of the time this will be true) and divide by N if you are working with all the data from an entire population.

B. **Weighted averages**

1. Situations occur where classes are assigned weights or different levels of relative importance.

    a. For example, in rating personnel at Data Tech, Inc. there might by possible values of 1 to 10 in a number of categories, such as prior experience, education level, appearance and attendance.

    b. However, some categories should be treated with more significance than others so we assign each a weight, w.

2. Suppose we assign a weight of 5 to the number of years a person worked at Data Tech, Inc. 7 to education level, 2 to appearance and 6 for attendance. The sum of the weights is 20. The formula for a weighted average $\bar{x}$.

$$\bar{x} = \frac{\sum x \cdot w}{\sum w}$$

3. To compute a weighted average for each employee in the company (and hence determine his salary level) multiply the score in each category by its assigned weight, then divide by the sum of the weights. In this case suppose Mike Scott had a score of 8 for his years in the company, a score of 9 for his education level, a score of 5 for his appearance and a score of 4 for his attendance during the past year. His weighted average would then be 8(5) +9(7) +2(5) +4(6) divided by 20 which is the sum of the weights. Putting this information in the form of a table makes it easier to compute.

4. The *weighted* average would therefore be 137÷20 =6.85.

Problem Solving Warm-Up

1. A sample of scores for the Advanced Placement Exam for the 1990 examination in Calculus BC are as follows: (Possible scores are 1,2,3,4 or 5 and college credits are usually awarded for scores of 3 or more.)

score	1	2	3	4	5
frequency	4964	2647	3256	926	1443

Using grouped data formulas, compute a) the sample mean and b) the sample standard deviation for these scores

Solution:

Construct a table with vertical columns I to VI. You will use only the first three columns compute the sample mean.

I	II	III
x	f	x·f
1	4964	4964
2	2647	5294
3	3256	9768
4	926	3704
5	1443	7215
	13236	30945

First compute the sample mean $\bar{x} = 30945 \div 13236 = 2.34$ ♦
To compute the sample standard deviation, fill in the remainder of the table.

I	II	III	IV	V	VI
x	f	x·f	x-$\bar{x}$	(x-$\bar{x}$)²	(x-$\bar{x}$)²f
1	4964	4964			
2	2647		-1.66	2.76	
3	3256				
4	926	3704	0.34	0.12	
5	1443				
	13236				

Some of the figures have been included. Fill in the blank cells that are not shaded with the missing numbers.

The sum in the memory of your calculator should be 20382.08. Remember that each deviation squared (column V) must be multiplied by its corresponding frequency (column II) to get the entry in column VI.

To compute the variance divide 20382.08. by 13235 (which is $\Sigma f-1$). $s^2 \approx 1.54$. Finally, the standard deviation is:

$$s = \sqrt{1.54} \approx 1.24$$

2.   A random sample of 120 executives at large company were asked how much time they spent driving to work each day. The results were as follows:

time (minutes)	frequency
1-20	45
21-40	18
41-60	34
61-80	23

For this problem, data has been grouped into 4 classes. Calculate the midpoint for each class. For example, the midpoint for the first class 1-20 is 10.5 (Add the class limits and divide by 2.) This will be the class mark and should be substituted for x (column I) in the computations. Find a)the mean and b) the standard deviation of the sample data.

Solution: Construct a table as follows.

	I	II	III	IV	V	VI
class	x	f	x·f	x-x̄	$(x-\bar{x})^2$	$(x-\bar{x})^2 f$
1-20	10.5	45	472.50	-25.83	667.19	30,023.55
21-40	30.5	18	549.00	-5.83	33.99	611.82
41-60	50.5	34	1,717.00	14.17	200.79	6,826.86
61-80	70.5	23	1,621.50	34.17	1,167.59	26,854.57
SUM		120	4,360.00			64,316.80

a) $\bar{x} = 4360 \div 120 = 36.33$

b)   Fill in the blank cells that are not shaded to compute the standard deviation. Note that when using these formulas, you must *first* compute the mean.

The sum of squares is 64316.80
The variance is $64316.80 \div 119 \approx 540.4773$.
Then, the standard deviation is: $s = \sqrt{540.4773} \approx 23.25$

3.   In a chemistry course, the final average is computed based on the following activities with the corresponding weights:

a)labs 20%   b)attendance 10%   c)midterm 30% and d)final exam 40%

Each of the following activities is graded on a 100 point scale. Calculate your weighted average if you have the following grades:

labs 73   attendance 97   midterm 75   and final exam 83.

Solution:

First construct a table:

category	x	w	x·w
labs	73	0.2	14.60
attendance	97	0.1	9.70
midterm	75	0.3	22.50
final	83	0.4	33.20
SUM		1.00	80.00

To calculate the weighted average, multiply each score by its corresponding weight, then add all these products. Finally, divide the sum by the total of the weights.
$\bar{x} = 80.00 \div 1.00 = 80.00$

Thinking About Statistics

1.   When computing a weighted average we use the formula $\bar{x} = \dfrac{\sum x \cdot w}{\sum w}$

Each data value is multiplied by its weight. The products are added. The sum of the products is divided by the sum of the weights.

Compare the formula for weighted averages to the one for the grouped data formula for a sample mean.

2.   When working with individual entry data in section 3.1 it was stated that the sum of the deviations from the mean (x-x̄) is always equal to zero. In this section, why do you usually **not** get zero if you add the column (x-x̄)? In order to be consistent with the statement in the first sentence, how would you have to adjust it for grouped data?

Selected Solutions Section 3.3

1.   Necessary calculations are shown in the table below: For column I, compute the midpoint of each class to obtain the class mark = x. Each entry in a class is in effect rounded to this value. For the first class x = (64 + 67)/2 = 65.5

	I	II	III	IV	V	VI
class	x	f	x·f	x-x̄	(x-x̄)²	(x-x̄)²·f
64-67	65.5	1	65.50	-4.86	23.62	23.62
68-71	69.5	38	2,641.00	-0.86	0.74	28.12
72-75	73.5	12	882.00	3.14	9.86	118.32
SUM		51	3,588.50			170.06

a)   To estimate the sample mean use only columns I, II and III.
Divide the sum from column III by the <u>total frequency</u>.
The sample mean x̄ ≈ 3588.50÷51 ≈ 70.36 ♦

b)   To estimate the sample standard deviation divide the sum from column IV by (n-1).
170.06 ÷ 50 ≈ 3.401.(This is the variance.) Finally, take the square root of the sample variance to get the sample standard deviation.

$$s - \sqrt{3.401} \approx 1.84 ♦$$

5.

class	I x	II f	III x·f	IV x-x̄	V (x-x̄)²	VI (x-x̄)²·f
14-17	15.5	122	1891.0	-21.11	445.63	54,366.86
18-24	21.0	80	1680.0	-15.61	243.67	19,493.60
25-44	34.5	159	5485.5	-2.11	4.45	707.55
45-64	54.5	106	5777.0	17.89	320.05	33,925.30
65-80	72.5	63	4567.5	35.89	1,288.09	81,149.67
SUM		**530**	**19401.0**			**189,642.98**

a) First estimate the sample mean. sample mean ≈ 19401/530 = 36.61 ♦

b) $s^2 \approx 189642.98/529 \approx = 358.4915$ = the sample variance. The standard deviation is:

$$s = \sqrt{358.4915} \approx 18.93♦$$

c) The coefficient of variation is 18.93/36.61 *100 = 51.71 ♦

9.

I x	II f	III x·f	IV x-x̄	V (x-x̄)²	VI (x-x̄)²f
3.5	2	7.00	-4.40	19.36	38.72
4.5	2	9.00	-3.40	11.56	23.12
5.5	4	22.00	-2.40	5.76	23.04
6.5	22	143.00	-1.40	1.96	43.12
7.5	64	480.00	-0.40	0.16	10.24
8.5	90	765.00	0.60	0.36	32.40
9.5	14	133.00	1.60	2.56	35.84
10.5	2	21.00	2.60	6.76	13.52
	200	**1,580**			**220.00**

a) Sample mean ≈1580 ÷200 ≈ 7.9 hours. ♦

b) s^2≈ 220 ÷ 199 ≈ 1.1055≈ sample variance. The sample standard deviation is:

$$s \text{-} \sqrt{1.1055} \approx 1.05 \quad hours \text{ ♦}$$

c) The coefficient of variation is $\dfrac{7.9}{1.05}$ (100) = 13.29 ♦

13.

I	II	III	IV	V	V
x	f	x·f	x-x̄	$(x-\bar{x})^2$	$(x-\bar{x})^2 f$
10	15	150	-18.17	330.15	4,952.25
20	19	380	-8.17	66.75	1,268.25
30	10	300	1.83	3.35	33.50
40	7	280	11.83	139.95	979.65
50	3	150	21.83	476.55	1,429.65
60	2	120	31.83	1,013.15	2,026.30
70	2	140	41.83	1,749.75	3,499.50
80	1	80	51.83	2,686.35	2,686.35
90	1	90	61.83	3,822.95	3,822.95
SUM	60	1690			20,698.40

a)   The sample mean x̄ = 1690÷60 =28.17 (rounded to hundredths) ♦

b)   The sample variance s^2=20698÷59 = 350.8203 ♦
        The sample standard deviation is:
$$s \text{-} \sqrt{350.8202} \approx 18.73 \text{ ♦}$$

17.   Set up a table, listing the activities in the left column.

Activity	x (score)	w (weight)	x·w
promptness	9	2	18.00
record keeping	7	3	21.00
appearance	6	1	6.00
bedside manner	10	4	40.00
SUM		**10.00**	**85.00**

Weighted Average = 85÷10 = 8.5 ♦

Answers to Thinking About Statistics

1.   The formulas for weighted average and for the mean of grouped data are similar.

Weighted Average   Mean of Grouped Data

$$\frac{\Sigma \, x \cdot w}{\Sigma w} \qquad\qquad \frac{\Sigma \, x \cdot f}{\Sigma f}$$

The only difference is that in *weighted averages* you are using a weight assigned to each category and in the *mean of grouped data* each data value is multiplied by the number of times it occurs. Thus a value which occurs more frequently should have more "influence", affect or *weight* in the computation of a mean.

2.   The sum of the deviations of all the scores is always zero. When you are working with grouped data, you must take the frequency of each score into account. Therefore we can say

$$\sum (x - \overline{x}) \cdot f = 0$$

This is consistent since with individual entry data since f = 1 for each score!

Section 3.4
Percentiles and Box-and-Whisker Plots

<u>Review</u>

I. **Percentiles**
    A. Used with data that are placed in order, smallest to largest.
    B. Measures the relative position of a data value (similar to the median).
    C. The data is divided into 100 equal parts, each part is called a percentile.
        1. The 85th percentile P_{85} is the score such that 85 parts are at or below and 15 parts are above.
        2. The 10th percentile P_{10} is the score such that 10 parts are at or below and 90 parts are above.
    D. There are 99 designations for percentiles, P_1, P_2, P_3,...P_{99}.
    E. Rules for exact computation may vary, consequently we will only be concerned with an interpretation of a percentile score which is already computed for us.

II. **Quartiles**
    A. Data is placed in numerical order lowest to highest.
    B. Measure of relative position.
    C. Data is divided into 4 equal parts.
        1. The first quartile Q_1 is the score at which 1 part is below and 3 parts above.
        2. The second quartile Q_2 is the score at which 2 parts are below and 2 above.
        3. The third quartile Q_3 is the score at which 3 parts are below and 1 part above.
    D. To evaluate quartiles
        1. Rank data smallest to largest.
        2. Compute the median. This will be the second quartile, Q_2.
        3. Consider the data values *below* (not including) the median. Compute the median of this set. This is Q_1.
        4. Similarly, find the median of the data which is *above* the median of the entire set. This is Q_3.
    E. Important equivalences
        1. Q_1=   median of lower half $\approx P_{25}$.
        2. Q_2=   median $\approx P_{50}$.
        3. Q_3=   median of upper half $\approx P_{75}$.

III.   **Interquartile range**
    A.   Measure of the spread of the middle half of the data.
    B.   Difference between the 3rd and 1st quartile values. Interquartile range = Q_3 - Q_1.
    C.   Not influenced by extreme values.

IV.   **Box-and -Whisker Plot**
    A.   Exploratory Data Analysis (EDA) tool.
    B.   Uses 5 key values from the entire data set.
        1.   Lowest value
        2. Q_1
        3.   The median (Q_2)
        4. Q_3
        5.   Highest value
    C.   To construct
        1.   Construct a number line. Be sure to preserve equal spacing between units.
        2.   Form a rectangular box with edges at the levels of Q_1 and Q_3 on your number line scale.
        3.   Draw a line in the box parallel to the edges at the level of the median value.
        4.   Place a dot at the highest score level and one at the lowest score level.
        5.   Draw a line from the box to each extreme value. These lines will look like whiskers.

Problem Solving Warm-Up

1.   You are managing a store at the mall and have recorded the value of the average sale for each of 27 randomly selected days in the last quarter. The data are:

           28 43 48 51 43 30 55 44 48 33 45 37 37 42
           27 47 42 23 46 39 20 45 38 19 17 35 45

    Make a box-and-whisker plot.

2.   The following is the value of the average sale for 22 randomly selected days for last year during the last quarter (same time as for problem 1 but in the previous year. The data are:

           37 23 34 22 55 33 20 19 28 47 17
           25 45 46 26 18 19 27 46 46 28 19

    Make a box-and whisker plot

Solutions:

1. The data in ranked order is:

17 19 20 23 27 28 **30** 33 35 37 37 38 39 **42**
42 43 43 44 45 45 **45** 46 47 48 48 51 55 .

The five number summary is as follows:

	<u>Rank = r</u>	<u>Value</u>
1.	Lowest Value r = 1	17♦
2.	Highest Value r = 27	55♦
3.	Since there are 27 values, the median will be in the (27+1)÷2 = 14th rank.	42♦
4.	The first quartile Q_2. There are 13 values below the median, the median for the lowest half is at the 7th rank.	30♦
5.	The third quartile Q_3. Count 7 scores above the median. The rank is 21.	45♦

2. The data ranked in order for problem 2 is:
17 18 19 19 19 **20** 22 23 25 26 27|28 28 33 34 37 **45** 46 46 46 47 55

The five number summary is as follows:

	<u>Rank</u>	<u>Value</u>
1.	Lowest Value r = 1	17♦
2.	Highest Value r = 22	55♦
3.	Since there are 22 values, the median will be in the (22+1)÷2=11.5 rank. {Mean of 11th and 12th rank}	27.5♦
4.	The first quartile Q_2. There are 11 values below the median, the median for the lowest half is at the 6th rank.	20♦
5.	The third quartile Q_3. Count 6 scores above the median. The rank is 17.	45♦

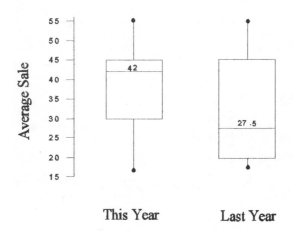

Thinking About Statistics

Compare and contrast the descriptions illustrated by the two box-and-whisker plots discussed in the Problem Solving Warm-Up section. In which year do you think the company is doing better?

Answers to Thinking About Statistics

In each of the two years there was a high value of 55 and a low of 17. The interquartile range for the second distribution (last year) is much larger than that for the first (this year). This year half the values are above 42 whereas last year half were above 27. The sales figures for problem 1 look better than those for problem 2. The company is doing better this year, assuming all other factors (inflation, fixed and variable costs to the company, etc.) are held constant.

Selected Solutions Section 3.4

1.   82% of the scores were at or below and 18% were above.

5.   a) The median is $574,769. This means 50% , made more than $574,769 (and 50% less).
b) The 90th percentile is $887,057, so 10% made more than this.
c) 90% -50% = 40%. 40% made between $574,769 and $887,057.

9.   Ranked in order the data are:

2   5   7   8   8   11   12   14   20   23 | 23   25   26   27   28   29   31   36   36   42

FOR THE PLOT
- low score= **2** ♦
- high score =**42** ♦
- median rank=(20+1)÷2 =10.5
  median value = **23** ♦
- there are 10 scores in the lower half, so the rank for Q_1=5.5 the value for Q_1 is **9.5.** ♦
- in the upper half, start with rank 11 and add 5.5 ranks to get to rank 15.5.
The value for Q_3 is **28.5.** ♦

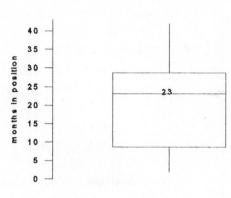

c) The interquartile range is 28.5-9.5 = 19. ♦

13) FOR THE PLOT
- low score= **0** ♦
- high score =**21** ♦
- median rank=(40+1)÷2 = 20.5
  median value = **7** ♦
- there are 20 scores in the lower half, so the rank for Q_1=10.5
the value for Q_1 is **5.** ♦
- in the upper half, start with rank21 and count 10.5 ranks.
  The value for Q_3 is **9.5.** ♦

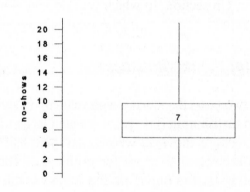

c) The interquartile range is 9.5-5 = 4.5 ♦

17.   a) From the ends of the whiskers we see that California has the lowest premium and Pennsylvania the highest.
b) Pennsylvania has the highest median premium.
c) California has the smallest range (difference between maximum and minimum) and Texas has the smallest interquartile range (smallest box).
d) The A boxplot corresponds to Texas, B to Pennsylvania and C to California.

Chapter 4

ELEMENTARY PROBABILITY THEORY

Section 4.1
What is Probability?

<u>*Review*</u>

I. Basic Terms
    A. A **statistical experiment** is an action from which an outcome, response or measurement is obtained.
        1. A gambler might roll a die and count the number of dots on top.
        2. A quality control officer, working for a company that manufactures radios, might select one radio from inventory (at random) and determine whether it is defective or not defective.
        3. A psychologist might give a Differential Aptitude Test (DAT) and determine a percentile score on the Verbal Reasoning subtest.
    B. A **sample space** is the set of possible outcomes of an experiment.
        1. outcomes for die roll = {1,2,3,4,5,6}
        2. outcomes for quality control = {defective, not defective.}
        3. outcomes for DAT = {1st percentile, 2nd percentile, 3rd percentile...99th percentile}
    C. An **event** is a subset of the sample space. It is usually denoted with a capital letter.
        1. Examples of events for the die roll:
            a. A = roll is a 4 = {4}
            b. B = roll is *at least* a five = {5,6}
            c. C = roll is an odd number = {1,3,5}
            d. D = roll is less than 9 ={1,2,3,4,5,6}

2.   Examples of events for radio quality control:
a.   Q = radio is defective
b.   R = radio is not defective
3.   Examples of events for the DAT (Differential Aptitude Test).
a.   S = score is 85th percentile = {85}.
b.   T = score is at least in the 90th percentile= {90,91,92,93,94,95,96,97,98,99}

D.   We will be interested in the **relative likelihood** of a specified event, say E.
1.   This is called the **probability** of event E.
2.   It denoted P(E) and read as "probability *of* E."
3.   The probability of event B as described earlier as "roll is at least a five" can be written as P(at least a five) or P(5 or 6) or simply P(B).

II.   Methods of determining P(E), read as the probability of an event E.
A.   Intuition
1.   I feel I have a 90% chance of getting the job I applied for.
2.   Lacks a scientific basis.
3.   Not used in statistical studies.
B.   Equally probable outcomes
1.   In the roll of a fair (unloaded) die, the outcomes 1,2,3,4,5,6 are equally probable.
2.   f = number of ways **favorable** to the event $P(E) = \dfrac{f}{n}$
n = **number** of outcomes in the sample space.
3.   Examples:
a. P(roll is a 4) = $\dfrac{1}{6}$
b. P(roll is at least a 5) = $\dfrac{2}{6}$ or $\dfrac{1}{3}$
c. P(roll is less than a 9) = $\dfrac{6}{6}$ = 1

C.   Relative frequency (statistical probability)
1.   From an inventory of 53 radios, 17 were found to be defective. A radio is selected at random. Find the probability it is defective.
f = the count of **favorable** outcomes (In this situation, being defective is a favorable outcome.) $P(E) = \dfrac{f}{n}$
n = **number** of trials in the sample
2.   Let Q=event that radio is defective.
3. $P(Q) = \dfrac{17}{53}$ or .32.

III.   Range of probability values

A.   If an event is *certain* to happen, it is assigned a probability of **1**.

1.   For example: The probability of the event G=roll on a die is less than a 15 = 1. We say P(G) =1.

2.   This happens because there are 6 favorable ways out of 6 outcomes $\frac{6}{6}$ = 1.

B.   If an event is *impossible*, it is assigned a probability of **0**.

1.   For example: Roll a die and let N = roll is a 9. There are 0 favorable ways out of 6 outcomes.

2.   Thus P(roll is a 9)= $\frac{0}{6}$ = 0.

$$0 \le P(E) \le 1$$

C.   All probability values range between 0 and 1 inclusive.

1.   Probability values can *never be negative*.

2.   Probability values can *never be greater than 1*.

IV.   **Complementary events** E'=not E

A.   The complement of an event E is an event denoted E'. This can be read as "not E" or "E complement."

B.   The event E' consists of all the possible outcomes from the sample space which are **not** in event E.

1.   If B = at least a five = 5 or 6= {5,6}
then B' = less than a five = 1 or 2 or 3 or 4 = {1,2,3,4})

2.   If Q = radio is defective, then Q' = radio is not defective.

$$P(E') + P(E) = 1$$

or equivalently,

$$P(E') = 1 - P(E)$$

3.   Thus P(B') = $1 - \frac{2}{6}$ = $\frac{4}{6}$.

4.   P(Q') = $1 - \frac{17}{53}$ = $\frac{53}{53} - \frac{17}{53}$ = $\frac{36}{53}$.

If you prefer to work in decimals, P(Q') = 1 - .32 = .68

Problem Solving Warm-Up

1.   You work in a hospital which must be staffed 7 days a week. Each week, you get one day off which is picked at random by your supervisor. Suppose one day of the week will be randomly picked for next week:

a.   List the sample space

_____

a.   {Mon., Tues., Wed., Thurs., Fri., Sat., Sun.}

b.   List the event A that you will have a day off on the weekend.

_____

b.   A = {Sat., Sun.}

c.   Find the probability that you will have a day off on the weekend.

_____

c. $P(A) = \dfrac{2}{7}$ or $.2857.$

d.   Describe the event "not A".

_____

d.   not A = A' = {Mon., Tues., Wed., Thurs., Fri.}

e.   Find the probability of "not A".

_____

e. $P(\text{not A}) = 1 - \dfrac{2}{7} = \dfrac{5}{7}$ or 1- .2857 = .7143

2.   A spokesperson for United Airlines said there is a growing demand among fliers for special meals (vegetarian, low fat diabetic etc.). Out of 60,000 meals they serve every day, 6,000 are special. A passenger is selected at random and asked what kind of meal he or she ate.

a.   List the sample space

_____

a.   {special meal, not special meal}.

b.   Let B= person orders a special meal. Find P(B).

_____

b. $P(B) = \dfrac{6000}{60000} = \dfrac{1}{10} = .1$

c.   Find P(not B).

_____

c. $P(\text{not B}) = \dfrac{9}{10} = .9$

Thinking About Statistics

A standard deck of cards has 52 cards which are separated into 4 suits: ♠spades, ♡hearts, ◇diamonds and ♣clubs.

Each suit has 13 cards : Ace, 2,3,4,5,6,7,8,9,10, Jack, Queen and King.

♡Hearts and ◇diamonds are red, ♠spades and ♣clubs are black.

Jacks, Queens and Kings are called face cards and are valued at 10 points each. The point value of each other card corresponds to the number on it. An ace is valued at one point.

One card is selected at random from the deck. For each of the following events:
a) Find the probability of that event.
b) Describe the complement of that event.
c) Find the probability of the complement.

1.   H = Card is a heart.
2.   K = Card is a King.
3.   F = Card is a face card.
4.   R = Card is red.
5.   S = The point value of the card is at least a 7.

Selected Solutions Section 4.1

1.   Probability is a measure of the relative likelihood of the occurrence of an event. Probabilities may be assigned by intuition, equally probable outcomes formula or by relative frequency formula for statistical probability.

3.   Since the probability of an event is always between 0 and 1 inclusive, b) 4.1 and h) 150% can**not** be probabilities because they are more than 1. d) -0.5 cannot be a probability since it is a negative number and as such is less than 0.

5.   P(successful removal of port-wine birthmark) = $\frac{33}{35}$ - .94♦
      note f=33 and n=35.

9.   a)   For 6 AM to 12 noon: 290 / 966 = .30,
            For 12 noon to 6 PM   135/966 = .14,
            For 6 PM to 12 Midnight   319 /966 = .33
      and For 12 Midnight to 6 AM   222 /966.= .23♦

      b)   .30 + .14 + .33 + .23 = 1. Yes! This is as it should be since we will assume each inventor responded to only one time interval and all 966 members are counted once in the table. The sample space consists of the 4 listed time intervals. ♦

13.   a) The sample space, consisting of equally likely outcomes if {1, 2, 3, 4, 5, 6}

       b) Assign each of the 6 outcomes a probability of $\frac{1}{6}$.

       $$\frac{1}{6} + \frac{1}{6} + \frac{1}{6} + \frac{1}{6} + \frac{1}{6} + \frac{1}{6} - \frac{6}{6} - 1$$

c) Being successful in getting a number less than 5 on a single throw can be achieved by getting a 1 or a 2 or a 3 or a 4. Since there are 4 ways of being successful out of the six possible ways, the probability is $\frac{4}{6}$.

d) Since there are 2 ways (rolling a 5 or a 6) of being successful out of the 6 possible ways, the probability of getting a 5 or a 6 on a single throw is $\frac{2}{6}$. Since the events in parts c and d are complementary, the probabilities add up to 1.

Answers to Thinking About Statistics

1. a) $P(H) = \frac{13}{52} = \frac{1}{4} = .25$

    b) $H' = $ Card is not a heart $=$ Card is a spade or a club, or a diamond.

    c) $P(H') = 1 - \frac{1}{4} = \frac{3}{4}$.

2. a) $P(K) = \frac{4}{52} = \frac{1}{13} = .0769$.

    b) $K' = $ Not a king $=$ Ace, 2, 3, 4, 5, 6, 7, 8, 9, 10, Jack or Queen.

    c) $P(K') = 1 - \frac{1}{13} = \frac{12}{13} = .9231$.

3. a) $P(F) = \frac{12}{52} = \frac{3}{13} = .2308$.

    b) $F' = $ Not a face card $=$ Ace, 2, 3, 4, 5, 6, 7, 8, 9, or 10.

    c) $P(F') = 1 - \frac{3}{13} = \frac{10}{13}. = .7692$

4. a) $P(R) = \frac{26}{52} = \frac{1}{2} = .5$

    b) $R' = $ not red $=$ black.

    c) $P(R') = 1 - \frac{1}{2} = \frac{1}{2} = .5$

5. a) $P(S) = \frac{28}{52} = \frac{7}{13} = .5385$.

    b) $S' = $ value is less than 7 $=$ Ace, 2, 3, 4, 5 or 6.

    c) $P(S') = 1 - \frac{7}{13} = \frac{6}{13} = .4615$.

Section 4.2
Some Probability Rules-Compound Events
<u>Review</u>

We have seen how to calculate the probability of simple events for a statistical experiment. Compound events are those which combine two or more simple events. Two connectives with which simple events are combined to produce compound events are **AND** and **OR**. It is essential to differentiate between them and to recognize special cases for each.

I.   The AND combination P(A and B)

    A.   Used when we are required to compute the probability of two events which occur together or in sequence. P(A AND B).

    B.   Look for words like AND, BOTH, TOGETHER and phrases which combine two traits like KING OF SPADES (king AND spade), AGGRESSIVE SALESPERSON (aggressive AND salesperson), MALE NURSE (male AND nurse), overworked teacher, paranoid schizophrenic, etc.

    C.   To select the correct formula we must first determine whether the events A and B are independent or dependent.

        1.   Two events A and B are **independent** if the occurrence (or non-occurrence) of event A does **<u>NOT</u>** affect the probability of event B.

        2.   For example: roll a die and flip a coin. A= die is a 4 B= coin is a tail. Whether the die is a 4 or the die is not a 4, $P(B) = \frac{1}{2}$.

            a.   When events are independent, use the simple multiplication rule:

            b.   Calculate P(A), calculate P(B) and **multiply** the two probabilities together.

$$P(A \text{ and } B) = P(A) \cdot P(B)$$

            c.   P(A and B)   = P(4 on die and tail on coin)
$$= P(A) \cdot P(B) = \frac{1}{6} \cdot \frac{1}{2} = \frac{1}{12}$$

        3.   Two events are **dependent** if the occurrence (or non-occurrence) of event A affects the probability of event B.

            a.   In the rule for dependent events , we must examine the probability that event B will occur under the condition that event A has occurred. This is called conditional probability and will be denoted P(B, given A). Some texts use P(B|A) to denote the probability of the occurrence of event B given that event A has occurred.

            b.   For example: in a jar containing 5 red marbles, 3 green and 2 blue you wish to draw 2 marbles without replacing the first before you draw the second. Find the probability that the first marble is red and the second is green.

                (1)   A = first marble is red and

                (2)   B = second marble is green.

P(second marble is green) *depends* on the color of the first marble.

   c.   When events are dependent use the following multiplication rule:

$$P(A \text{ and } B) = P(A) \cdot P(B, \text{ given } A)$$

        (1)   Calculate P(A).
        (2)   Then assume that event A has occurred.
        (3)   Make the necessary adjustments to the sample space and calculate P(B, given A).
        (4)   Multiply these two values.

   d.   P(first marble is red **and** second marble is green).
        (1)   P(first marble is red) = 5 /10 =1/2 =.5.
        (2)   Now assume the red marble has been removed.
        (3)   This leaves the sample space with 4 red 3 green and 2 blue. We calculate getting a green marble in *this* sample space to be 3 / 9. Thus, P(second marble is green, given first marble is red)= 3 / 9.
        (4)   Finally, P(A and B) = $\dfrac{5}{10} \cdot \dfrac{3}{9} = \dfrac{15}{90} = \dfrac{1}{6} = .167$.

   D.   For most AND situations we will have to use intuition to determine whether two events are *independent* (and consequently, which of the two multiplication formulas to use). However, with sufficient information, we can determine whether two events are independent. We know that if two events are independent, P(A and B) = P(A) ·P(B). The converse of this is also true. *If P(A) · P(B) = P(A and B)* **then** the events A and B are independent.

   E.   *When events are independent, P(B) is the same as P(B, given A).* The chances that event B occurs is the same regardless of whether event A has occurred or not. To decide whether two events, A and B are independent:
     1.   Evaluate P(B)
     2.   Evaluate P(B, given A)
     3.   When the two results are equal, the events are independent.
     4.   When the two results are not equal, the events are dependent.

II.   The OR combination P(A or B).

   A.   The question concerns the probability of either of two (or more) events occurring. When we say " A or B" we include the possibility of just A, just B or both A and B.
   B.   Look for key words like OR, EITHER or phrases like AT LEAST ONE.
   C.   To select the correct formula we must first determine whether or not the events A and B are **Mutually Exclusive**.

     1.   A and B are **mutually exclusive** events if they cannot both occur within the

same trial or an experiment.

2.   If A occurs then B can **not** occur and vice-versa.

3.   In other words, the occurrence of event A *excludes* the occurrence of event B.

4.   For example: draw a card from a deck.

    a.   A = card is a ten

    b.   B = card is a king.

    c.   Once we know the card is a ten, it can *not* be a king. Thus the events are mutually exclusive.

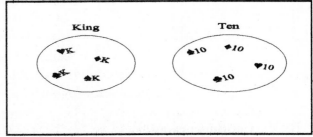

Mutually Exclusive Events

5.   When events are mutually exclusive, use the *simple* addition rule. Find the individual probabilities of A and of B and **add** .

$$P(A\,or\,B) = P(A) + P(B)$$

6.   P(ten or king) = P(ten) + P(king) = $\dfrac{4}{52} + \dfrac{4}{52} = \dfrac{8}{52} = .1538$.

D.   A and B are **non-mutually exclusive** if both events may occur within the same trial of an experiment.

1.   For example: draw a card from a deck

    a.   A = card is a ten

    b.   B = card is a diamond.

    c.   Even though we know the card is a ten, it may or may not be a diamond as well. The events ten and diamond are **not** mutually exclusive.

    d.   Use the addition rule for non-mutually exclusive events.

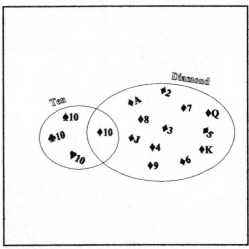

Non-Mutually Exclusive Events

$$P(A\,or\,B) = P(A) + P(B) - P(A\,and\,B)$$

        (1)   Calculate the individual probabilities of A and of B.

        (2)   Calculate the probability of "A and B".

        (3)   Add the probability of A to the probability of B and *subtract*

71

the probability that they both occur, P(A and B).

(4)   P(ten or diamond) = P(ten) + P(diamond) - P(ten and diamond) = $\frac{4}{52} + \frac{13}{52} - \frac{1}{52} = \frac{16}{52} = .3077$.

(5)   There are 16 cards out of the total of 52 which are *either* a ten or a diamond or both. Note that one card, the ten of diamonds is counted in the "ten" category as well as in the "diamond" category. In order not to count it twice, we subtract.

6.   *When events are mutually exclusive, P(A and B) =0*. The probability that both events occur together is 0.

III.   **Contingency tables**

   A.   When each respondent is cross-referenced by two traits, the data can be displayed in a contingency table.

   B.   The following is a result of a market research opinion poll, testing the reaction of people to Flakey Cereal in supermarkets in three different cities. People taste tested Flakey Cereal and answered the question "Would you buy Flakey Cereal?"

   C.

	Fort Worth	Dallas	Chicago	Row Totals
Yes (Y)	100	150	150	400
No (N)	125	130	95	350
Undecided (U)	75	170	5	250
Column totals	300	450	250	1000

1.   Responses to question are listed by rows.
2.   Locations are listed by column(up and down).
3.   There are 9 cells in which the number of respondents is recorded.
4.   The last column contains the total for each row
5.   The last row contains the total for each column.
6.   Notice that in the lower right corner, row total=column total.

D.   To answer a simple probability question

   1. $P(A) =$ <u>total in row with trait A</u>

                     total in sample

or

   2. $P(B) =$ <u>total in column with trait B</u>

                     total in sample

E.   To answer a probability question with the AND combination, locate trait A and locate trait B.

   1.   If one trait is in a row and one is in a column, there will be a cell where the two traits intersect.

   2. $P(A \text{ and } B) =$ <u>number in the intersecting cell</u>

                     total in sample

   3.   If both traits are in rows or both traits are in columns then there is no intersecting cell and $P(A \text{ and } B) = 0$.

   4.   If you prefer using a formula, you must use the one for dependent events, since you usually do not know whether the traits are independent or dependent. *It's easier to answer the question directly from the table.*

F.   To answer a probability question with the OR combination.

   1.   If both traits are in rows or both traits are in columns, the events A and B are mutually exclusive. To compute $P(A \text{ or } B)$ add the total in row A to the total in row B then divide this by the total in the sample. Likewise, if both traits are in columns, add the total in column A to the total in column B and divide this by the total in the sample. Your result will be the same if you use the formula $P(A \text{ or } B) = P(A) + P(B)$.

   2.   If one trait is in a row and the other is in a column, then the traits are *not* mutually exclusive. In this case to compute $P(A \text{ or } B)$, add the total of row A to the total of column B and *subtract the number in the intersecting cell.* Divide this result by the total in the sample. Your result will be the same if you use the formula: $P(A \text{ or } B) = P(A) + P(B) - P(A \text{ and } B)$.

G.   **Conditional probability** $P(B, \text{ given } A)$

   1.   To answer a question such as find the probability that the person is from Dallas, GIVEN the person responded no, you need only consider the row of respondents who answered no. (Since a NO response is given, we are no longer concerned with people who had other responses.) The revised sample space looks like:

	Ft. Worth	Dallas	Chicago	row total
No (N)	125	130	95	350

P(Dallas, given No) = $\frac{130}{350}$ = number in cell in "No" row which are from Dallas divided by the total who responded "No".

2.   To find the probability that a person responded No GIVEN that the person is from Dallas, we need only consider the column of responses from Dallas.

	Dallas
yes	150
no	130
undecided	170
column total	450

P(no, given Dallas) = $\frac{130}{450}$. The number in the Dallas column who responded no divided by the total in the Dallas column.

H.   Common phrases
1.   **"Neither"** means not A <u>and</u> not B. When events are independent then P(neither A or B) =P(not A)·P(not B).   Remember that P(not A)= 1-P(A).
2.   **"None"** means not any and applies to a situation where there are more than two events. When events are independent, P(none) = P(not A)· P(not B) ·P(not C) etc.
3.   **"At least one"** means one or <u>more</u>. When a problem has two events A and B then at least one means A or B or both and the complement of "at least one" is "neither". When a problem has more than two events, the complement of "at least one" is "none".
     a.   P(at least one) = 1 - P(neither) for two events.
     b.   P(at least one) = 1 - P(none) for more than two events.

Problem Solving Warm-Up

For each problem
a)   Determine what the events are.
b)   Decide whether to use the "and" combination, the "or" combination or the complement rule.
c)   Before choosing the correct formula, ask one of the following questions:
    1. For the AND combination: ARE THE EVENTS INDEPENDENT?
    2. For the OR combination: ARE THE EVENTS MUTUALLY EXCLUSIVE?
d)   Answer the question from part c and write down the appropriate formula.
e)   Finally, answer the probability question.

For problems 1-3:   Two marbles are drawn without replacement from a bowl containing 7 red, 4 blue and 9 yellow marbles.

1.   What is the probability that both are red?

_____

a)   Events are: A=first is red
                            B=second is red.
b)   This is an "and" combination (the first is red AND the second is red.)
c)   To determine the correct formula, we need to know "are the events independent or dependent?"
d)   The events are <u>dependent</u> since the first marble is not replaced before the second marble is drawn.
e)   Using the formula
        P(A and B) = P(A)·P(B, given A)
        P(First is red)= 7/20
        P(Second is red, given first is red) = 6/19 (since one red marble is gone leaving 6 reds out of a new total of 19.

P(**both** are red)= $\frac{7}{20} \cdot \frac{6}{19} = \frac{21}{190} = .1105$.

2.   What is the probability neither is red?

_____

This is an AND combination translating to the first is not red and the second is not red.
Are the events independent? No, since the first marble is not replaced before drawing the second.   P(first marble is not red)=13 / 20.
P(second marble is not red, given the first is not red) = 12 / 19.
Using the multiplication rule we get
P(neither is red)= $\frac{13}{20} \cdot \frac{12}{19} = \frac{39}{95} = .4105$.

3.   What is the probability at least one is red?

        _____

The complement to "at least one" is "neither". We can use the complement rule and get P(at least one is red) =1-P(neither is red)= $1-\frac{39}{95}=\frac{95}{95}-\frac{39}{95}=\frac{56}{95}$.

We could also compute 1-.4105 = .5895 and get an equivalent answer.

For problems 4-6: A card is drawn from a standard deck of 52 cards. (See section 4.1, Thinking About Statistics for a description of a standard deck.)

4.   What is the probability it is a 4 or a 5?

        _____

The events are:
A = card is a 4;   B = card is a 5.
This is an OR combination.
Are the events mutually exclusive? Yes, since a card cannot be both a 4 and a 5 at the same time.
Use the simple addition rule.
P(A or B) = P(A) +P(B)
$P(4\ or\ 5) = \frac{4}{52}+\frac{4}{52}=\frac{8}{52}=\frac{2}{13}=.1538$

5.   What is the probability it is neither a four or a five.

        _____

This is the complement to problem 4. The card is NOT a "4 or 5". $1-\frac{2}{13}=\frac{11}{13}=.8461$.

6.   Find the probability it is a 4 or it is red

        _____.

This is an OR combination.
Are the events mutually exclusive? No, since a card can be a 4 as well as red at the same time.
Use the addition rule to compute as follows:
P(A or B)=P(A)+P(B) -P(A and B)
P(A)=4 / 52 and P(B)=26/ 52
P(A and B)=2 /52 (2 red 4's).
$P(4\ or\ red)= \frac{4}{52}+\frac{26}{52}-\frac{2}{52}=\frac{28}{52}=.5385$.

For problems 7-9: Two dice are rolled and the sum of the dice is noted.

7.   What is the probability the sum is a 7 or 11?

This is an OR combination.
Are the events mutually exclusive? Yes, since a roll cannot be both a 7 and an 11 at the same

_____

time. Use the simple addition rule: P(A or B)= P(A) +P(B).

Thus P(7 or 11)= $\frac{6}{36} + \frac{2}{36} = \frac{8}{36} = .2222$.

8. What is the probability it is at least a ten.

_____

This is an OR combination. At least a ten means 10 OR 11 OR 12. These three outcomes are mutually exclusive, so we may add their probabilities. P(at least a ten) = $\frac{3}{36} + \frac{2}{36} + \frac{1}{36} = \frac{6}{36} = .1667$

9. What is the probability the sum is less than a ten?

_____

This is the complement to problem 8. P(less than a ten)=1 -P(at least a ten) = $1 - \frac{6}{36} = \frac{30}{36}$. In decimals, 1-.1667 = .8333.

For problems 10-12:   At Studymore University 46% of the students are female and 13% of the females are psychology majors. 9% of all the students are psychology majors. A student is picked at random.

10. Find the probability that the person is a female psychology major.

_____

This is an AND combination. Are the events independent? NO, since the probability of being a psychology major among females (.13) is different than the probability of being a psychology major among all students(.09). .09 ≠ .13

P(female and psychology major) = P(female)·P(psychology major, given female) =(.46)(.13)=.0598

11. Find the probability the person is a female or a psychology major.

_____

This is the OR combination. Are events mutually exclusive? No since a person can be in both categories. P(female or psychology major)=P(female) + P(psychology major)-P(female psychology major)= .46+.09-.0598 = .4902

77

For problems 12-17:   Use the contingency table below to answer the questions.
Respondents in three cities were asked whether they would buy a new breakfast cereal that was being taste tested.

	Fort Worth	Dallas	Chicago	Row Totals
Yes (Y)	100	150	150	400
No (N)	125	130	95	350
Undecided (U)	75	170	5	250
Column totals	300	450	250	1000

12.   What is the probability a person responded yes?

Total in YES row =400 and total in sample=1000. Answer: $\frac{400}{1000}$ = .4

13.   What is the probability the person is from Dallas?

Total in Dallas row = 450 and total in sample =1000. Ans. $\frac{450}{1000}$ = .45

14.   What is the probability the person responded yes and is from Dallas?

Categories intersect. The number in the intersecting cell is 150. Ans. $\frac{150}{1000}$ = .15 .

15.   What is the probability the person responded yes or is from Chicago?

Categories are not mutually exclusive. Answer=.4 + .45 - .15 =.7. There are 450 from Dallas and 400 who responded yes, however 150 of these are in both categories leaving 700 individuals in Dallas or responding yes. 700 / 1000=.7

16.   What is the probability the person responded yes given they are from Dallas?.

Only refer to the Dallas column. Answer: 150 /450=.33

17.   What is the probability the person is from Dallas given they responded yes?   Only refer to the yes row. Ans. $\frac{150}{400} = .375$.

_____

Thinking About Statistics

1. When answering an AND combination with a formula (multiplication rules) it is essential to know whether or not the events are INDEPENDENT.

P(A AND B) Are events Independent?

P(A OR B) Are events Mutually Exclusive?

When answering an OR combination (addition rules) it is essential to know whether or not events are MUTUALLY EXCLUSIVE.

When answering an OR combination, it is NOT necessary to know whether events are independent or dependent, only if whether they are mutually exclusive or not.

Consider the following events.

M = A person is male.
B = A person has brown eyes.
N = A person is a full time nurse.
E = A person is less than 8 years old.

ARE THE EVENTS INDEPENDENT ?

	Male	Brown Eyes	Nurse
Brown Eyes		▨	▨
Nurse			▨
Under 8			

ARE THE EVENTS MUTUALLY EXCLUSIVE?

	Male	Brown Eyes	Nurse
Brown Eyes		▨	▨
Nurse			▨
Under 8			

From the list of events:

a) Find two events which are mutually exclusive.

b) Find two events which are non-mutually exclusive.

c) Find two events which are independent.

d) Find two events which are not independent (they are dependent).

e) Find two events which are independent as well as mutually exclusive.

f) Find two events which are non-mutually exclusive and are also dependent.

g) Find two events which are non-mutually exclusive and are also independent.

h) Two events which are mutually exclusive must be dependent. Why?

2. When using a contingency table, the probability of events A and B both occurring is given by:

P(A and B) = <u>number in the intersecting cell</u>.

total in sample

Explain why this is equivalent to the formula for

P(A and B) when events are dependent.

$$P(A\ and\ B) = P(A) \cdot P(B,\ given\ A)$$

Selected Solutions Section 4.2

1. a) OR combination. The outcomes are mutually exclusive since a candy cannot be both orange and tan (i.e. each candy is only one color).
        Answer .15 +.05 = .20♦

    b) Outcomes are mutually exclusive. Answer .20 +.20 =.40 ♦

    c) Complement rule: 1-.30 = .70 ♦

    You could also use the direct method by saying "not brown" = orange OR green OR red OR yellow OR tan. Then the probability of not brown (since these categories are mutually exclusive)=.15 + .10 +.20 +.20 +.05 = .70 ♦

3. a) OR combination- Events are Non-mutually exclusive.
        A card *can* be both an ace and a heart at the same time.
        P(Ace or heart)=P(Ace) + P(heart) - P(ace of hearts)= $\frac{4}{52} + \frac{13}{52} - \frac{1}{52} = \frac{16}{52}$ = .3077 ♦

    b) OR combination-events are not mutually exclusive since a card can be both a heart and red at the same time.
        P (heart or red) =P(heart) +P(red) -P(heart and red) = $\frac{13}{52} + \frac{26}{52} - \frac{13}{52} = \frac{26}{52}$ = .5.♦

    c) OR The events are mutually exclusive since a card cannot be both a 2 as well as a 10.

        P(2 or 10) = $\frac{4}{52} + \frac{4}{52} = \frac{8}{52}$ = .1538 .♦

    d) Complement rule: 1-P(diamond) = $1 - \frac{13}{52} = \frac{39}{52}$ = .75

5. a) The outcomes on the two dice are independent since the outcome on the green die does not affect the outcome on the red one. In an AND combination, we will use the simple multiplication rule.

    b) P(5 on green die) · P(3 on red die)= $\frac{1}{6} \cdot \frac{1}{6} = \frac{1}{36}$ = .0278 ♦

    c) P(3 on green die) · P(5 on red die)= $\frac{1}{6} \cdot \frac{1}{6} = \frac{1}{36}$ = .0278 ♦

    d) The overall question is an OR combination. The events are mutually exclusive so we can add the probabilities. P(5 on green die and 3 on red die) + P(3 on red die and 5 on green die) = $\frac{1}{36} + \frac{1}{36} = \frac{2}{36}$ = .0555 ♦

7. a) First compute the ways of getting a 6. We will write P(1 on first die and 5 on second) as P(1,5). the ordered pairs which are ways you can add up to 6 on a die are (1,5) (2,4) (3,3) (4,2) and (5,1). There are 5 ways to get a six out of 36.
        P(sum is a 6)=5 / 36 =.1389 ♦
        Note that to a statistician, the ordered pair (2,4) is different from the ordered pair (4,2). (To a gambler it is not.)

    b) Sum of 4 happens on (1,3) (2,2) and (3,1). Thus there are three ways out of 36 to roll a sum of 4.

P(sum is 4)=3 / 36 = .08333 ♦

c) This is an OR combination. The outcomes of sum of a 4 and sum of a 6 on the same roll are mutually exclusive.

P(sum is 4 or 6)= $\frac{5}{36} + \frac{3}{36} = \frac{8}{36} = .2162$ ♦

9. a) This is an AND combination. The events of drawing the first card and drawing the second are *not* independent, since the first card is not replaced in the deck after it is drawn. ♦

b) The probability of drawing a king on the second card *depends* on what happened on the first. When drawing the first card there are 4 aces out of 52. P(ace on first card) = 4 / 52. We assume that the first card is an ace. Since we do not replace the ace that was drawn, we have 51 cards left and 4 of them are kings. P(king on second card, given ace on the first) = 4 / 51.   Answer $\frac{4}{52} \cdot \frac{4}{51} = \frac{4}{663} = .0060$ ♦

c) In this situation the order is reversed, though analysis is the same as in part a). The Answer is $\frac{4}{663} = .0060$ ♦

d) This is an OR combination where the outcomes are mutually exclusive, so we add $\frac{4}{663} + \frac{4}{663} = \frac{8}{663}$. Or using the decimal equivalents .0060 +.0060 = .0120 ♦

11. a) When the first card is replaced, the outcomes are independent. It doesn't matter which card is drawn for the first action since it's replaced before the second action occurs.

b) P(ace on first card)=4/52 P(king on second card)=4 / 52. Using the multiplication rule for the AND combination we multiply to get: $\frac{4}{52} \cdot \frac{4}{52} = \frac{1}{169} = .0059$ ♦

c) P(King on first card AND Ace on second) = $\frac{4}{52} \cdot \frac{4}{52} = \frac{1}{169} = .0059$ ♦

d) P(Ace and King in either order) = $\frac{1}{169} + \frac{1}{169} = \frac{2}{169} = .0118$ ♦

13. a) OR combination. Since all categories are mutually exclusive (no child is represented by more than one age category) add 27% + 14% + 22% = 63% ♦

b) OR combination. Adding the probabilities of the categories, we get 15% +22% + 27% +14% = 78%. An easier method is to use the rule of complementary events. That is the probability of *not* being 12 years or younger is being 13 or over. The probability of being 13 or over is 22%. So the probability of *not* being 13 and over is 1-22% = 78%.♦

c) OR combination. Add the probability of being in the 6-9 year category to that of being in the 10-12 year category to get 27% + 14% = 41%. ♦

d) OR combination with mutually exclusive categories. Add 22% + 27% = 49%. ♦

If the category for 'children' goes to age 18, then there are more 'children' in the 6 year span including 13-18 years than there are in the three year span 10-12 years. ♦

17. First let's symbolize the given information:

P(person wears eyeglasses) = 56%.

P(Person wears contacts) = 3.6%

P(woman, given wears glasses) = 55.4%

P(man, given wears contacts) = 44.6%

P(woman, given wears contacts) =63.1%

P(man, given wears contacts) = 36.9%

a) Translate to "a woman ***and*** wears glasses". Use the multiplication rule and multiple P(person wears eyeglasses) times P(woman, given wears glasses) = (56%)(55.4%) = (.56)(.554) = .31 or 31%. ♦

b) Translate to "a man ***and*** wears glasses". Use the multiplication rule and multiple P(person wears eyeglasses) times P(man, given wears glasses) = (56%)(44.6%) = (.56)(.446) = .25 or 25%. ♦

c) Translate to "a woman ***and*** wears contacts". Multiply P(wears contacts) times P(woman, given wears contacts = 3.6% 63.1% = (.036)(.631) = .02 = 2%.♦

d) Translate to "a man ***and*** wears contacts".multiply P(wears contacts) P(man, given wears contacts. = 3.6% 36.9% = (.036)(.369) = .01 = 1%.♦

e) First compute P(person wears contacts or glasses). In this problem we are asked to assume that they are mutually exclusive since it says assume no one wears both glasses and contacts. Adding the probabilities 56% + 3.6% = 59.6% of the population wears either glasses or contacts. Now use the complement rule to find the probability that the person does not wear either: 100% - 59.6% or 40.4%, or (in decimal form) 1 - .596 = .404 ♦

21.

	Favor Fa	Neutral N	Oppose O	Row total
Students S	353	75	191	619
Faculty F	11	5	18	34
Column total	364	80	209	653

a)   P(Fa) = $\dfrac{\text{total in Fa column}}{\text{total in sample}}$ = $\dfrac{364}{653}$ =.5574 ♦

P(Fa, given F)is computed by just examining the F row.

	Favor FA	Neutral N	Oppose O	row total
Faculty F	11	5	18	34

Number in faculty who are in Favor = 11. Total Faculty =34. P(Fa, given F) = $\dfrac{11}{34}$ ‑ .3235♦

In the same manner, examine the row of Students. The number of students who favor is 353 and the total number of students is 619. P(Fa, given S) = $\frac{353}{619}$ = .5703 ♦

b) from the table:

$$P(F \text{ and } Fa) = \frac{number\ in\ both\ F\ column\ and\ Fa\ row}{total\ number\ in\ sample} = \frac{11}{653} = .0168$$

To compute by formula ***assume the variables are not independent***:

$$P(F \text{ and } Fa) = P(F) \times P(Fa, given\ F) = \frac{34}{653} \times \frac{11}{34} = \frac{11}{653}$$

c)   If the events are independent P(Fa)=P(Fa, given F).. We have computed P(Fa) = 364/ 653 = .5574   and P(Fa, given F) = 11 /34 =.3235

Since .5574 ≠ .3235, the events are not independent, they are dependent events. ♦

d)   P(S, given O) Of those who responded "Opposed", what's the probability one is a student?

$$\frac{Number\ of\ Students\ in\ column\ O}{total\ in\ O\ column} = \frac{191}{209} = .9139 ♦$$

P(S, given N)= $\frac{number\ of\ students\ in\ N\ column}{total\ number\ in\ N\ column} = \frac{75}{80} = .9375 ♦$

e)   P(S and Fa) = $\frac{number\ in\ cell\ where\ S\ row\ intersects\ Fa\ column}{total\ number\ in\ the\ sample}$

$$= \frac{353}{653} = .5406 ♦$$

P(S and O) = $\frac{191}{653}$ = .2925 ♦

f)   P(S) = $\frac{number\ in\ row\ S}{total\ in\ sample} = \frac{619}{653} = .9479 ♦$

P(S, given Fa) $= \frac{number\ of\ students\ in\ Fa\ column}{total\ number\ in\ Fa\ column} = \frac{353}{364} = .9698 ♦$

since .9479 ≠ .9698 the events are *not independent*, they are dependent.

g)   Fa and O are mutually exclusive events. A person cannot be both in the favor column as well as the oppose column. Therefore we can use the simple addition rule and compute: P(Fa or O) = $\frac{364}{653} + \frac{209}{653} = \frac{573}{653}$ = .8775 ♦

25a)   P(A) = $\frac{total\ number\ in\ column\ A}{total\ in\ sample} = \frac{697}{1153} = .6045$ ♦

P(A, given G) = $\dfrac{\text{Number in A that are also in row G}}{\text{Number in row G}}$ = $\dfrac{406}{511}$ = .7945 ♦

P(A, given D) = $\dfrac{\text{Number in A that are also in row D}}{\text{number in row D}}$ = $\dfrac{291}{642}$ = .4533 ♦

b) P(B) = $\dfrac{\text{total number in column B}}{\text{total in sample}}$ = . $\dfrac{456}{1153}$ = .3955 ♦

P(B, given G) = $\dfrac{\text{Number in B that are also in row G}}{\text{number in row G}}$ = $\dfrac{105}{511}$ = .2055 ♦

P(B, given D) = $\dfrac{\text{Number in B that are also in row D}}{\text{number in row D}}$ = $\dfrac{351}{642}$ = .5467 ♦

c)   P (G) = $\dfrac{\text{total number in row G}}{\text{total in sample}}$ = $\dfrac{511}{1153}$ = .4432 ♦

P(G, given A) = $\dfrac{\text{Number in G that are also in column A}}{\text{number in column A}}$ = $\dfrac{406}{697}$ = .5811 ♦

P(G, given B) = $\dfrac{\text{Number in G that are also in column B}}{\text{number in column B}}$ = $\dfrac{105}{456}$ = .2303 ♦

d)   P (D) = $\dfrac{\text{total number in row D}}{\text{total in sample}}$ = $\dfrac{642}{1153}$ = .5568 ♦

P(D, given A) = $\dfrac{\text{Number in D that are also in column A}}{\text{number in column A}}$ = $\dfrac{291}{697}$ = .4175 ♦

P(D, given B) = $\dfrac{\text{Number in D that are also in column B}}{\text{number in column B}}$ = $\dfrac{351}{456}$ = .7697 ♦

e)   From the table: P(G and A) = $\dfrac{\text{Number cell in row G and Column A}}{\text{Total in sample}}$ = $\dfrac{406}{1153}$ = .3521 ♦

Or, using the multiplication rule for dependent events:

P(G and A) = P(G)× P(A, given G) = $(\dfrac{511}{1153})(\dfrac{406}{511})$ = $\dfrac{406}{1153}$ = .3521 ♦

To compute P(D or B) use the addition formula for events that are not mutually exclusive . Don't forget to subtract P(D and B) so that the college dropouts from below upper middle income level are not counted twice.

P(D or B) = P(D) + P(B) - P(D and B) = $\dfrac{642}{1153}$ + $\dfrac{456}{1153}$ - $\dfrac{351}{1153}$ = $\dfrac{747}{1153}$ = .6479 ♦

f)   The events are not independent. P(G) is not equal to P(G, given A).

g)   The events B and D are not mutually exclusive since there are 351 people in the sample that belong to both categories. (Being in the below upper middle income bracket does not exclude a person from being a college dropout.) ◆

27.   A = grosses over 93,000 in first year
       B = grosses over 93,000 in second year

a)   P(A)=P(profit in the first year) = .65 = P(A). ◆

b)   P(B)=P(profit in the second year)= .71 = P(B). ◆

c)   P(B, given A) =P(profit in second year, given profit in first year) = .87 ◆

d)   AND combination. Are events independent? No the events are not independent since P(B)= .71 but P(B, given A) =.87. We use the multiplication rule, but be careful which factors to choose. P(A and B) =.65 · .87 = .5655◆

e)   OR combination. Are events mutually exclusive? No since a store can be *both* successful in the first year as well as in the second year.
      P(A or B) = P(A) + P(B) -P(A and B)= .65 +.71 -.5655= .7945. ◆

      Be sure to subtract P(A and B) thus accounting for the stores that were successful in the first year AND in the second.
      Note that if you do not subtract, you will get an answer which is more than 1.

f)   P(store will not be closed after two years) = .7945 ◆
      Using the rule for complementary events: P(store will be closed after two years)
      = 1- P(store will not be closed after two years) = 1-.7945 = .2055. ◆

29.   From the given information we know:
       a)P(A) = 8% b)P(B) = 8% and c) P(B, given A) = 23% ◆
       d) to find P(A and B) use the multiplication rule for dependent events. (We know the events are dependent since P(B) is not equal to P(B, given A)).
       P(A and B) = P(A) × P(B, given A) = (.08) (.23) = .0184◆
       e) to find P(A or B) use the addition formula for non-mutually exclusive events. We know the events are not mutually exclusive because there are customers who make claims in the first and in the second year. P(A or B) = .08 + .08 -.0184 = .1416 ◆

31.   In a medical test, a result of "positive" indicates that you have the disease being tested for, and a result of "negative" indicates that you do not have the disease. Most tests, however can give erroneous answers and for example, a person who actually does not have a disease, can have a positive result on a test. This is sometimes called a false positive.

P(Positive test, given a person has TB) = .82   (a true positive)

P(Positive test, given a person does not have TB) =.09 (there is a 9% chance of a false positive.)

P(TB) = .04 (note that the events of having TB and testing positive are dependent.)

a)   P(have TB and a positive test) = P(TB) ·P(positive test, given TB) =(.04)·(.82) = .0328 ♦

b)   Using complement rule P(not TB) = 1- P(TB)=1-.04=.96♦

c)   P(Not TB and a positive test)=P(not TB) · P(positive test, given person does not have TB) =(.96)(.09) = .0864 ♦

Answers to Thinking About Statistics

ARE THE EVENTS INDEPENDENT?

	Male	Brown Eyes	Nurse
Brown Eyes	yes		
Nurse	no	yes	
Under 8	yes	yes	no

ARE THE EVENTS MUTUALLY EXCLUSIVE?

	Male	Brown Eyes	Nurse
Brown Eyes	no		
Nurse	no	no	
Under 8	no	no	yes

From the list of events:
a)   Being a full time nurse and being less than 8 years old are mutually exclusive.
b)   Being male and having brown eyes are non-mutually exclusive.
      Being male and being a full time nurse are non-mutually exclusive.

Having brown eyes and being less than 8 years old are non-mutually exclusive.

c)   Being male and having brown eye are independent.

Being male and being less than 8 years old are independent.

d)   Being male and being a full time nurse are not independent (dependent).

A person is a full time nurse and being less than 8 years old are not independent.

e)   None, if events are mutually exclusive, they must be dependent.

f)   Being male and being a full time nurse are non-mutually exclusive and are also dependent. (The categories are non-mutually exclusive since there are male nurses. However, at this time there are fewer male nurses in the population than female nurses.)

g)   Having brown eyes and being less than 8 years old are non-mutually exclusive and are also independent.

h)   Two events which are mutually exclusive must be dependent. If two events are mutually exclusive they can not both occur in the same trial hence, P(A and B) =0. When events are independent P(A and B) = P(A) ·P(B).

But, generally, P(A) · P(B) ≠ 0.

P(A and B) ≠ P(A)· P(B) so events which are mutually exclusive MUST be dependent.

2. The formula for computing the probability of A and B occurring, when A and B are dependent events is: P(A and B) = P(A) P(B, given A).

In a contingency table:

$$P(A) = \frac{Total\ in\ row\ A}{Total\ in\ sample}$$

and $$P(B, given\ A) = \frac{Number\ in\ cell\ intersecting\ row\ A\ and\ column\ B}{Total\ in\ row\ A}.$$

Multiplying the two probabilities together, we get:

$$\frac{Total\ in\ row\ A}{Total\ in\ sample} \times \frac{Number\ in\ cell\ intersecting\ row\ A\ and\ column\ B}{Total\ in\ row\ A}$$

And, after cancelling the factor "Total in row A", we then get.

$$\frac{Number\ in\ cell\ intersecting\ row\ A\ and\ column\ B}{Total\ in\ sample}$$

Section 4.3
Trees and Counting Techniques

Review

As we have seen, formulas for probability involve <u>counting</u> the number of favorable outcomes to an event and <u>counting</u> the total number of outcomes. To compute the probability of an event, we then divide the number of favorable outcomes by the total number of outcomes. Methods of counting are described below:

I.   **Tree diagram** (Used to illustrate sequential actions.)

    A.   Start from a point ● at the left of your diagram and draw as many lines (branches) as there are choices for the first action.

    B.   From the point at the end of each 1st level branch draw as many branches as there are ways the second action can be done.

    C.   From the point at the end of each 2nd level branch, construct as many branches as there are choices for a 3rd action etc. Continue for as many actions specified.

    D.   The number of branches which are furthest to the right corresponds to the number of ways the sequential acts can be performed in **specified order.** They may now be listed.

    E.   To compute the probability for each specified outcome:

        1.   Compute at the first level, the probability of the act occurring in that specific way.

        2.   Move along that branch to the right but when you get to the second level branch, you must take into account whatever action is indicated on the first level of that particular branch.

        3.   At this stage, you will be computing a *conditional* probability. The probability of being on the second level of the particular branch GIVEN that the action described in the first branch occurred.

        4.   Continue with conditional probabilities until you reach the right most branch of that sequence.

        5.   To compute the probability of the specified act, *multiply* the probabilities along the branch.

    F.   Repeat the steps in E. for each branch of your tree, and compute the probability of each sequential outcome. *The sum of these probabilities will always be 1.*

II.   The **multiplication rule of counting**

    A.   Used to determine the number of ways two or more actions can occur **in a sequence**.

    B.   If the first action can be done in 5 ways and the 2nd action can be done in 3 ways, the first action AND the second action can be performed in sequence $5 \cdot 3 = 15$ ways.

        1.   Think of the branches of a tree diagram. There will be 5 branches drawn from the starting point and then for **each** of the 5 branches, there will be 3 branches drawn from it. This will give a total of 15 branches.

2.   For example: There are 5 courses you can select for a 9 am class and 3 courses for a 10 am class. You can select a 9 am class and *then* a 10 am class in 15 ways.

C.   Suppose a first action can be performed in 4 ways, a second action in 7 ways and a third in 2 ways.

    1.   Using the multiplication rule the first action AND the second action AND the third action can be performed in 4·7·2=56 ways.

    2.   Note if you were to construct a tree diagram, you would have 56 branches at the right.

    3.   For example: In the restaurant where you work there are 4 choices for soup, 7 choices for a main course and 2 choices for desert. A patron who eats there every night, would like to know how many different meals he could have. The answer is 4· 7 · 2 = 56.

III.   Counting the number of ways to **arrange** a set of n members.

A.   Your first choice can be made in n ways. That is, you can choose <u>any</u> of the n members of the set.

B.   The first member that was selected is removed , so you can make your second choice in (n-1) ways.

C.   Now 2 choices have been removed, so the third choice can be made in (n-2) ways and so on until you get to the last choice which can be made in only 1 way (the way that is left after the others have been removed).

D.   Using the multiplication rule, since you are making a first choice AND a second choice AND a third choice etc., the actions can be performed in sequence
    $n(n-1)(n-2)...(1)$ ways.

E.   The product obtained from all the integers 1 to n is called "n factorial" and is denoted n!. Many calculators have a key x! which will compute this function. *Therefore, the number of ways n objects can be arranged in order is n!*

F.   How many ways can 7 different books be arranged on a shelf?   Answer:7! = 7·6·5·4·3·2·1 = 5040.

G.   How many ways can 6 people be ranked in order? Answer: 6!= 6·5·4·3·2·1· = 720 ways.

H.   For convenience, we <u>define</u> 0! = 1.

IV.   Sometimes we want to determine how many ways we can choose and arrange not a whole set, but a specified number of members from that set.

A.   For example: We have 7 books and wish to select 3 to be read in order (1st, 2nd and 3rd book to be read.) How many ways can this be done?

    1.   We could use the multiplication rule which says we have 7 choices for the first book, 6 choices for the 2nd book and 5 choices for the third book so we have 7·6·5 = 210 choices to read 3 of the 7 books in order.

2.   The number of ways that r (being a whole number which is less than or equal to n) elements out of a set of n elements can be arrange is called a PERMUTATION of n objects using r. This is denoted as $P_{n,r}$ where n gives the total number in the set and r gives how many you are using.

$$P_{n,r} = \frac{n!}{(n-r)!}$$

a. $P_{7,3} = \dfrac{7!}{(7-3)!} = \dfrac{7!}{4!} = \dfrac{7 \cdot 6 \cdot 5 \cdot 4 \cdot 3 \cdot 2 \cdot 1 \cdot}{4 \cdot 3 \cdot 2 \cdot 1} = 210$

b. $P_{9,3} = \dfrac{9!}{(9-3)!} = \dfrac{9!}{6!} = 504$

There are also situations for which we wish to determine the number of ways an r-member subset can be formed from a set with n members. In this situation, *the order of selection is immaterial.*

B.   This is called a **combination** of n elements using r and is denoted $C_{n,r}$.

1.   There are 10 people in a club. We wish to know how many ways we can select a committee (where order does not matter) consisting of 4 people. n=10, r=4 and we compute :

$$C_{n,r} = \frac{n!}{r!(n-r)!}$$

$$C_{10,4} = \frac{(10!)}{4!(10-4)!} = \frac{10!}{4!6!} = 210$$

Problem Solving Warm-Up

Calculate the number of ways each of the following can be done. Then answer the corresponding probability question.

1.   Your company routes all materials from N.Y. to Chicago, then from Chicago to Denver and then from Denver to L.A. There are 4 routes from N.Y. to Chicago, 6 routes from Chicago to Denver and 3 routes from Denver to L.A. How many possible routes are there from N.Y. to L.A.? What is the probability that one specified route is taken?

1.   Use the multiplication principle.

Since there are 4 ways to perform the first action and 6 ways to perform the second and 3 ways to perform the third, there are $4 \cdot 6 \cdot 3$ = 72 possible routes.

The probability that one specified route is taken is $\dfrac{1}{72}$ = .0139 .

2.   You are supervisor of nurses and have 12 nurses working for you. In how many ways can you choose 4 to have the weekend off? What is the probability that 4 specific individuals will have the weekend off?

_____

_____

2.   In this problem, the order does not matter, so we will use a combination. n=12, r=4

$$C_{12,4} = \frac{12!}{4!(12-4)!} \quad \frac{12!}{4!8!} = 495$$

The probability that 4 specific individuals will have the weekend off is 1/ 495=.0020, since you are only interested in one specific combination of four people, from 495 possible combinations.

3.   You are still in charge of 12 nurses and must assign one to be head of the first floor ward, one to be head of the second floor ward, one for the third floor and one for the fourth. In how many ways can this be done. What is the probability that the assignments are made in one specified order?

_____

The order of assignments is significant, so we must use a permutation formula to count the number of ways. n=12, r=4

$$P_{12,4} = \frac{12!}{(12-4)!} = \frac{12!}{8!} = 11880.$$

The probability that the assignment is given in one specified order is $\frac{1}{11880} = .00008$.

Thinking About Statistics

Why is the name "combination lock" a misnomer?

Selected Solutions Section 4.3

1. When you flip a coin three times, there are 8 sequences that can occur. These are shown in the tree diagram.

b) There are 3 of the sequence in which there are <u>exactly</u> 2 heads. HHT, HTH and THH.

c) The probability that you will get exactly 2 heads when you toss a coin 3 times is $\frac{3}{8}$ = .375♦

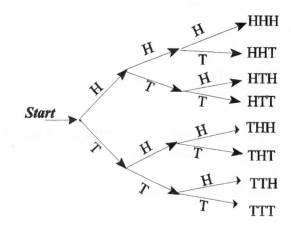

5.   The tree diagram is like the one in problem one, except that there are T and F labels on each choice. Since there is only one sequence that will contain all three correct answers, the probability of guessing all three questions correctly is $\frac{1}{8}$. ♦

7. $4! = 4 \cdot 3 \cdot 2 \cdot 1 = 24$ sequences to be tested. ♦

9   a.   You have 52 ways of drawing a card from the first deck and 52 ways of drawing a card from the second deck. Using the multiplication principle you will have $52 \cdot 52$ =2704 ways of drawing the cards as specified. ♦

   b)   You have 4 ways to draw a king from the first deck and 4 ways to draw a king from the second so you have $4 \cdot 4 = 16$ ways of drawing a king from each deck.♦

   c)   P(drawing 2 kings) = $\frac{16}{2704}$ = .0059 ♦

13. $P_{5,2} = \frac{5!}{(5-2)!} = \frac{5!}{2!3!} = 20$ $C_{5,2} = \frac{5!}{2!(5-2)!} = \frac{5!}{2!3!} = 10.$

21.   Order is important for this situation since the nursing positions are different (possibly having different salaries, responsibilities etc.) $P_{15,3} = \frac{15!}{(15-3)!} = \frac{15!}{12!} = 2730.$

use n=15 and r=12. remember r ≤ n.

27.   Order is not important here, so use a combination formula.
n= 15, r=5

$$C_{15,5} = \frac{15!}{5!\,(15-5)!} = 3003 \; \blacklozenge$$

29.   There is a total of 12 people in the applicant pool and the order of selection is not important, so we can use a combination.

$$C_{12,6} = \frac{12!}{6!\,6!} = 924 \; \blacklozenge$$

n=12 , r= 6

b)   There are 7 women (again order does not matter so we use a combination)

$$C_{7,6} = \frac{7!}{6!\,1!} = 7 \; \blacklozenge$$

There are 7 ways to choose 6 women out of 7 (think of the ways to choose leaving one out) and 924 ways to choose 6 people out of 12.

The probability that the trainee class will consist entirely of women is $\frac{7}{924} = .0076.$ $\blacklozenge$

Answer to Thinking About Statistics

1.   An important feature of a combination lock is the **order** of the numbers used to unlock it. In a mathematical combination, order is *not* important. So, the next time you have to buy a lock, ask for a "permutation" lock.

Section 4.4
Introduction to Random Variables and Probability Distributions

Review

I.   **Random variable** x

A.   x represents a ***numerical*** outcome which could be a count or a measurement in a statistical experiment.

1.   For example: Take a multiple choice test with 20 questions. Your raw score will be the number of correct responses.

a.   x = number of correct answers (raw score)

b.   We can list the values for x: 0,1,2,3...20.

c.   a possible value for the random variable is x = 18.

2.   For example: Measure the mileage you drive between your home and your job.

a.   x = number of miles you drive

b.   We cannot list the possible responses here since all decimal numbers are possible.

c.   A possible value for the random variable is x=26.835 miles.

B.   The term *random* is used because the particular value it takes in one trial of an experiment occurs by chance.

II.   Types of random variables

A.   **Discrete random variables**

1.   Values can be listed.

2.   Usually determined by a <u>counting</u> process.

3.   A discrete random variable takes on only certain values.

4.   The only values are usually integers, however, an exception would be a shoe size which could be 6, 6½, 7, 7½ etc. Note however that a shoe size could not be 7.23.

B.   **Continuous random variables**

1.   Possible values cannot be put in a list since there are an uncountably infinite many.

2.   Usually determined by a <u>measuring</u> process.

3.   All measures in an interval (including decimals and fractions) are candidates

for replacement.
4.   No value is skipped.

III.   Probability distribution for a *discrete* random variable.
   A.   List each value x that may occur in the experiment and assign the probability of its occurrence P(x).

$$P(x) = \frac{number\ of\ times\ x\ has\ occured}{total\ number\ of\ times\ the\ experiment\ is\ performed}$$

   B.   The *sum* of all the simple probabilities is 1. $\Sigma\ P(x) = 1$
   C.   The **expected value** of a discrete probability distribution (also called the mean) is denoted μ.

$$\mu = \sum x \cdot P(x)$$

   1.   To calculate μ, make a table
      a.   List the values of x in a vertical column I
      b.   List the corresponding probabilities in vertical column II.
      c.   In vertical column III, calculate the product of each value of x times its probability.
      d.   The expected value of x is the sum of the products listed in column III.
   D.   The **standard deviation** of an probability distribution is denoted σ.
      1.   Since we use the same table in which we have calculated the expected value, columns $\quad \sigma = \sqrt{\Sigma\ (x-\mu)^2 P(x)}$
      I. and II. already are formed and have x and P(x) entries.
      2.   Subtract the mean μ from each value of x, thus computing the deviations (x-μ). Form a vertical column IV for these deviations.
      3.   Square each deviation and form vertical column V. for (x-μ)^2, the deviations squared.
      4.   Multiply each deviation squared by the corresponding probability from column II. Put these products into vertical column VI.
      5.   Add the entries in column VI.
      6.   Find the square root.
   E.   The computation for σ is quicker if you do the computations across each horizontal row, having your calculator save the entry in column VI in its memory. Use the sum function in your calculator memory to add column VI.

IV.   Probability distribution of a *continuous* random variable.

A.   Since all the possible values of the random variable x cannot be listed for a continuous variable, it would be impossible to form a table such as we did for a discrete random variable.

B.   With a continuous random variable, we deal with the probability that x occurs within an *interval* of numbers. At this time we will not be required to evaluate these probabilities, but will deal with them in later chapters.

C.   To compute the expected value μ and the standard deviation σ in a continuous probability distribution, it would be necessary to use mathematics which is beyond the level of this course. Therefore, when they are discussed in later chapters, we will be given the results of these computations.

V.   Graph of a probability distribution of a discrete random variable.

A.   The graph is a histogram.

B.   Mark the horizontal axis so that the width of each bar is one unit. x will be the label of this axis.

C.   Mark the vertical axis with P(x), the probability of x.

D.   The vertical axis will only have numbers on the interval from 0 to 1, inclusive, so look for the highest probability that occurs in a distribution and mark the scale accordingly. P(x) is also referred to as the *relative frequency*, so the histogram will be the same as discussed in Chapter 2.

E.   Construct each bar so that the random variable value is at the center of the bar. Each bar will be a rectangle with a width of 1 unit and a height which corresponds to the probability of that particular variable.

VI.   Interesting features for a probability histogram of a discrete random variable.

A.   Each bar is a rectangle and as such its area can be computed by the formula: Area = (width) · (height).

B.   When the width of the bar =1, the area = (1)· (height) = height of the rectangle. This is the probability for that particular value of x in the distribution.

C.   ***The area of each rectangle = probability that x is the value which is marked at the center of the base of the rectangle.***

D.   The total area of all the bars = 1.

E.   The expected value, μ will be at a point on the horizontal axis around which the distribution will appear "balanced".

F.   From Chebyshev's Theorem, we know that *at least* 75% of the area will be within 2 standard deviations of the mean. i.e. between the values of μ - 2σ and μ + 2σ and *at least* 89% of the area will be within 3 standard deviations of the mean.

Problem Solving Warm-Up

Identify each of the following as either a discrete or continuous random variable.

1. The number of people who are in a car.

    Discrete-The number of people in a car are *counted. The values can be listed, 0,1,2,3 etc.*

    _____

2. The number of miles you drive in one week.

    Continuous-The number of miles is *measured. The values can not all be listed.*
    x could possibly take on values like 87.59 or 132.45 etc. Your odometer does not skip any values.

    _____

3. Weight of a box of cereal

    Continuous. The number of ounces is measured. Any value is possible, including decimals.

    _____

4. The number of boxes of cereal you buy in a year.

    Discrete-The number of boxes is counted. Possible values can be listed. We assume you do not buy fractional parts of boxes.

    _____

5. Length of time you spend for lunch.

    Continuous-The value is measured on a clock and no value is skipped.

    _____

6. The number of patients on a psychiatric ward in one day.

    Discrete-The value is a count variable.

    _____

7. The volume of blood which is transfused during an operation.

    Continuous-The volume is measured. No values are skipped.

    _____

8. In a personality inventory test for passive-aggressive traits, the possible scores are 1=extremely passive 2=moderately passive 3=neither 4=moderately aggressive 5=extremely aggressive. The test was administered to a group of 110 people and the results were as

follows.

x (score)	1	2	3	4	5
f (freq.)	19	23	32	26	10

Construct a probability distribution table and compute the expected value (the mean) and the standard deviation. Use a histogram to graph the probability distribution.

Solution: Complete the following table. Check with those in the table that follows.

I	II	III	IV	V	VI	VII
x	f	P(x)	x·P(x)	x-μ	(x-μ)²	(x-μ)²·P(x)
1	19					
2	23					
3	32					
4	26					
5	10					
Σ	110					

After you have made the correct entries, your table should look like the following one: Remember that $P(x) = \frac{f}{110}$ since $\Sigma f = n = 110$.

I	II	III	IV	V	VI	VII
x	f	P(x)	x·P(x)	x-μ	(x-μ)²	(x-μ)²·P(x)
1	19	0.1727	0.1727	-1.8700	3.4969	0.6039
2	23	0.2091	0.4182	-0.8700	0.7569	0.1583
3	32	0.2909	0.8727	0.1300	0.0169	0.0049
4	26	0.2364	0.9456	1.1300	1.2769	0.3019
5	10	0.0909	0.4545	2.1300	4.5369	0.4124
Σ	110	1.0000	2.8637			1.4814

The expected value is 2.87♦ The standard deviation is:

$$s - \sqrt{1.4762} \approx 1.22$$

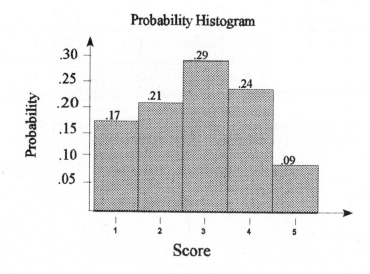

Probability Histogram

Thinking About Statistics

In a game you roll 2 dice. You win $5 if the sum of the dice is 3, 7 or 11. You lose $3 if the sum is 4,5,8,9 or 10. For any other roll, you do not win or lose anything. What is the expected value for this game? Hint, let x = amount won or lost on a roll of the dice. List the values for x as 5, -3 or 0.

Selected Solutions Section 4.4

1. a) Discrete. Fatalities are counted 0,1,2,3 etc. You cannot have a fractional number of fatalities.
    b) Continuous. This is a measured value. You cannot go from 160 yards to 161 yards without travelling every distance in that interval for example: 160.2347 yards.
    c) Continuous. A measured value. Time does not jump-the variable can take on every value in an interval.
    d) Discrete. A count variable
    e) Continuous. A measured variable.
    f) Discrete. A count variable. Values can be listed.

5. The relative frequencies are calculated for each value of x by dividing the number of times that value occurred (f) by the total number in the sample. The results are listed in the table below under P(x).

I	II	III	IV	V	VI
x	P(x)	x·P(x)	x - μ	(x-μ)²	(x-μ)²·P(x)
1	0.3090	0.3090	-1.0400	1.0816	0.3342
2	0.3541	0.7082	-0.0400	0.0016	0.0006
3	0.3276	0.9829	0.9600	0.9216	0.3020
4	0.0092	0.0369	1.9600	3.8416	0.0354
Σ	1.0000	2.0371			0.6722

    a) The respective relative frequencies are .3090, .3541, .3276 and .0092 for the 1st, 2nd,and 3rd periods and OT.♦

c)   To compute μ, we let OT= period 4. The expected value is 2.04. This value would be interpreted as most of the goals are scored in the 2nd period.♦

d)   To compute the standard deviation find the square root of the sum of the last column.

$$\sigma - \sqrt{.672} - .82 \,♦$$

e)   A goal is most likely to be scored in the 2nd period, since .3541 is the highest individual probability. Using the complement rule, we can compute the probability that a goal was **not** score in the 2nd period is 1-.3541 =.6459 ♦

9.

I	II	III	IV	V	VI
x	P(x)	x·P(x)	x - μ	(x-μ)²	(x-μ)²·P(x)
1	0.02	0.02	-3.98	15.8404	0.3168
2	0.07	0.14	-2.98	8.8804	0.6216
3	0.15	0.45	-1.98	3.9204	0.5881
4	0.18	0.72	-0.98	0.9604	0.1729
5	0.21	1.05	0.02	0.0004	0.0001
6	0.16	0.96	1.02	1.0404	0.1665
7	0.10	0.70	2.02	4.0804	0.4080
8	0.06	0.48	3.02	9.1204	0.5472
9	0.04	0.36	4.02	16.1604	0.6464
10	0.01	0.10	5.02	25.2004	0.2520
Σ	1.00	4.98			3.7196

a) The probabilities as x goes from 1 to 10 are:
(reading down column II)   .02, .07, .15, .18, .21, .16, .10, .06, .04, and .01 ♦
The distribution is skewed right.

b) Add the probabilities of failing in the first, second and third years.
.02 +.07+.15 =.24 ♦

c) Add the probabilities of failing in year 5, 6, 7 8 9 or 10

.21+ .16+ .10+ .06+ .04+.01 = .58 ♦

Probability Histogram

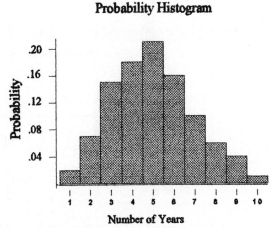

d) μ = 4.98 (From the sum in column III.). For businesses that fail, the expected number of years is 4.98 (almost 5). ♦

e) From the frequency distribution table,

Σ (x-μ)²·P(x)= 3.7196.

$$\sigma = \sqrt{3.7196} \approx 1.929 \; ♦$$

13. a) Let x=amount of money won. There are only two values for x. x=2479.16 (if he wins, he gets the value of the trip) or x=0 (if he doesn't win). ♦

 b) The probability he wins is $\frac{10}{1792}$ = .0056. The probability he does not win is 1 - .0056 =.9944.♦

 c) We get the expected earnings by μ = ΣxP(x) =(2479.16)(.0056) +0(.9944)= 14.88. Since he bought 10 tickets for $4 each, he paid out $40. Thus money he paid out minus money he expects to receive equals his contribution. 40 - 14.88 =$25.12. He has effectively contributed $25.12 to the museum.♦

Answers to Thinking About Statistics

The values of x represent the amount of money won or lost. Notice that the random variable can be a negative number or zero as well as a positive.

x=5 if you roll a 3,7 or 11,   **x=-3** if you roll a 4,5,8,9 or 10 **x=0** on other rolls. (2,6 or 12)

P(x=5)   =P(sum is 3 or 7 or 11) = $\frac{2}{36} + \frac{6}{36} + \frac{2}{36}$ = $\frac{10}{36}$ = .2778

P(x=-3)   =P(sum is 4 or 5 or 8 or 9 or 10) = $\frac{3}{36} + \frac{4}{36} + \frac{5}{36} + \frac{4}{36} + \frac{3}{36}$ = $\frac{19}{36}$ = .5227

P(x=0)   =1-(.2778 +.5277) = .1945 using complement rule. You could get this also by direct computation of P(sum is 2 or 6 or 12) which are the possible rolls not already listed.

103

x	P(x)	x·P(x)
5	0.2778	1.3890
-3	0.5277	-1.5831
0	0.1945	0.0000
Σ	1	-0.1941

The expected value is Σ x· P(x) = -.1941. This means your average *loss* per game you play is a little more than 19 cents. If you play this game 100 times, you can expect to lose $19.41. This game is not *fair* since you expect to lose. If the expected value is negative, you expect to lose and if it is positive you expect to win. A fair game is one in which the expected value is 0. Try to compute the expected value of a new game in which you win $5 for a sum of 3,7 or 11, you lose $3 for a sum of 4,5,8 or 9 and you break even for all other rolls.

Games at a casino are designed so that they have a negative expected value.

Chapter 5

THE BINOMIAL PROBABILITY DISTRIBUTION AND RELATED TOPICS

Section 5.1
Binomial Experiments

Review

In the previous chapter we looked at statistical experiments and computed the probabilities of specified events. We will now examine a particular type of statistical experiment called a **binomial experiment.**

I.   Characteristics of a binomial experiment
    A.   The same action is repeated
        1.   Conditions for repetition must be identical.
        2.   One trial must be independent of all others. (The results of one trial cannot affect another.)
        3.   The number of trials is n.
    B.   A binomial experiment must have 2 outcomes
        1.   Success (which is defined in the problem)
        2.   Failure (all outcomes except those defined as success).
    C.   On an individual trial
        1. $P(success) = p$
        2. $P(failure) = q$
        3. $q = 1 - p$ (They are complementary events)
    D.   The number of trials that are successful is denoted r where $r \leq n$.

II.   Problems for section 5.1 will only concern

    A.   Whether a given experiment is or is not binomial

    B.   If it is binomial, define the action that constitutes a "trial."

    C.   If it is binomial, identify the values for n, p, and q and the range of values for r.

        1.   n = number of trials

        2.   p = probability that an individual trial is "successful."

        3.   q = probability that an individual trial is a "failure."

        4.   r = the exact number of trials (out of n) that are "successful." The value of r can range from 0 (no successes out of the n trials) to n (each of the n trials is a success.)

III.   An important problem, beginning in Section 5.2

    A.   Compute the *probability* of **exactly** r successes out of n trials.

    B.   The first step will be to identify the components, n, p, q and r (or range of values for r).

Problem Solving Warm-Up

For each of the following,

a)   State whether it is a binomial experiment or not.

b)   If it is a binomial, describe "Success" and "Failure" and

c)   Identify values for n, p, q and the range of values for r.

1.   *U.S.A. Today* reported July 27, 1990 that 70% of the people questioned said that they watched less T.V. than they did a year ago, 22% said they watch the same amount and 8% said they watch more. Find the probability out of a randomly selected group of 5 that exactly 3 will say they watch less T.V. this year than last.

    a)   This is a binomial experiment.

    b)   "Success" = watch less T.V. this year than last.
"Failure"= watch the same or more T.V. than last year.

    c)   n = 5 (total number in sample)
p= .70 (probability that one person will say they watch less T.V. this year than last.
q = .30 (1 - .70)
r = 3 (number of "successes")

2.   There are 20 m&m's candies in a dish. 8 are brown, 3 red, 5 green and 4 yellow. Two candies are picked from the dish at random. What is the probability that both are red?

    This is *not* a binomial experiment since the trials are not independent. The probability that the first candy is red is 3/20. Once this candy is removed from the dish, the probability that the second is red is 2/19. The probability that both are red is $3/20 \cdot 2/19 = 3/190$.

3.   A multiple choice test is given which has 10 questions. Each question has 4 choices. You did not study and have no clue as to any of the questions, so you have to randomly guess each answer. What is the probability you guess exactly 6 correctly. (So you get a passing grade!)

a)   This is a binomial experiment.
b)   "Success" = guessing the answer correctly.
       "Failure" = guessing incorrectly.
c)   n = 10 (number of "trials").
       p = .25 (since there are 4 choices, you have 1/4 = .25 probability of guessing each question correctly.
       q = .75 (1-.25)
       r = 6

Thinking About Statistics

Look in several newspapers or magazines to find some reports about statistical studies. Identify each as a binomial study or not.

Selected Solutions Section 5.1

1.   This is a binomial experiment. A trial = a room call.
       "Success" is defined as a nurse responding to a call within 3 minutes.
       "Failure" is he or she does not respond within 3 minutes.
       Assume that the trials are independent i.e. that response to one patient's call does not affect the response to another's.
       n = 73 ♦ r = 62 ♦ p = .80 ♦ q = .20 ♦

5.   This is not binomial since there are 3 outcomes (Japanese, Spanish and Other).

7.   Although there are 2 outcomes the experiment is not binomial since the first straw is not replaced before the second one is drawn so the trials are not independent (conditions are not identical.)

9.   This is a binomial experiment. A trial is examining a claim and determining whether the

claim is made by a single male under 25 years of age.

"Success" = claim is made be a single male under 25 years of age and "Failure" = claim is made by someone other than a single male under 25. (A female or a person 25 or over.) n =619 ♦ r = ranges from 45 and 50 inclusive. r = 45, 46, 47, 48, 49 and 50. ♦ p = .075 ♦ q = .925♦

13.   This is a binomial experiment. A trial is examining the records of a home burglary and determining whether it has been solved. Success = burglary has been solved. Failure= burglary has not been solved. n = 300, p = .14, q = .86 and r ranges from 0 to 40. r = 0, 1, 2, ...40.

Answer to Thinking About Statistics

Answers will, of course, vary. Many medical studies are done as binomial experiments.

Section 5.2
The Binomial Distribution

Review

I.   The basic problem is to *find the probability of getting **exactly** r successes out of n trials.*
   A.   In a binomial experiment we use r as the random variable.
      1.   r *counts* the number of successful outcomes.
      2.   r is a discrete random variable.
      3.   For each experiment, the possible values of r can be listed, r = 0,1,2,3,...n. The values range from r=0 (no successful outcomes i.e. all failures) to r=n (all outcomes are successful.)
   B.   The probability of getting exactly 0 successes (all failures) is denoted P(0), the probability of getting exactly 1 success and the rest failures is denoted P(1) and so on.
      1.   Since the categories of no successes, exactly one success, exactly two successes etc are mutually exclusive, we can add their probabilities to answer a question using the OR combination.
      2.   The sum of all the probabilities =1. P(0) + P(1) + P(2) +P(3) + ...P(n) = 1.

I.   Methods of determining the probability of r successes out of n trials.
A.   Formula (may be optional): $P(r) = C_{n,r} p^r q^{n-r}$

1.   To find the probability of exactly 3 successes from 7 trials where p= .35.
   a.   n = 7, r = 3, p = .35 and q = .65
         (q is the complement of p) $P(3) = C_{7,3} (.35)^3 (.65)^4$
   b.   The value of $C_{7,3}$ can be
         determined from the combination formula $C_{n,r} = \dfrac{n!}{r!(n-r)!}$
         where n! = n(n-1)(n-2) ...1.

   c.   From the Table of Binomial Coefficients in Appendix II.
   d.   Using a calculator with the built-in combinations function.
   e. $C_{7,3}$ = 35. This means if you have a set of 7 objects there are 35
         different ways of choosing exactly 3 to be successful.
   f.   P(3) = 35 (.007653) = .268.

B.   Table of Binomial Probabilities found in Appendix II of your text.
1.   Results of the formula for selected values of n, r and p are listed in table
      form.
2.   Construction of table
   a.   In the left most column, values of n (the number of trials) are listed
         from n=2 to n = 20.
   b.   Next to each n, in a parallel column is a list of possible values for r
         = the number of successes. Next to n =3 the possible values of r are
         listed as 0,1,2 or 3. Next to n = 10 the possible values of r are listed
         as 0,1,2,3,4,5,6,7,8,9, or 10.
   c.   Across the top are various values for p = the probability of success
         on an individual trial. Remember, q = 1 - p.
3.   To determine the probability of exactly 3 successes out of 7 trials where p=
      .35, first find 7 under the n column. Then go one column to the right to
      locate r=3. Go across the page until you are under p=.35. The entry here is
      .268, which is the same value we got when the formula was used.
4.   If the values of n and p are ones that are included in the table, it is only
      necessary to locate the correct entry to find the probability of exactly r
      successes out of n trials. For most people, this is preferable to using the
      formula.
C.   For questions that involve the OR combination, you can break the outcomes into
      mutually exclusive events and use the simple addition rule.
1.   For n = 7 and p = .35, find the probability of at least 3 successes.
   a.   This is an OR combination. Remember that "at least 3" means _3 or
         more_ which is translated to r = 3 OR r = 4 OR r = 5 OR r = 6 OR r

= 7. P(at least 3) = P(3) + P(4) + P(5) + P(6) + P(7). Reading from the table, we get .268 + .144 + .047 + .008 + .001 = .468.

2.   For n = 7 and p = .35, find the probability of at least 1 success. We could of course add the probabilities for r=1, 2, 3, 4, 5, 6 and 7, however it is easier in this situation to use the complement rule. Remember that the complement of at least one success is "no successes". P(no successes) = P(0) = .049. Therefore, P(at least one success) = 1 - .049 = .951.

Problem Solving Warm-Up

1.   In section 5.1 we began to set-up the following problem: *U.S.A. Today* reported that 70% of the people questioned said that they watched less T.V. than they did a year ago, 22% said they watch the same amount and 8% said they watch more.

a)   Find the probability that in a randomly selected group of 5 people, exactly 3 will say they watch less T.V. this year than last.

Use the Binomial Tables. Read down the left hand column to locate n =5. Then across the top to find p = .70.

r	P(r)
0	.002
1	.028
2	.132
3	.309
4	.360
5	.168

a)   P(3) = .309

b)   Find the probability that between 2 and 4 (inclusive) people will say they watched less T.V. this year than last year.

b)   P(between 2 and 4 inclusive) = P(2)+ P(3) + P(4) = .132 +.309+.360 =.801

c)   Find the probability that at least one will say they watched less T.V. this year than last year.

c)   P(at least one) could be computed by adding the probabilities for r=1,2,3,4 and 5. However, since r=0 is the complement of r=1 or 2 or 3 or 4 or 5, it is easier to compute P(at least 1)

110

$= 1 - .002 = .998.$ $(.002 = P(0)$ from table).

Hint: If you are required to find the probability of at least one success, it's easier to use the rule of complements. That is, find the probability of no successes and subtract this result from 1.

Thinking About Statistics

In many classes learning the formula to compute binomial probabilities may be optional. If this is the case, your instructor will avoid any problems where you could not use the binomial table of probabilities and thus were forced to use the formula. Identify several situations in which the table would not be of use. With a calculator or computer software package, the formula become simple to use.

Selected Solutions Section 5.2

1.   For this problem , a trial consists of a flip of a quarter, success is "quarter lands on heads" so failure is "quarter does not land on heads" (or equivalently, "quarter lands on tails"). Since the quarter is flipped 3 times, $n = 3$. The value of $p = \frac{1}{2} = .5$ since there are 2 outcomes, heads and tails, and each is equally probable. $q = \frac{1}{2}$ using complement rule $1 - \frac{1}{2} = \frac{1}{2}$ or $1 - .5 = .5$ ♦

   a)   Using the formula: $P(x) = C_{n,r} p^r q^{n-r}$

   $$P(r=3) = C_{3,3} (.5)^3 (.5)^0 = \frac{3!}{3!0!} (.125)(1) = 1(.125)(1) = .125 ♦$$

   To obtain the probability directly from the binomial table, go down to $n = 3$ then $r = 3$ and across to $p = .5$.
   $P(r=3) = .125$ ♦
   b)   Using the formula:
   $$P(r=2) = C_{3,2} (.5)^2 (.5)^1 = \frac{3!}{2!1!} (.25)(.5) = 3(.25)(.5) = .375 ♦$$

   From the table, $P(2) = .375$ ♦
   c) $P(2$ or more$)$ means $= P(2$ or $3) = P(2) + P(3)$ using addition rule for mutually exclusive outcomes $= .500$ Note that the formula must be used twice (once for $r = 2$ and once for $r = 3$) and the results added together to determine the answer.♦

d)   Since success is defined as landing on heads, we must first translate the problem to focus on the number of heads. Getting 3 tails is equivalent to getting 0 heads. Using the formula:

$$P(r=0) = C_{3,0} (.5)^0 (.5)^3 - \frac{3!}{0!3!} (1)(.125) - 1(.125)(1) - .125$$

From the binomial probability table, P(0) = .125 ♦

5.   To perform a trial, catch a trout with a fly and then release it. Success is "the trout lives". Failure is "the trout dies". From the information in the problem p = .90 so q = .10.
a) n = 8 . To find the probability six or more live, add the probabilities corresponding to r = 6, r = 7 and r = 8. Thus adding .149 + .383 + .430 we get .962 ♦.
To find the probability that they all live use r = 8. From the tables P(r = 8) = .430 ♦
No more than one dies means that either 0 dies or 1 dies. This is equivalent to 8 lives or 7 lives. So we must find the probability that either 7 or 8 lives. We do so by adding the probabilities for r = 7 and r = 8 and get .813 ♦

b) For this part, n = 15. To find the probability that 12 or more live, add the probabilities for r = 12, 13, 14 and 15. That is, .129 +.267 + .343 +.206 = .945 ♦
To find the probability that they all live, look up the entry for r = 15. P(r = 15) = .206 ♦
No more than 2 die means 0 or 1 or 2 dies. This is equivalent to 15, 14 or 13 lives. To find the probability that 15 or 14 or 13 lives, add the probabilities from the table. .267 +.343 + .206 = .816 ♦

9.   A trial consists of examining the day's receipts. Success occurs when the gross receipts are at least $2,200 and failure is when they are lower.
a) Use n = 7, p = .85 and r = 5, 6, 7. Add the probabilities given in the table. .210 +.396+ .321 = .927 ♦
b) Use n = 10, p = .85 and r = 5, 6, 7, 8, 9, 10.. Adding the corresponding probabilities we get .998 An easier way is to use the rule of complements. The probability of being successful less than 5 days is .001. Subtracting this from 1 we get .999. ♦
c) Use n = 5, p = .85, r = 0, 1, 2. .000 + .002.+.024 = .026 ♦
d) Use n = 10, p = .85, r = 0, 1, 2, 3, 4, 5, 6. Add the probabilities listed in the binomial table to get .049 ♦

13.   a) Use n = 15 and p = .75. To find the probability that 10 or more marketing personnel are extroverts, use r = 10, 11, ... 15. So .165+.225+.225+.156+.067+.013 = .851 ♦
To find the probability that 5 or more marketing personnel are extroverts use n = 15, p = .75 and r = 5, 6, 7, 8, 9, 10, 11, 12, 13, 14,15 and add the corresponding probabilities. From the table we see it's easier to use the complement rule. Since the probability that less than 5 are introverts is 0 (rounded to the nearest .001), then the probability of 5 or more introverts in this group is very close to1. ♦
The probability that all are extroverts (r= 15) is .013. ♦

b) Use n = 5, p = .60 and r = 0. From the table, the probability is .010 (1%) ♦
For 3 or more introverts, use n = 5, p = .60 and r = 3, 4, 5. .346+.259+.078 = .683 ♦
All introverts means n = 5, r = 5. The probability is .078 ♦

17. For this problem , n = 6 and p = .75. (Success is finding a den with 5 or more pups.)
 a) r = 0, 1, 2. Add the probabilities: .000 +.004 +.033 = .037 ♦
 b) r = 4, 5, 6, Add the probabilities:.297+ .356+ .178 = .831 ♦
 c) r = 6. The probability that this occurs is .178 ♦
 d) r = 0. The probability that this occurs is 0. Yes, assuming that p = .75, there is virtually no chance of this occurring. Therefore you might suspect that there has been a change and p < .75. ♦

21. For all parts of this problem, n = 5 and p = .30. Assume the trials are independent.
 a) r = 0. The probability is .168 ♦
 b) r = 5. The probability is .002 ♦
 c) r = 2, 3, 4, 5. Adding .309+ .132 + .028 +.002 = .471
 Using the complement rule, 1 - (.168+.360) we get .472. The slight difference in answer is due to round-offs. Either answer is acceptable.♦
 d) r = 2, 3, 4. Adding the probabilities, we get 309 +.132+.028 = .469 ♦

Answers to Thinking About Statistics

The table would not be of use if the given value of p were, for example, .07, .33 or .78. The binomial probabilities for any experiment in which the number of trials exceeds 20 could not be evaluated with this table. In a later chapter we will examine an additional method for evaluating these probabilities.

Section 5.3
Additional Properties of the Binomial Distribution
Review

I.   Graph of a Binomial Distribution
 A.   A probability histogram
 B.   Each bar represents a value of r, the random variable which *counts* the number of successes. The horizontal axis is marked "r".

1. The midpoints of the bars are marked 0,1,2,3...n. These whole numbers are the class marks.
2. Bars extend ½ unit below the class mark and ½ unit above the class mark, making the bars one unit wide.
3. For example, for r=3 the midpoint is at 3 and the bar extends on the horizontal axis from 2.5 to 3.5.

C. The vertical axis is marked P(r) or relative frequency.
1. The height of each bar corresponds to the probability that r takes on that particular value.

D. The area of each bar = (width)·(height) =(1)·(height) =(1)·(probability) = probability.

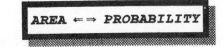
AREA ⇐ ⇒ PROBABILITY

E. The total area of all bars = 1 since the total probability = 1.

F. Shape
1. With p = .5, the histogram is perfectly symmetric.
2. The closer the value of p is to 0 the more the histogram is skewed to the left (longer tail on the left.)
3. The closer the value of p is to 1 the more the histogram is skewed to the right.
4. When n (the number of trials) gets larger, the histogram gets more symmetric.

II. Other Features
A. As in all probability distributions, the mean or expected value is the balance point.
B. The binomial distribution's special properties allow for an easier formula to compute the expected value, the variance and the standard deviation.

1. To compute the mean of a binomial distribution simply multiply the number of trials by the probability of success on one trial use $\mu = \mathbf{np}$.

2. The variance of a binomial distribution is found by $\sigma^2 = \mathbf{npq}$ so the standard deviation of a binomial distribution is computed by $\sigma = \sqrt{\mathbf{npq}}$

To compute the standard deviation of a binomial distribution multiply the number of trials times the probability of success on one trial times the probability f failure on one trial and then take the square root.

III.   Application of the binomial distribution.
   A.   Useful in determining the probability of meeting certain quotas or specifications under success/failure conditions.
   B.   For these problems, you'll be determining the value of n (the number of trials) necessary to meet the given quotas.

Problem Solving Warm-Up

1. Construct a probability histogram for the binomial distribution with n=5 ,p=.70

   Before making a histogram, examine the distribution from Appendix II. We need 6 bars for r=0, 1, 2, 3, 4, and 5.

The highest bar will be at .360 (for r= 4).

r	P(r)
0	.002
1	.028
2	.132
3	.309
4	.360
5	.168

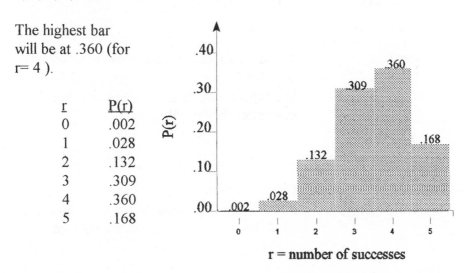

r = number of successes

2. In Upjohn Pharmaceutical clinical trials, 60% of those men tested remained bald after using Rogain, an anti-baldness cream. The cream will be tested on 5 men who have "male pattern" baldness.

a)   Find the probability P(r) of r successes (remaining bald) for r ranging from 0 to 5.

r	P(r)
0	0.010
1	0.077
2	0.230
3	0.346
4	0.259
5	0.078

n=5 p=.60

b)   What is the expected number μ of men in this group who will remain bald?

Using the formula for the mean of a binomial distribution μ = np, we get μ = 5(.60) = 3. We expect 3 of the five men to remain bald even after they use Rogain.

c)   What is the standard deviation σ?

Using the formula for the binomial distribution, first compute npq=(5)(.60)(.40) =1.2. To get σ, we take the square root. σ= 1.095

3.   You are manager of a telemarketing company. Each call has a 40% chance of making a sale. How many calls would you need to be 95% sure of making at least one sale?

This type of problem differs from the others since the unknown is the sample size, n. To help understand the problem look at the binomial distribution when p=.40 and n=2. The probability that at least one sale will be made is P(1) +P(2) = .480 + .160 = .640. i.e. with 2 calls you are 64% sure of making at least one sale. Make a table for various values of n, adding the probabilities for P(1) +P(2)+...+P(n). The answer to the problem will be found when you find the total to be at least .95.

Fill in the probability values in the following table. For each entry, the value of p= .40 and the value of r (starting with r=1 and continuing to r = n) is given on the right. Add the values for each column and stop when the sum of probabilities in a column is at least .95.

r	n=2	n=3	n=4	n=5	n=6
1					
2					
3					
4					
5					
6					
Sum					

Your entries (taken from the binomial table in your text) should look like:

r	n=2	n=3	n=4	n=5	n=6
1	0.480	0.432	0.346	0.259	0.187
2	0.160	0.288	0.346	0.346	0.311
3		0.064	0.154	0.230	0.276
4			0.026	0.077	0.138
5				0.010	0.037
6					0.004
Sum	0.640	0.784	0.872	0.922	0.953

When n =6 the total probability (which is .953) is *at least* .95. With 6 calls you can be 95% sure of at least one sale when 6 or more calls are made.

Thinking About Statistics

Draw a card from a deck of 52 and replace it noting the suit. Repeat this experiment 5 times. What is the expected number of clubs? What is the standard deviation of this binomial probability distribution?

a)   Use the formulas for μ and σ of a **binomial distribution** discussed in this section.
b)   Review the formulas for μ and σ of a **probability distribution** discussed in chapter 4.
c)   Compare the answers from parts a and b.

Selected Solutions Section 5.3

1 a)   p = .50

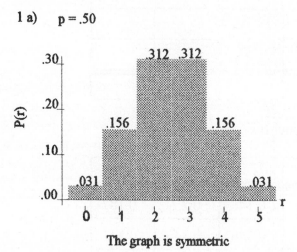

The graph is symmetric

1 b)   p = .25

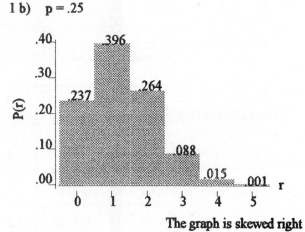

The graph is skewed right

d) The histogram for p = .50 is perfectly symmetric while the histograms for p = .25 and for p = .75 are mirror images of each other.

1 c)   p = .75

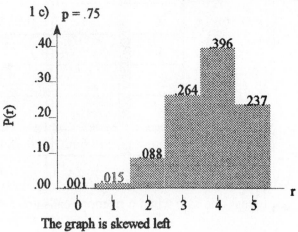

The graph is skewed left

e) If the probability of success is .73, it would be skewed left since it would be similar to the histogram for p = .75. We would expect histograms for values of p that are greater than .5 to be skewed left and those for values of p less than .5 to be skewed right.

5.   a) The histogram is to the right. n = 6 and p = .70

b) The mean of this distribution is given by $\mu = np = 6(.70) = 4.2$ friends. ♦

The standard deviation is

$$\sigma = \sqrt{npq}$$
$$= \sqrt{6\,(.70)\,(.30)}$$
$$= \sqrt{1.26} = 1.12 \; friends \; ♦$$

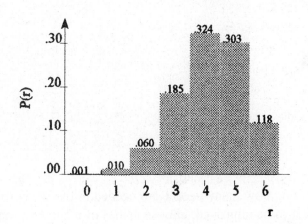

You would expect about 4 friends to be found. ♦

c) Enter the values for p = .70 for various values of n. Since we need at least 2, start with r= 2.

r	n=2	n=3	n=4	n=5	n=6
2	.490	.441	.265	.132	.060
3		.343	.410	.309	.185
4			.240	.360	.324
5				.168	.303
6					.118
sum	0.490	0.784	0.915	0.969	0.990

For n = 2, 3, 4, and 5 the probability of at least 2 successes is less than .97. With n = 6 we are more than 97% sure of getting at least 2 (2 or more) successes. ♦

9.   a) The histogram is on the following page.
b) $\mu = np = 8(.25) = 2$ ♦

c) $\sigma = \sqrt{npq} = \sqrt{8\,(.25)\,(.75)} = \sqrt{1.5} = 1.22$

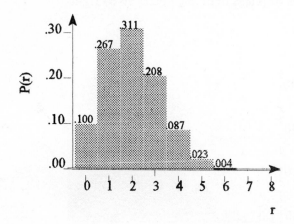

c) To find how many people are needed in the study to be 99% sure that at least one believes the product to be improved, choose values of n and add the probabilities for r = 1,2,3,...n. Since this sum increases as n increases, stop when the sum of probabilities in a column is at least .99. Some results are in the table that follows:

r	n=6	n=8	n=10	n=11	n=12	n=16	n=20
1	0.356	.267	.188	.155	.127	.053	.003
2	0.297	.311	.282	.258	.232	.134	.021
3	0.132	.208	.250	.258	.258	.208	.067
4	0.033	.087	.146	.172	.194	.225	.134
5	0.004	.023	.058	.080	.103	.180	.190
6	0.000	.004	.016	.027	.040	.110	.202
7		.000	.003	.006	.011	.052	.169
8		.000	.000	.001	.002	.020	.112
9			.000	.000	.000	.006	.061
10			.000	.000	.000	.001	.027
11				.000	.000	.000	.010
12					.000	.000	.003
13						.000	.001
Sum	0.822	0.900	0.943	0.957	0.967	0.989	1.000

Using only the tables in the text, we conclude that the required number is between 16 and 20. An alternate way (and probably easier) is to use the complement rule. The complement of "at least one success" is "no successes". We can look up P(r) for r =0 in the chart for various values of n or we can use the binomial formula. Since the table in the text does not list the binomial probabilities from n = 17, 18 and 19, we can compute them with the binomial probability formula.:
For n = 17, r = 0 and p = .25 $P(r=0) = C_{17,0}(.25)^0(.75)^{17} = 1(1)(.00752) = .00752$

Therefore the probability that at least one believes the product to be improved is 1-.00752 = .99248. With n = 17 we are 99% sure that at least one believes the product to be improved. ♦

13.   In this problem we have to find n, the number of trials so that we are 90% sure that there will be at least one success. The value of p = .10, so q is .90. Instead of adding the probabilities of r= 1, 2, 3, ...n we can compute the probability that r = 0 and use the complement rule. (Recall that the complement of "at least one successful trial" is "no successful trial". Probability of success on at least one being be 90% of higher is equivalent to probability of r = 0 being less than 10%. From the binomial table we see that

for n = 20, P(0) = .122 which would mean the probability for its complement is .878. Trying n = 21 with the formula we get $C_{21,0}$ $(.10)^0(.90)^{21}$ = .10942. Sine this is not going to make the complementary event have a probability higher than 90%, try n = 22. $C_{22,0}$ $(.10)^0(.90)^{22}$ = .09848. This means the probability of the complementary event is .90152. n =22 meets the conditions in the problem. ♦

17.   We have to find n, the number of radar stations required such that P(at least one will detect an enemy plane) ≥ .98. If a single radar station is in use the probability that it will detect an enemy station is .65, so p=.65. We'll use the complement rule by first finding P(0) for various values of n. We wish to find the value of n such that P(0) ≤ .02. (Using the complement rule 1 - .98 =.02)

n	P(0)	P(at least one) = 1 - P(0)
1	.35	.65 (this is given in the problem)
2	.123	.877
3	.043	.957
4	.015	.985 *

Thus if we have 4 radar stations, the probability that *at least one* (1 or 2 or 3 or 4) will detect an enemy plane is .985. This satisfies the requirements of the problem that the probability must be higher than .98.
The expected value when n = 4 is: μ = 4(.65) = 2.6 ♦

21.   In this problem, we are given p = .75. We want n the minimum number of players the athletic director must contact so that the probability of at least 6 successful recruits is .90 or more.

Starting with n=6 and reading from the Binomial Tables in Appendix II,
we get P(6 or more) = P(6) = .178
For n=7, P(6 or more) = P(6 or 7) = .367 + .201 = .568
for n=8, P(6 or more) = P(6 or 7 or 8) = .311 + .267 + .100 = .678
for n=9, P(6 or more) = P(6 or 7 or 8 or 9) = .234 + .300+ .255+ .075 = .834.
for n=10,P(6 or more) = P(6 or 7 or...10) = .146 + .250 +.282 + .188 +.056 =.922
If he contacts 10 recruits, he has a probability of .922 of 6 or more successes. This satisfies the requirement that there be more than a 90% probability of getting 6 or more successful recruits. ♦

If he contacts eight players, the *expected number* that will be successfully recruited is μ = 8(.75) = 6.

If he contacts 10 players, he *expects* (10)(.75) = 7.5 to be successful. However, if he contacts 10, there's more than a 90% (actually 92.2%) probability that he will be successful with 6 or more.

Answers to Thinking about Statistics

a) Using formulas for a binomial distribution, n= 5, p=.25 (since there are 13 clubs out of 52 cards) and q =.75 (1-.25).

$\mu = np = 5(.25) = 1.25$ $\sigma = \sqrt{npq} = \sqrt{5(.25)(.75)} = \sqrt{.9375} = .97.$

b) Using formulas for a general probability distribution, we construct a table, Using r in place of x, the formulas will look like: $\mu = \sum r \cdot P(r)$

and $\sigma = \sqrt{(r-\mu)^2 \cdot P(r)}$

I	II	III	IV	V	VI
r	P(r)	r·P(r)	r-μ	(r-μ)²	(r-μ)²P(r)
0	0.237	0.000000	-1.250000	1.562500	0.370313
1	0.396	0.396000	-0.250000	0.062500	0.024750
2	0.264	0.528000	0.750000	0.562500	0.148500
3	0.088	0.264000	1.750000	3.062500	0.269500
4	0.015	0.060000	2.750000	7.562500	0.113438
5	0.001	0.005000	3.750000	14.062500	0.014063
		1.253000			0.940564

From the table, we compute $\mu = \Sigma \, r \cdot P(r) = 1.25$ to two decimal places.

Next find the variance which is the sum of the last column and is equal to .9406. The standard deviation is: $\sigma = \sqrt{.9406} = .97$

c) The answers whether done with the binomial formula or done with the general probability formulas are equivalent.

When working with a binomial experiment, although is would be correct to use the general probability distribution formula, it is certainly quicker and easier to use the binomial distribution formulas. However to compute the mean and standard deviation for a probability distribution which is not binomial, you must learn and use the longer formulas. ♦

Section 5.4

The Geometric and Poisson Probability Distributions

This section describes two more examples of probability distributions. As with the binomial distribution, the random variable for these distributions is discrete.

I.   The Geometric Distribution
      A.   Binomial trials are repeated until the first time success is achieved.
      B.   The random variable n represents the trial on which the first success is reached.
      C.   The values of n can be listed 1,2,3...
      D.   To find the probability of the first success occurring in trial number n, use:

      $$P(n) = p(1-p)^{n-1}$$ p is the probability of success for each trial and n is the number of the trial on which the first success occurs.

      E.   For example, if the first success occurs on the 5th trial, there is failure on the 1st, 2nd, 3rd and 4th trial and success on the 5th. Since the trials are independent, we can use the multiplication formula to calculate the probability of this occurring. The factors will be q q q q p or q^4p. Since (1-p) =q, the formula becomes $(1-p)^4p$.
      F.   Note that whatever the value is for n, there will be (n-1) failures and then 1 success.

II.   The Poisson Probability Distribution
       A.   Conditions for use:
             1.   The random variable r represents a count of the number of times an event occurs within a unit of given unit time or space.
                   a.   (unit of time) The number of hospital admissions in an hour.
                   b.   (product unit)The number of defects in a product part.
                   c.   (unit of space) The number of particles of CO_2 in one cubic foot.
             2.   The probability that an event occurs in a given unit of time or space is the same for all units.

3.   The number of events that occur in one unit of time or space is independent of the number that occur in other units.

4.   The mean (or expected) number of events in each unit is denoted by the Greek letter lambda, λ.

B.   We are interested in calculating the probability of r occurrences within the given unit of time or space.

$$P(r) = \frac{e^{-\lambda}\lambda^r}{r!}$$

r = the number of occurrences = 0, 1, 2,...
λ = the mean number of occurrences in the time or space unit
e = a constant number which can be rounded to 2.7183.

Most calculators have a key marked e^x. (On many it's over the ln key.)

1.   Probability values for selected values of λ and r are found in Table 5 of Appendix 2.

III.   Poisson Approximation to the Binomial Probability Distribution.

A.   When the number of trials is large and the probability of success on an individual trial is small (a rare event) then the binomial distribution can be approximated by that of the Poisson. This means that you can use the simpler formula for computing the Poisson probability when the following conditions are verified.

1. $n \geq 100$ and
2. $np < 10$
3.   The distribution of the binomial r (the number that counts the number of successes) can be approximated by a Poisson distribution with $\lambda = np$.

Problem Solving Warm-Up

1. In previous sections, we've been examining the binomial experiment for which *U.S.A. Today* reported that 70% of the people questioned said that they watched less T.V. than they did a year ago, 22% said they watch the same amount and 8% said they watch more.

a)Calculate the probability that the first time a person responds he or she watches less T.V. now than a year ago occurs on the third interview.

This is a geometric distribution with p = .70 so (1-p) = .30 and n = 3. Using the formula:

$$P(n) = p(1-p)^{n-1} = .70(.30)^2 = .063$$

b) Calculate the probability that the first time a person says he or she watches

Calculate the probabilities for n = 1, 2 and add it to the probability n = 3 calculated in part a.

less T.V. will occur on or before the third interview.

$P(n = 1) = .70(.30)^0 = .70$
$P(n = 2) = .70(.30)^1 = .21$
so $.70 + .21 + .063 = .973$

c) Calculate the probability that the first time a person says he or she watches T.V. less occurs after the first three interviews.

This event is the complement to the one in part b. Using the rule for complementary events we get $1 - .973 = .027$. There's a probability of .027 that the first "success" will come after the third interview.

2. During the rush hour periods, an average of five cars arrive at a highway tollgate every minute.

a) Find the probability that during the rush hour period, exactly 7 cars will arrive in a one-minute period.

The variable that counts the number of cars during a 1 minute period has a Poisson distribution. Use the formula for Poisson probabilities with $\lambda = 5$ and $r = 7$..

$$P(r) = \frac{e^{-\lambda}\lambda^r}{r!}$$

$$= \frac{e^{-5}5^7}{7!} = \frac{.0067(78125)}{5040} = .1044$$

b. What is the probability that 6 or 7 cars will arrive during a 1 minute period.

b. Compute the probability of exactly 6 cars arriving during a 1 minute period and add the result to the answer in part a..

$$P(r) = \frac{e^{-5}5^6}{6!} = \frac{.0067(15625)}{720} = .1462$$

$.1044 + .1462 = .2506$

Thinking about Statistics

1.The following situations are taken from the Chapter Review problems in your main text. In each case a random variable is described. Determine whether the random variable has a binomial, a geometric or a Poisson distribution. Justify your answer.

a) It is known that 80% of all guinea pigs injected with a certain culture will contract red blood cell anemia. 10 guinea pigs are injected with the culture. Let r be the number of guinea pigs that contract red blood cell anemia.

b) In a large theater audience you'll hear about 11 coughs per minute. Let r be the number of coughs in a one minute period.

c) An experiment consists of tossing a coin a specified number of times and recording the outcomes. Let n be the toss when the first head occurs.

2. The Poisson distribution is a discrete probability distribution. The mean (expected value) is denoted λ. The variance σ^2 of the distribution is equal to the mean.

Selected Solutions Section 5.4

1.   a) Since the random variable n represents the number of the trial in a binomial experiment where the first success is reached, the geometric distributions appropriate. The formula is $P(n) = p(1 - p)^{n-1}$.For this problem p = .77 and 1-p = .23 so use $P(n) = .77(.23)^{n-1}$. ♦

b) Note that it is really not necessary to use the formula for n = 1 since the probability is .77. However, using the formula we get $.77(.23)^0 = .77(1) = .77$. ♦

c) Use n = 2. P(n=2) = .77(.23) = .1771 (note that this is one success and one failure) ♦

d) First compute the probability that she passes in less than 3 tries (the complement of 3 or more). Add the results of parts a and b (which determined the probability she first passes in the 1st try or in the 2nd.) to get .77 + .1771 =.9471. Using the complement rule, the probability Susan needs 3 or more tries to pass is 1 - .9471 = .0529. ♦

5.   The random variable has a geometric distribution. The formula is $P(n) = p(1 - p)^{n-1}$.

b)Use p = .71: P(n =1) = .71 and P(n=2) = .71(.29) = .2059. The probability that the first success comes in the 1st or the 2nd try is .71 +.2059 = .9159. Using the rule for complements, the probability that the first success is reached in the 3rd trial or later is 1 - .9159 = .0841. ♦

c) Use p = .83:   P(n =1) = .83 and P(n=2) = .83(.17) = .1411. The probability that the first success comes in the 1st or the 2nd try is .83 +.1411 = .9711. Using the rule for complements, the probability that the first success is reached in the 3rd trial or later is 1 - .9711 = .0289. ♦

9.   a) The experiment counts the number of successes that occur in a fixed interval of time, this number is the same for all time intervals and assuming independence between different time intervals, the Poisson distribution is appropriate for the random variable r. We are given that the frequency of grooming is approximately 1.7 for each 10 minutes. So in a 30 minute period the number of times one otter grooms another is 3 (1.7) = 5.1, which means λ = 5.1. Since parts b and c will require the probability values for r = 0, 1, 2, 3, 4, 5 and 6, we'll compute them first (or find them in a Poisson table of values with λ = 5.1.)

$$P(r) = \frac{e^{-\lambda}\lambda^r}{r!}$$

$$P(0) = \frac{e^{-5.1}(5.1)^0}{0!} = .006097 \qquad P(1) = \frac{e^{-5.1}(5.1)^1}{1!} = .031093$$

$$P(2) = \frac{e^{-5.1}(5.1)^2}{2!} = .079288 \qquad P(3) = \frac{e^{-5.1}(5.1)^3}{3!} = .079288$$

$$P(4) = \frac{e^{-5.1}(5.1)^4}{4!} = .171857 \qquad P(5) = \frac{e^{-5.1}(5.1)^5}{5!} = .175294$$

$$P(6) = \frac{e^{-5.1}(5.1)^6}{6!} = .108557$$

Entering the results in a table, we get:

r	P(r)
0	0.0061
1	0.0311
2	0.0793
3	0.1348
4	0.1719
5	0.1753
6	0.1490

b) P(r = 4) = .1719 ♦
P(r = 5) = .1753 ♦
P(r = 6) = .1490 ♦

c) Compute the probability of the complementary event, that the otter will groom less than 4 times during the 30 minute period. Adding the probabilities for r = 0, 1, 2 or 3 times we get: .0061+.0311+ .0793+ .1348 = .2513. The probability that r is 4 or more is than 1 - .2513 = .7487. ♦

d) The probability r is less than 4 is .2513 as shown in part c. ♦

13.   a) The variable r counts the number of times an event occurs within a fixed period of time. Gales occur relatively infrequently. Assuming the probability of the gale occurring is the same for all time units and that the number of gales for each time unit is independent of the number of gales in another time unit, the Poisson distribution is appropriate to use.

b) The probability the gale force wind occurs within a given hour is $\frac{1}{60}$, so the expected number of occurrences in 108 hours is $108\left(\frac{1}{60}\right) = 1.8$ ♦

Using $\lambda = 1.8$ and r = 0, 1, 2, 3 4 and 5 we can compute (using the Poisson formula) or use the following table to determine the required probabilities:

r	P(r)
0	0.1653
1	0.2975
2	0.2678
3	0.1607
4	0.0723
5	0.0260

b) P(r =2) = .2678 ♦
P(r =3) = .1607 ♦
P(r =4) = .0723 ♦
P(r < 2) = P(r = 0 or 1)= .1653 +.2975 = .4628 ♦

c) P(r = 3 or 4 or 5) = P(r=3) +P(r=4)+ P(r=5) = .1607 +.0723 +.0260 = .2590 ♦
P(r<3) =P(r = 0 or 1 or2) = .1653 +.2975+ .2678 = .7603 ♦

17.   Since the variable r counts the number of occurrences (repeat offenders) out of a given unit (1000 convicted drunk drivers who toured the morgue), the probability of occurrence is the same for all units and the events between units are independent, the Poisson distribution may be used. since p = 1/569, λ = 1000 (1/569) = 1.8. ♦

b) Since the value of λ = 1.8 is the same as that for problem 13, we can use the values that have been listed there. P(r = 0) = .1653 ♦

c) P(r >1) = 1 - P (r= 0 or 1). = 1 - (.1653 +.2975) = 1 -.4628 = .5372. ♦
d) P(r >2) = 1 - P (r = 0 or 1 or 2) = 1 - (.1653 +.2975 + 2678) = 1 -.7303 = .2697 ♦
e) P(r >3) = 1 - P (r = 0 or 1 or 2 or 3) = 1 - (.1653 +.2975 + .2678 +.1607) = 1 -.8913 = .1087 ♦

21.   a) Some preliminary computations: 1 - p = 1 - .02 = .98 and n - r = 100 - 2 = 98. Using the binomial formula: P(2) = $C_{100,2}(.02)^2$ $(.98)^{98}$ = 4950(.02)^2 $(.98)^{98})$ = .2734 ♦

b) λ = np = 100(.02) = 2. Using the Poisson formula P(2) = $\frac{e^{-2} 2^2}{2!}$ = .2707 ♦

c) Comparing the results of parts b and c we see that they both round off to 27%. It appears in this situation the Poisson distribution is a good approximation for the binomial since $n \geq 100$ and $np = 100\,(.02) = 2 < 10$.♦.

d) Some preliminary computations: $1 - p = 1 - .02 = .98$ and $n - r = 100 - 3 = 97$. Using the binomial formula: $P(3) = C_{100,3}(.02)^3\,(.98)^{97} = 161{,}700(.02)^3\,(.98)^{97} = .1822$ ♦

Using the Poisson formula $P(3) = \dfrac{e^{-2}\,2^3}{3\,!} \approx .1804$ ♦

Comparing the results from the binomial and Poisson formulas, they both round off the 18%. The Poisson distribution provides a good approximation for the binomial for this situation.

Answers to Thinking about Statistics

1. This is a binomial experiment since there are a fixed number (10) of independent trials and the variable is counting the number os successes out of the 10 trials.

2. This is a Poisson probability distribution since there are a fixed number of occurrences during a time period. The variable r counts the number of occurrences during the time period.

3. This is a geometric distribution since a binomial experiment is repeated until success is reached. The first success is on the nth trial.

Chapter 6

NORMAL DISTRIBUTIONS

Section 6.1
Graphs of Normal Probability Distributions

Review

I.   Why we study **normal probability distributions.**
      A.   They describe the pattern for the distribution of measurements we often investigate in statistics. For example:
            1.   Heights of adult females in U. S.
            2.   Life spans (in hours) of batteries.
            3.   Weight of the contents of a box of cereal marked 20 oz.
            4.   Measures of Intelligence Quotients (I.Q.).
            5.   Lengths of diameters of oranges.
            6.   Average daily temperatures in Philadelphia.
            7.   Times it takes for individuals to finish a psychological test.
      B.   There are numerous applications of a normal probability distribution.
            1.   In quality control (discussion is later in chapter)
            2.   For approximating a binomial distribution when the number of trials is high. (topic covered in Chapter 7)
            3.   Essential in the study of sampling theory (covered in Chapter 7).

II.   Features of a Normal Probability Distribution curve.

      A.   Bell Shaped
      B.   Symmetric about the mean
      C.   The curve never touches the horizontal axis but gets closer and closer to it as x gets further and further

away from the mean. (In technical terms, the curve is asymptotic to the horizontal axis.)

D.   The mean = the median = the mode.

III.   Areas under Normal Probability Distribution curves.

A.   The total area between the curve and the horizontal axis is =1.

B.   The area to the right of the mean is .5 and the area to the left of the mean is .5. (since curve is symmetric)

C.   The area of the region bounded by the curve on top, vertical lines at the left and right and the horizontal axis below corresponds to the probability that the variable x will fall within that specified interval on the x axis..   **AREA** ⟵ ⟹ **PROBABILITY**

D.   **Empirical rule** for Area under any Normal Probability Distribution curve.

1.   Approximately 68% of the area under the curve falls in the center of the curve between the values μ - 1σ and μ + 1σ.

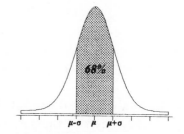

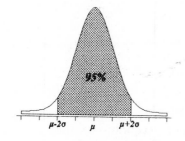

2.   Approximately 95% of the area under the curve falls between μ - 2σ and μ + 2σ.

3.   Approximately 99.7% (*almost all*) of the area under the curve falls between μ - 3σ and μ +3σ.

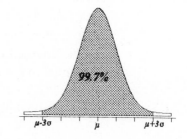

132

IV.   Significance of the mean and the standard deviation of a normal distribution curve.
    A.   The mean can be equal to any number.
        1.   It is the center value of the curve.
        2.   It divides the distribution into 2 halves, so it is equal to the median of the distribution as well.
        3.   It is the highest point on the curve, so it is equal to the mode.
    B.   The value of the standard deviation can be any positive number.
        1.   It gives information about the spread (or variability) of the data.
        2.   If the standard deviation is small, the curve is less spread out.
        3.   If the standard deviation is larger, the curve is more spread out.
        4.   The curve is cupped downward between $\mu - 1\sigma$ and $\mu + 1\sigma$.
        5.   There is a transition point at $\mu - 1\sigma$ and another at $\mu + 1\sigma$. (Remember that the curve is symmetric, so whatever happens on one side of the mean will happen on the other.)
        6.   After the transition point on either side of the mean, the curve changes to a upward cup as it gets closer and closer to the horizontal axis (but remember, it never touches this axis.)

V.   The use of the Normal Distribution in Quality Control
    A.   Control charts are used to provide warning signals to detect processes that are possibly 'out of statistical control'.
    B.   Used when individual measurements of a variable x are normally distributed.
    C.   Description of a control chart.
        1.   Horizontal scale represents numbers in a time sequence
        2.   Vertical scale represents the variable measure.
        3.   Center line is drawn corresponding to the mean of the population of values being measured.
            a.   Obtained from past measurements. Or
            b.   Obtained from specifications or "target values".

        4.   Control limits are set.
            a.   Upper Control limit (UCL) is set at 3 standard deviations above the mean.
            b.   Lower Control Limit (LCL) is set at 3 standard deviations below the mean.
    D.   Out of Control Warning Signals
        1.   At least one point falls above the UCL or below the LCL.
        2.   There is a run of 9 points on one side of the center line.
        3.   At least 2 out of 3 consecutive points lie beyond the 2 standard deviation level on the same side of the center line.

Problem Solving Warm-Up

1. Each of the variables in the left hand column of the table has a normal probability distribution with the given mean μ and standard deviation σ. Use the empirical rule to complete the table.

variable	μ	σ	68% falls between	95% falls between	99.7% falls between
Heights of adult females	65"	2.5"			
Contents of a box of cereal	20 oz.	.2 oz			
Life span of a battery	1000 hrs.	50 hrs.			
Measure of I.Q.	100	15			
Diameter of engine part	3"	.05"			

Check your answers in the table that follows.

To complete the column for 68% falls between, use μ - 1σ to μ + 1σ for each row.

To complete the column for 95% use μ - 2σ to μ + 2σ for each row.

To complete the column for 99.7% use μ - 3σ to μ + 3σ for each row.

variable	μ	σ	68% falls between	95% falls between	99.7% falls between
Heights of adult females	65"	2.5"	62.5 - 67.5	60 - 70	57.5 - 72.5
Contents of a box of cereal	20 oz.	.2 oz	19.8 - 20.2	19.6 - 20.4	19.4 - 20.6
Life span of a battery	1000 hrs.	50 hrs.	950 - 1050	900 - 1100	850 - 1150
Measure of I.Q.	100	15	85 - 115	70 - 130	55 - 145
Diameter of engine part	3"	.05"	2.95 - 3.05	2.90 - 3.10	2.85 - 3.15

2.   Use the empirical rule, together with the symmetry of the normal distribution to calculate how much of the area under the curve is between the vertical lines at the positions below. Use the following diagram as a guide.

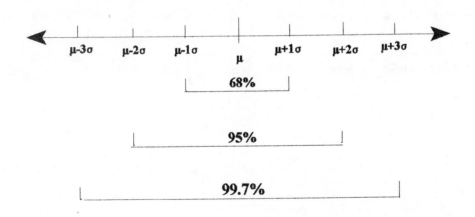

a)   μ and μ + 1σ

_____

b)   μ - 1σ and μ

_____

a) Half of 68% is 34%. Approximately 34% of the area under the curve is between the mean and one standard deviation above it.

b) 34% (using the symmetry of the curve).

c) μ and $\mu + 2\sigma$

_____

c) Half of 95% = 47.5%. Approximately 47.5% of the area falls between the mean and 2 standard deviations above it.

d) $\mu - 3\sigma$ and μ

_____

d) Half of 99.7% = 49.85%

e) $\mu - 1\sigma$ and $\mu + 2\sigma$

_____

e) We know that 34% of the area falls between $\mu - 1\sigma$ and μ. We also know that 47.5% falls between μ and $\mu + 2\sigma$. Adding these areas we get 81.5%.

f) $\mu + 1\sigma$ and $\mu + 3\sigma$

_____

f) We know that 34% of the area falls between μ and $\mu + 1\sigma$. Also, 49.85% of the area falls between μ and $\mu + 3\sigma$. However, these areas overlap. To get the area between them, we subtract 49.85% - 34% = 15.85%.

g) $\mu - 3\sigma$ and $\mu - 1\sigma$

_____

g) The answer, 15.85% is the same as part f, since the curve is symmetric.

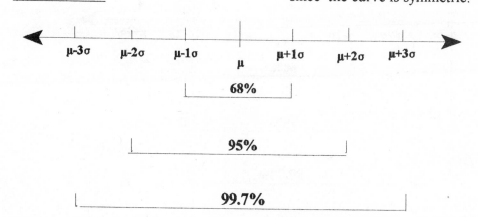

3.   Intelligence Quotient (IQ) is normally distributed with $\mu = 100$ and $\sigma = 15$. Fill in the values that correspond to the standard deviation marks on the number line and find the probability a person picked at random out of the general population has an IQ is in the given interval.

a)   Between 100 and 115?

_____

a) The mean is 100.
$115 = \mu + 1\sigma$ so the probability corresponds to the area under the curve in this interval. Since the area in this interval is 34%, the probability that a person will have an IQ in this interval is .34.

b)   Between 85 and 130?

_____

b) $85 = \mu - 1\sigma$
   $130 = \mu + 2\sigma$
In this interval is 34% + 47.5% =81.5% of the curve. Therefore, the probability of having an IQ between 85 and 130 is .815.

c)   Between 130 and 145?

_____

c) $130 = \mu + 2\sigma$
   $145 = \mu + 3\sigma$
Since these areas overlap, we subtract 49.85% - 47.5% = 2.35%. The probability of having an IQ in this interval is .0235.

d)   Over 130?

_____

d) $130 = \mu + 2\sigma$
We know that there is an area of 47.5% between the mean and $\mu + 2\sigma$. Since the area to the right of the mean = 50%, we can subtract 50% - 47.5% = 2.5% to get the area to the right of $\mu + 2\sigma$. The probability of having an IQ higher than 130 is .025.

e)   Less than 55?

_____

e) $55 = \mu - 3\sigma$
There is an area of 49.85% between the mean and $\mu - 3\sigma$. Since 50% of the curve is to the left of the mean, we subtract .50-.4985 = .0015 which is   the probability of having an IQ below 55.

3.   You are in charge of Quality Control for a manufacturing company that produces parts for automobiles. A specific gear has been designed to have a diameter of 3". We have learned that

the standard deviation for this gear is .2"

The following 10 measures were taken from a random sample of gears which came off the production line one day. Make a control chart for the measures given below. Does this indicate that the measures are "in control?"

part	1	2	3	4	5	6	7	8	9	10
diam.	2.9	2.6	3.1	3.5	2.8	2.9	3.4	3.2	2.7	3.3

To make a control chart, draw a horizontal center line at the mean = 3".

Control Chart

Draw horizontal lines at "control limits" at $\mu + 3\sigma$ and $\mu - 3\sigma$
LCL = 3 - 3(.02) = 2.4 and
UCL = 3 + 3(.02) = 3.6.

Draw horizontal lines at $\mu + 2\sigma$ and $\mu - 2\sigma$ (At 2.6 and 3.4)

Plot the data in sequential order.

Observation Number

Check for warning signals.
1. Do any points fall beyond the LCL and the UCL 3 standard deviation limits? No.
2. Is there a run of 9 points on one side of the center line? No.
3. Is there an instance of 2 out of 3 points beyond the 2 standard deviation limits on the same side of the Center Line? No.

Since the answer is No to all the warning signals, the process appears to be in statistical control.

One week later, the process was checked again and the following data were obtained. Make a control chart and test to see if the process remain "in control." Compare your results with the chart that follows.

part	1	2	3	4	5	6	7	8	9	10
diameter	2.9	3.5	2.8	3.5	3.2	2.8	3.4	3.2	3.9	3.3

Check for warning signals.
1. Do any points fall beyond the LCL and the UCL 3 standard deviation limits? Yes. Observation

number 9 is beyond the 3 sigma control limit.

2. Is there a run of 9 points on one side of the center line? No.

3. Is there an instance of 2 out of 3 points beyond the 2 standard deviation limits on the same side of the Center Line? Yes. two out of three of the points for observations numbers 3, 4 and 5.

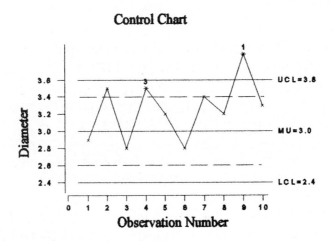

Thinking About Statistics

How does Chebyshev's Theorem relate to the Empirical Rule? What are the differences between them?

Selected Solutions Section 6.1

1.   None of the four curves in this problem resemble a normal distribution curve.
   a)   Is skewed to the left, therefore it is not symmetric.
   b)   The graph passes through the horizontal axis. In a normal distribution curve, the graph never touches it.
   c)   This curve has 3 peaks. The normal distribution curve has only one peak.
   d)   The normal distribution curve is a smooth curve. The curve shown is in the shape of a histogram.

5.   a)   Since the curve is symmetric about the mean, .50 of the curve is to the left of the mean. (.50 is to the right.) ♦
   b)   Approximately .68 falls within 1 standard deviation of the mean. ♦
   c)   From the empirical rule we know 99.7% falls between $\mu - 3\sigma$ and $\mu + 3\sigma$. ♦

9.   We are given that $\mu =$ year 1243 and $\sigma = 36$ years. Mark the line in standard deviation units as shown. On the following page.

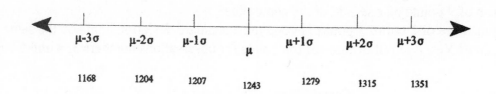

a)   About 68% of the data will fall within 1 standard deviation of the mean of 1243.
$\mu - 1\sigma = 1243 - 36 = 1207$ and $\mu + 1\sigma = 1243 + 36 = 1279$. ♦

b)   About 95% of the data will fall within 2 standard deviations of the mean.
$\mu - 2\sigma = 1243 - 2(36) = 1171$ and $\mu + 2\sigma = 1243 + 2(36) = 1315$. ♦

c) Almost all (99.7%) will fall within 3 standard deviations of the mean.
$\mu - 3\sigma = 1243 - 3(36) = 1135$ and $\mu + 3\sigma = 1243 + 3(36) = 1351$. ♦

13.   a)   Verify with your calculator.
   b)   68% should fall within $\mu \pm 1\sigma$. $\mu = 9.8\%$ and $\sigma = 3.8\%$ so $\mu - 1\sigma = 9.8\% - 3.8\% = 6.0$ % and $\mu + 1\sigma = 9.8\% + 3.8\% = 13.6\%$. 68% should fall between 6.0% and 13.6%.♦

   c)   95% should fall within 2 standard deviations of μ. So $\mu - 2\sigma = 9.8\% - 2(3.8\%) = 2.2\%$ and $\mu + 2\sigma = 9.8\% + 2(3.8\%) = 17.4\%$. Limits are 2.2% and 17.4%. ♦

   d)   100 - 95% = 5% the stocks will be outside the limits of $\pm 2\sigma$, and since the curve is symmetric, 2.5% of the time they will be over 2 from the mean. Likewise 32% (1-68%) the stocks will fall outside the boundaries of $\pm 1\ \sigma$, so 16% of the time they will be over 1σ from the mean. ♦

17. The Center Line is at 615.1. The UCL and the LCL at 3 standard deviations are at 581.5 and 648.7, respectively. The 2 standard deviation limits are at 592.7 and 637.5. ♦

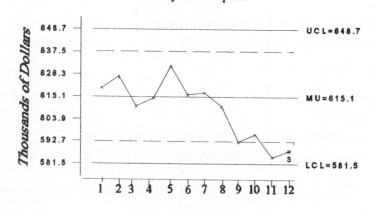

Monthly Loan Requests

From the control chart, it appears that the local business economy is cooling down since the trend is going downward. All values fall within the 3 standard deviation limits, but the last 2 out of 3 points fall beyond the 2

140

Monthly Loan Requests

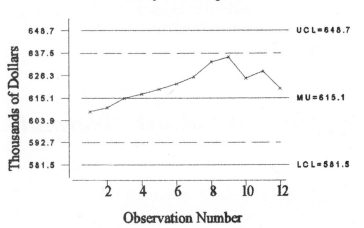

standard deviation line on the same side of the center line. This is a warning sign to indicate that the process may be heading out of control.

b) The control chart for the second 12 month period indicates that the local business economy is heating up. There are 9 points above the center line which may indicate a warning for an "out of control" trend. (type 3 signal)

21. The Center Line for this control chart should be at the mean = 28 tickets. The LCL and the UCL should be drawn at 13 and at 48. The 2 standard deviation control limits are at 18 and 43. All three out -of-control warnings are present. The first observation shows there is an unusually high number of tickets for the month.

Speeding Tickets

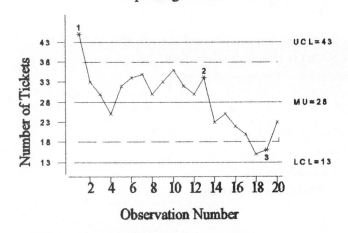

There are also 9 points in a row on the same side of the center line. Finally, the last 2 out of 3 points are beyond the 2 standard deviation control limits on the same side of the center line.

Answers to Thinking About Statistics

Chebyshev's Theorem states that for *any* distribution:

a)   AT LEAST 75% of the area under the curve is within 2σ of the mean.

The Empirical Rule gives specific areas under the **Normal Distribution** curve.

a)   Approximately 95% of the area under the Normal Distribution curve is within 2σ of the mean.

b)   AT LEAST 89% of the area under the curve is within 3σ of the mean.

b)   Approximately 99.7% of the area under the Normal Distribution curve is within 3σ of the mean.

c)   AT LEAST 93.75% of the area under the curve is within 4σ of the mean.

Section 6.2
Standard Units and the Standard Normal Distribution

Review

I.   The *standard score, z.*

   A.   A standard score makes it possible to *compare scores from different distributions with different means and different standard deviations.*

   B.   It is measured in standard deviation units.

   C.   To compute a z-score.

   1.   Find the difference between the x score and the mean of the distribution, μ. (x - μ) is called the deviation.

   $$z = \frac{x - \mu}{\sigma}$$

   2.   Divide the deviation by σ the standard deviation.

   D.   Possible values of z.

   1.   z can be any number, positive, negative or zero.

   2.   z = 0 occurs when x = μ. (Note then x - μ = 0.)

   3.   z is positive when x is above the mean.

   4.   z is negative when x is below the mean.

II.   To find an x value when its corresponding z-score is known.

   A.   We start with the formula for z,

   $$z = \frac{x - \mu}{\sigma}$$

   B.   To solve for x, multiply both sides by σ,

   $$z\sigma = x - \mu$$

   C.   Then add μ to both sides. We get a formula which we use to find x when we know z, μ and σ.

   $$x = \mu + z\sigma$$

III.   If x is a variable that has a *normal distribution*, then the corresponding z-scores will have a *normal distribution* called the **Standard Normal distribution** with:

   A.   The mean of the standard normal distribution is zero. μ = 0.

   B.   The standard deviation is one. σ = 1.

Problem Solving Warm-Up

1. Doug scored a 57 on the Miller Analogies Test which has a mean of 50 and a standard deviation of 5. Kathy scored 120 on the WISC (intelligence test) which has a mean of 100 and a standard deviation of 15. Compare their scores. Who had a better score?

   _____

   _____

$$z = \frac{x-\mu}{\sigma}$$

1. To compare the 2 scores, first convert each to a standard z-score. In the Distribution of Doug's test, $\mu=50$ and $\sigma=5$. Substitute x=57 to get the equivalent z score .

$$z = \frac{57-50}{5} = 1.4$$

For Kathy's test, $\mu=100$ and $\sigma=15$. x=120 so

$$z = \frac{120-100}{15} = 1.33$$

Doug's z score (1.4) is higher than Kathy's (1.33). Doug's score is better.

2. If x is a normally distributed variable with a mean of 5 and a standard deviation of .7, convert the following x intervals to z intervals.
   a) $5.3 \leq x \leq 6$

   _____

   _____

2. To convert to an interval of z scores, we must convert each endpoint of the given interval. Use $\mu = 5$ and $\sigma = .7$ for each part.

$$a) \quad z_L = \frac{5.3-5}{.7} = .43$$

$$z_R = \frac{6-5}{.7} = 1.43$$

The z interval is $.43 \leq z \leq 1.43$

   b) $4.2 \leq x \leq 4.8$

   _____

   _____

$$b) \quad z_L = \frac{4.2-5}{.7} = -1.14$$

$$z_R = \frac{4.8-5}{.7} = -.29$$

The z interval is $-1.14 \leq z \leq -.29$

   c) $4.2 \leq x \leq 6$

   _____

c) Using the z scores we have already computed, we can convert this interval to the

_____

| equivalent z interval
$-1.14 \le z \le 1.43$

d) $x \le 5.3$

d) $z \le .43$

_____

3.   The life span of a TopVolt brand Battery is normally distributed with a mean of 1000 hours and standard deviation of 50 hours. Given the following z intervals, convert to the equivalent x intervals.

a) $-1.7 \le z \le 2.1$

_____

b) $-2.8 \le z \le -.6$

c) $z \le -3$

_____

3. To convert from z scores to x scores use the formula $x = \mu + z\sigma$.
In this problem substitute $\mu = 1000$ and $\sigma = 50$.

a) $x_L = 1000 + (-1.7)(50) = 915$
$\quad x_R = 1000 + (2.1)(50) = 1105$
$\qquad$ the equivalent x interval is
$\qquad 915 \le x \le 1105$

b) $x_L = 1000 + (-2.8)(50) = 860$
$\quad x_R = 1000 + (-.6)(50) = 970$
$\qquad$ the equivalent x interval is
$\qquad 860 \le x \le 970$

c) $x = 1000 + (-3)(50) = 850$.
Note that from the Empirical Rule, *nearly all* the batteries should last for more than 850 hours.

Thinking About Statistics

Each of the following standard scores has been converted from an x value. Describe what each indicates about that x value.

    1. $z = 0$ 2. $z = 4.2$ 3. $z = -.49$

Selected Solutions

1.   a)   A positive z score indicates that the score is above the mean. Robert, Jan and Linda had positive x scores. ♦

b)   A z score of 0 indicates a score that is exactly equal to the mean. Joel's score was equal to the mean. ♦

c)   A negative z score indicates a score that is below the mean. John and Susan had negative z scores. ♦

d)   To compute the exam score (x) for each, we use the formula

$$x = \mu + z \cdot (\sigma)$$

Robert $x = 150 + (1.10)(20) = 172$ ♦
Jan $x = 150 + (1.70)(20) = 184$ ♦
Susan $x = 150 + (-2.00)(20) = 110$ ♦
Joel $x = 150 + (0.00)(20) = 150$ ♦
John $x = 150 + (-0.80)(20) = 134$ ♦
Linda $x = 150 + (1.60)(20) = 182$ ♦

Note that the students who had negative z scores had scores were less than 150. Examine the formula carefully to see why this happens.

5.   To convert an interval of x values to an interval of z scores, use the conversion formula for each endpoints. Use $73 = \mu$ and $5 = \sigma$.

$$z = \frac{x - \mu}{\sigma}$$

$$z_L = \frac{53 - 73}{5} = -4 \quad and \quad z_R = \frac{93 - 73}{5} = 4$$

a) The z interval is
   $-4 \le z \le 4$ ♦

$$z = \frac{65 - 73}{5} = \frac{-8}{5} = -1.6$$

b) The z interval is $z < -1.6$ ♦

$$z = \frac{78 - 73}{5} = \frac{5}{5} = 1$$

c) The z interval is $z < 1$ ♦

To convert from z scores into equivalent x values use $x = \mu + z\sigma$.

d) $x = 73 + 1.75(5) = 81.75$ The x interval is $x < 81.75°F$ ◆

e) $x = 73 + -1.90(5) = 63.5$ The x interval is $x < 63.5°F$ ◆

f) $x = 73 + -1.80(5) = 64$ and $x = 73 + 1.65(5) = 81.25$ The x interval is $64°F < x < 81.25°F$ ◆

9. To convert from an x interval to a z interval, use the formula at the right for each endpoint.

$$z = \frac{x - \mu}{\sigma}$$

$z = \dfrac{4.5 - 4.8}{.3} = -1.0$ a) $-1.0 < z$ (or $z > -1.0$) ◆

$z = \dfrac{4.2 - 4.8}{.3} = -2.0$ b) $z < -2.0$ ◆

$z_L = \dfrac{4.0 - 4.8}{.3} = -2.67$ and $z_R = \dfrac{5.5 - 4.8}{.3} = 2.33$ c) $-2.67 < z < 2.33$ ◆

To convert from a z interval to an interval of x values, use the formula $x = \mu + z\sigma$ for each endpoint. (z represents a standard score and x a score on that particular test.)

d) $x = 4.8 + (-1.44)(.3) = 3.936$ The equivalent x interval is $x < -1.44$ ◆

e) $x = 4.8 + (1.28)(.3) = 5.2$ The x interval is $5.2 < x$ ◆

f) $x_L = 4.8 + (-2.25)(.3) = 4.1$ and $x_R = 4.8 + (-1.00)(.3) = 4.5$
        The x interval is $4.1 < x < 4.5$ ◆

g)   A count of 5.9 or higher is equivalent to a standard score interval of $z > 3.67$. The probability of obtaining such a count is less than .0002 (found by .5 - .4898). A red blood cell count of 5.9 or higher would be considered unusually high for a healthy female. ◆

13.   a) Although Walter's dollar amount was lower than that of Niko, he might have a more difficult district to work in. The values can only be compared using standard scores.

b) For Niko   For Walter

$z = \dfrac{31600 - 27520}{2450} = 1.665$ $z = \dfrac{30950 - 24170}{2670} = 2.539$

Walter's standard score is higher than Niko's.

c)   Walter. His standard score was higher.

Answers to Thinking About Statistics

1.   A z score of 0 indicates that the x score is precisely equal to the mean. In a normal distribution this would also indicate that half the population was above this x score and half was below.

2.   A z score of 4.2 is *extremely* high. The raw score is 4.2 standard deviations above the mean. Only a minuscule percentage of the population will score above this.

3.   A z score of -.49 is slightly below the mean, but within one standard deviation of the mean so it is not exceptional.

Section 6.3
Areas Under the Standard Normal Curve

Review

When we studied probability histograms for discrete variables, we saw that the *area* inside a bar corresponded to the *probability* that the value of the variable fell at the value representing that bar. The normal distribution is a probability distribution that can be used to describe many continuous random variables. Although we can not find the probability that the variable is equal to one specific value (since that probability is virtually 0), we can determine the probability that the variable falls within an *interval of values*. The computations for the areas are well beyond the scope of your text, but an area table has been provided for this purpose.

Since there are an infinite number of normal probability distribution graphs, each having a different mean and a different standard deviation, it would be impossible to provide tables for all of them. Instead, we can convert intervals for any normal distribution into equivalent intervals under the standard normal curve and use area values provided for the standard normal distribution.

I.   Properties of the Standard Normal Probability Distribution curve
   A.   It is marked off in standard z units. Each z unit designates one standard deviation. A z-score of 1.23 is 1.23 standard deviations *above* the mean. A z-score of -2.34 is 2.34 standard deviation *below* the mean.
   B.   The mean is at $z = 0$.

147

C.   The standard deviation is 1.

D.   The total area under the curve = 1. (As it is with ALL probability distribution curves.)

    1.   The area to the right of z = 0 is .5.

    2.   The area to the left of z = 0 is .5.

II.   Use of tables to read areas under a Standard Normal Distribution curve

A.   We know some rough approximations of areas from the Empirical Rule.

    1.   Approximately 68% falls between 1 standard deviation below and 1 standard deviation above the mean. In a standard normal curve we can say between z = -1 and z = 1. This indicates that approximately 34% falls between the mean (z = 0) and 1 standard deviation above it (z = 1).

    2.   Approximately 95% falls between z = -2 and z = 2, indicating approximately 47.5% falls between z = 0 and z = 2.

    3.   Approximately 99.7% or almost all falls between z = -3 and z = 3 indicating approximately 49.85% falls between z = 0 and z = 3.

B.   Reasons to use a table

    1.   We often need a more precise measure for these particular values.

    2.   We will need area measures for values of z other than 1, 2 and 3 such as 1.52 or -2.94.

III.   Features of table found inside back cover of your text

A.   Only area values corresponding to positive z scores are included. Since the curve is symmetric, the areas to the left of the mean (negative z scores) are identical to their mirror image areas on the right side of the mean. It is not necessary to double the size of the table.

B.   The given area value is the area which is below the curve within the interval between z = 0 and z = specified number.

C.   Any other areas have to be computed with reference to these values.

IV.   Structure of the table (Refer to the table while reading.)

A.   The z values are listed down the left hand column ranging in increments of tenths from z = 0.0 to z = 5.0.

B.   The area values are found in the main portion of the table. The area values increase from .0000 at z = 0 to .4999997 (*almost* .5) at z = 5.

C.   Across the top are .00 .01 .02 to .09 which allow us to read the corresponding areas for z values expressed to two decimal places.

D.   For example: Find the area under the curve between the mean and z = 1.73

Use the following excerpt from the table of the Standard Normal distribution

z	.00	.01	.02	.03
0.0	.0000	.0040	.0080	.0120↓
0.1				.0517↓
0.2				.0910↓
↓				.1293↓
1.6				↓
1.7	.4554→	.4564→	.4573→	**.4582**

Read down the z column to 1.7 go across this row and read the entry which is underneath .03 at the top. The entry which is in this cell gives us the area under the standard normal curve between the mean and z = 1.73.

E.   For example: Find the z score on the right half of the curve so that 42% of the curve falls between this particular z score and the mean.

Use the table of the Standard Normal Distribution found inside the front cover of the Brase text. Note that the z scores are read down the left hand column and across the top row. The areas that are listed in the center portion of the table represent the area falling between the given z-score and the mean.

z	.00	.01	.02	.03
0.0	.0000	.0040↑	.0080	
0.1	.0398	↑		
0.2				
1.4	.4192 ←←	←.4207		
	←			

Since the area values are found in the large lower right hand portion of the table, look there for the entry which is closest to .4200. (Note that the entries are in numerical order.)

From the table we see that the area between the mean (z=0) and z = 1.40 is .4192, the area between the mean and z = 1.41 is .4207 and the area between the mean and z = 1.42 is .4222. .4207 is the closest entry to the required .4200, so we read the z score which corresponds to it. First read to the left to see 1.4 in the z column and then look up to the top of the column which contains .4207 and read .01. The answer is z = 1.41.

F.   To determine areas under the Standard Normal curve, 8 different situations, labeled A to H will be described together with the appropriate method for finding the required area. Later you will be given a set of area problems and asked to match them with situations A to H.

Note that if you draw a normal distribution curve for each problem, it is not necessary to memorize these techniques. Try to understand *why* they work.

Area values given in the Normal Distribution table represent the area bounded on the left by a vertical line drawn at the mean (z = 0), on the right by a vertical line at the given z score, above by the curve and below by the horizontal axis. To determine any other areas, some arithmetic computation may be necessary. In the diagram below, the shaded region corresponds to the area value found in the table in your text.

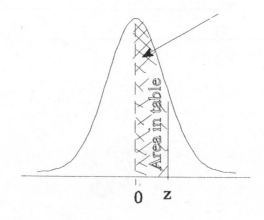

Examine how various areas under a normal curve are computed.

A. Between z = 0 and a specified positive z-score. B. Between z = 0 and a specified negative z-score

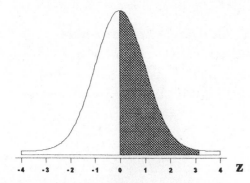

This is always the area given in the table.

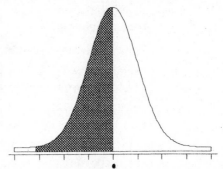

Look up corresponding area for positive z-score

C. Between a negative z-score and a positive one

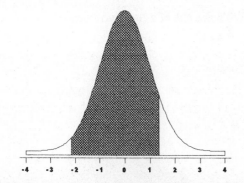

Add the two areas you obtain from the table.

D. Between two z-scores with the same sign

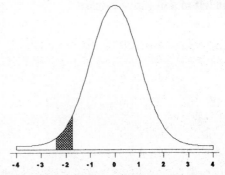

Subtract the smaller area from the larger.

E. To the right of a positive z score.

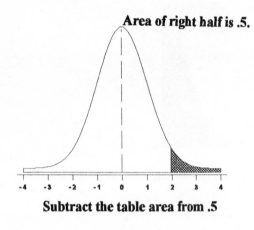

Area of right half is .5.

Subtract the table area from .5

F. To the right of a negative z-score

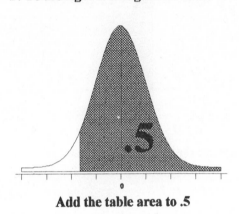

Add the table area to .5

G. To the left of a negative z-score

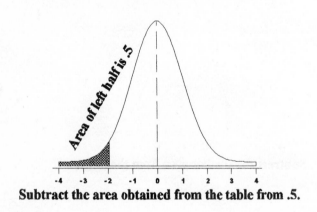

Area of left half is .5

Subtract the area obtained from the table from .5.

H. To the left of a positive z-score

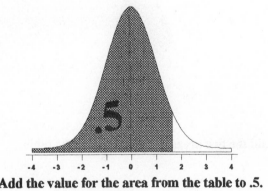

Add the value for the area from the table to .5.

Problem Solving Warm-Up

For each of the following area questions, draw your own normal distribution curve, shade the given areas and match the situation with the graphs drawn labeled A to H in the review section. It is a good idea to draw a standard normal curve and shade the appropriate area for each problem you do in the future. This helps to visualize the situation and eliminates the necessity for memorizing.

1.   Area between $z = 0$ and $z = \quad -1.75$.

_____

2.   Area between $z = 2.63$ and $z = 3.02$

_____

3.   Area between $z = -1.75$ and $z = 2.63$

_____

4.   Area to the right of $z = 2.63$

_____

5.   Area between $z = -2.63$ and $z = -3.02$

_____

6.   Area to the left of $z = 2.63$

_____

7.   Between $z = 0$ and $z = .27$

_____

8.   Area to the left of $z = -3.02$

_____

1. Situation B: Area = .4599

2. Situation D: Since both z scores are on the same side of the mean, we subtract. Area = .4987 - .4957 = .0030.

3. Situation C: Since the z scores are on opposite sides of the mean we add the areas: Area = .4599 + .4957 = .9556.

4. Situation E: We subtract .5 - .4957 = .0043.

5. Situation D: Since both are on the same side of the mean we subtract. The answer .0030 is the same as that for question 2 since the curve is symmetric.

6. Situation H: .5 + .4957 = .9957. Compare this with the answer to question 4.

7. Situation A: Look up on the table,(but be careful <u>not</u> to look up z = 2.7 instead). Area = .1064.

8. Situation G: Subtract .5 - .4987 = .0013.

For each of the following draw a standard normal curve, shade the appropriate area and then determine the probability that z falls in the given interval.

9.   P(-2.43 ≤ z≤ 1.65)

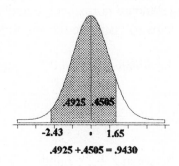

.4925 +.4505 = .9430

10.   P(-1.96 ≤z ≤-1.45)

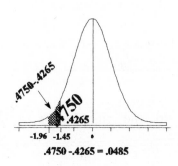

.4750 -.4265 = .0485

11.   P(z ≥1.96)

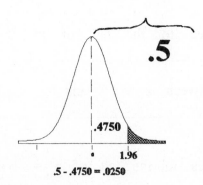

.5 - .4750 = .0250

12.   P(z≥0)

_____

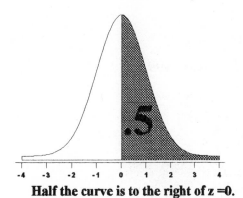

Half the curve is to the right of z =0.

13.   P(z ≤ -2.58)

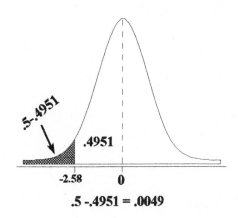

.5 -.4951 = .0049

Thinking About Statistics

P(z ≥ 1.96) is the same as P(z > 1.96). Why is the answer the same for a "greater than or equal to" inequality as it is for a strictly "greater than" inequality?

Selected Solutions Section 6.3

1.   Ans. .4993

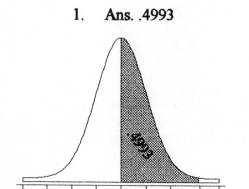

Look up the area on the table corresponding to the z-score.

5. Ans. .4854+.4099 = .8653

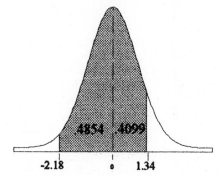

z-scores have opposite signs, so add the areas.

9. Ans. .0306

.4922

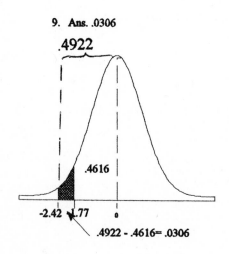

.4922 - .4616= .0306

13. Ans: .5 - .4357 = .0643

Area of right half is .5.

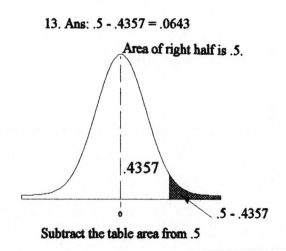

.5 - .4357

Subtract the table area from .5

17. Ans: .3888 + .5 = .8888

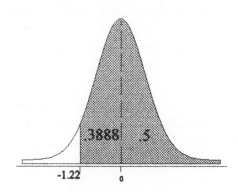

25. Ans: .1736 + .4968 = .6704

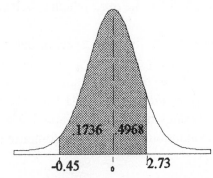

z-scores are opposite sign so add areas

27. Ans: .4854 - .1628 = .3226

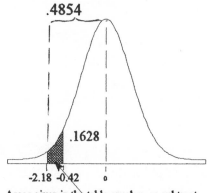

Areas given in the table overlap, so subtract

31. The area of the left half of the curve is .5

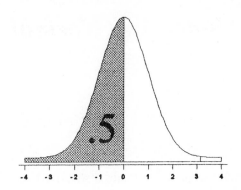

35. P(ż ≤ -.013) = .5 - .0517 = .4483 See curve G in the review section.

39. P (z ≤ 1.20) = .5 + .3849 = .8849. See curve H in the review section.

Answers to Thinking About Statistics

P(z > 1.96) corresponds to the *area* which is below the curve and to the right of the vertical line at 1.96.

P(z≥ 1.96) corresponds to the *area* which is below the curve and to the right of the vertical line at 1.96 + the *area* above the point at z = 1.96. Since the area above the point at z = 1.96 is 0 (there is no width), the answers to both probability questions is the same, .0250.

Technically, the *probability* that z = 1.96 is 0 since the z variable is continuous and can be any decimal number. (values of 1.9643286 and 1.9584085 are also possible). When we compute the probability for a continuous variable, we compute the probability that the variable is *within a given interval*.

Section 6.4

Areas Under Any Normal Curve

Review

I.   Problem: Given a normally distributed variable x with a mean μ and a standard deviation σ, find the probability that the value of x will fall in a specified interval.

   A.   Earlier in this chapter we saw how to solve the following:

   1.   Given a normally distributed variable x with its mean and standard deviation, convert it to a standard normal z score.

   2.   Find the probability that a z score will fall within a specified z interval.

   B.   To solve the stated problem, we will combine the techniques learned earlier in the chapter.

   1.   The x values will be given in the problem, along with values for the mean and the standard deviation. First convert each to its equivalent z-score, and write as a z interval.

$$z = \frac{x-\mu}{\sigma}$$

   2.   Now that you have an equivalent z score interval, use the standard normal distribution table to determine the area (hence probability). The probability that z is within the computed z interval *is the same as* the probability that x is within the given x interval.

C. The standard normal distribution curve table makes it possible to compute areas within any normal distribution curve. This means we only need one table of area values!

II. Problem: Given a specified area (a probability) under a standard normal curve find the z score boundaries which form the vertical line borders of the area region under that curve.
   A. This is the reverse of the problem posed in I. Here we know the **area** and need to find the z score.
   B. Start by drawing a standard normal distribution curve and shade the region whose area is described in the problem.
   C. If this region is not precisely one that is between the mean and a z score, use the given information to determine which area is the one that is between the mean and the unknown z score. (This is the area value which is listed in the table and must be used as a reference.)
   D. Look in the main body of the table for the closest area to the one you have determined for part C.
   E. Determine the corresponding z score by looking across to the left hand column for the one's and tenth's place of the z score and up to the top of the table for the hundredths place.

III. Given a specified area (probability) under a normal distribution curve with variable x, determine the x boundaries which define the area.
   A. Follow steps A to E from the problem in II.
   B. Using the formula shown convert the z score you found into an x value.
   $$x = \mu + z\sigma$$
   C. This procedure is used, for instance, when you are required to :
      1. Determine the length of time you should guarantee a product.
      2. Determine cut-off scores for a test when, for example you want to select the top 10% of the population.

IV. Hints for successful solution of these problems:
   A. Clearly list all the values given in the problem with appropriate labels, such as μ, σ, x or z.
   B. Determine what is the unknown. (What is the problem asking you to do?)
   C. Write down the appropriate formula. All computation must be done with the standard normal scores.
   D. Draw a standard normal distribution curve and shade to help visualize the problem.

Problem Solving Warm-Up

1. If x is a normally distributed variable with a mean of 30 and a standard deviation of 6, find the following probabilities:

a) P(x > 30)

_____
_____

a) The z score which corresponds to x = 30 is z = 0, since μ = 30. It is a good idea to reference all your z scores to the mean. Before you start to convert x scores to z scores in this problem you should realize that any x value above 30 will have a positive z score and any x value below 30 will have a negative z score. P(x > 30) = P(z > 0) = .5

b) P(22 < x < 35)

_____
_____

b) For x = 22
$$z_L = \frac{22-30}{6} = -1.33$$

For x = 35
$$z_R = \frac{35-30}{6} = .83$$

So to find P(22 < x < 35) find the corresponding P(-1.33 < z < .83) = .4082 + .2967 = .7049

c) P(33 < x < 37)

_____
_____

c) For x = 33
$$z_L = \frac{33-30}{6} = .5$$

For x = 37
$$z_R = \frac{37-30}{6} = 1.17$$

P(33 < x < 37) =
P(.5 < z < 1.17)

$$= .3790 - .1915 = .1875$$

2. The assembly times required for the manufacturing of a certain product are normally distributed with a mean of 400 seconds and a standard deviation of 50 seconds. An item is selected at random. Find the probability that its assembly time is :

a) between 288 and 400 seconds

a) $\mu = 400$; $\sigma = 50$ For x=288

$$z_L = \frac{288-400}{50} = -2.24$$

For x=400

$$z_R = \frac{400-400}{50} = 0$$

$P(288 < x < 400) =$
$P(-2.24 < z < 0) = .4875$

b) Greater than 492 seconds

b)

$$z = \frac{492-400}{50} = 1.84$$

$$P(x > 492) = P(z > 1.84)$$
$$= .5 - .4671 = .0329$$

c) between 360 and 440 seconds

c)

$$z_L = \frac{360-400}{50} = -.8$$

$$z_R = \frac{440-400}{50} = .8$$

$P(360 < x < 440) = \quad P(-.8 < z < .8)$
$= .2881 + .2881 = .5762$

d) Less than 420 seconds

d)

$$z = \frac{420-400}{50} = .4$$

$P(x < 420) = P(z < .4)$
$= .5 + .1554 = .6554$

3.   Let z be the standard normal variable. Shade each or the given curves appropriately. Find the value of z which fits each of the following conditions.

a).50 of the curve lies to the right of z.

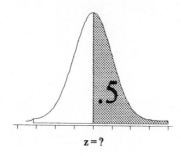

z = ?

a)   We know 50% lies to the right of the mean and so z = 0 at the mean. 50% of the curve lies to the right of z= 0..

_____

_____

b)   Area of .3479 is between z and the mean.

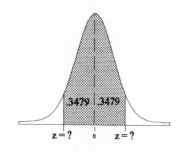

z = ?   0   z = ?

b)   In this case z could be on either side of the mean. Looking up an area of .3749 we see it corresponds to z = 1.15. Ans. z = -1.15 or z = 1.15

c) 5% of the curve lies to the left of z.

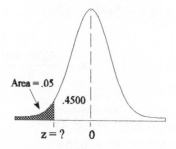

Area = .05

.4500

z = ?   0

c)   We can see that our z score is on the negative side of the curve. If 5% lies to the left of z then 45% falls between z and the mean. Looking up in the area portion for the entry closest to .4500 we see that .4500 falls directly in between .4495 and .4505. When an area is exactly in the middle, we take the midpoint of -1.64 and -1.65 and chose z = -1.645.

d) 10% of the curve is to the left of z.

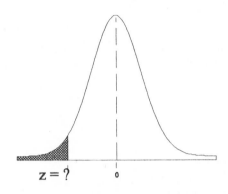

z = ? 0

d) This z score is on the positive half of the curve. In reference to the mean we look for a z score which has 40% area between itself and the mean. The closest area entry to .4000 is .3997 so z = 1.28

) Find z such that 95% of the curve falls between -z and z.

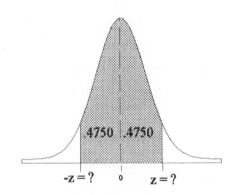

4750 4750

-z = ? 0 z = ?

e) Since our table only includes half of the curve, we look equivalently for the z score which defines an area of 47.5% or .4750 between itself and the mean. We find z = 1.96. 95% of the curve falls between z= -1.96 and z = 1.96 . Recall the Empirical Rule which said *approximately* 95% of the area in a normal probability distribution curve falls between z = ± 2. The z scores of ±1.96 are more precise.

4. The length of time employees have been working at a specific company is normally distributed with a mean of 15 years and a standard deviation of 5.2 years. The CEO has decided that 5% of the employees will have to receive lay-off notices. These notices will go to the individuals with the least seniority at the company. Find the number of years which will determine the lowest 5% of this distribution. Anyone at the company this number of years or less would then receive a lay off notice.

4. $\mu = 15$ yrs. ; $\sigma = 5.2$ yrs.

First find the z score for which 5% of the distribution lies to the left (is less than) z. From problem 3c above, we see that
z = -1.645.
We now use the formula $x = \mu + z\sigma$ and solve for x. x= 15 + (-1.645)(5.2) = 6.45. Thus, if a person has been working at this company 6.45 years or less, they should expect a lay off notice.

Thinking About Statistics

In a large section of a Western Civilization course, test grades are normally distributed with a mean of 70 and a standard deviation of 7. Grades are to be assigned according to the following rule. Find the numerical limits for each letter grade.

grade	boundaries
A	Top 10%
B	Between the top 10% and 30% .
C	Scores between the top 30% and the bottom 30%
D	Between the bottom 10% and 30%.
F	Bottom 10%

Selected Solutions Section 6.4

1. We are given an interval of x values where x is a normally distributed variable. We are also given the mean and the standard deviation of the x distribution. The problem is to find the indicated probability.

    Listing the given information with the appropriate labels

    $$\mu = 4 \qquad \sigma = 2$$

    We must now find the z scores which are equivalent to the left and right hand endpoints of the interval. Use the formula shown. $z = \dfrac{x - \mu}{\sigma}$

    The question is equivalent to

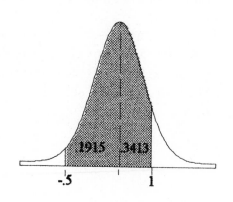

    $$\text{- 6:} \quad z_R = \frac{6 - 4}{2} = 1$$

    $P(-.5 \le z \le 1)$. We draw a standard normal distribution graph, shading the required area. As we can see from the drawing, we get the answer by adding the areas.

    $$.1915 + .3413 = .5328 \blacklozenge$$

    $P(3 \le x \le 6) = P(-.5 \le z \le 1) = .5328 \blacklozenge$

164

5. $\mu = 15$ $\sigma = 3.2$

$$z_L = \frac{8-15}{3.2} = -2.19 \quad and$$

$$z_R = \frac{12-15}{3.2} = -.94$$

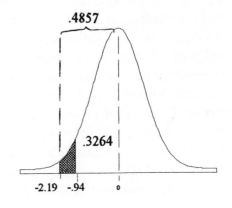

$P(8 \le x \le 12) = P(-2.19 \le z \le -.94) =$
$.4857 - .3264 = .1593$ ♦

$$z = \frac{90-100}{15} = -.67$$

9. $\mu = 100$; $\sigma = 15$; x =90P(x≥ 90) =
P(z≥ -.67) = .7486 ♦

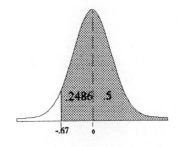

13.   We are required to find the negative value for
z such that the area between the unknown z
score and the mean is .4200. From the area
values found in the center of the table, the
closest value is .4207. Read the z-score found
at the left as 1.4 and up the column to .01.
Since the required value is negative, the z
score is z = -1.41 ♦

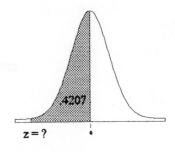

17. We are asked to find the z score so that 8% of the curve is to the right of it. Draw a standard normal curve and shade the given region. Since the table is set up for area values of area which are between the mean (z =0) and the value of z (which at this point is unknown), we have to translate the problem so that we can read the answer from the table. We know the entire area to the right of the mean is .5, so we subtract .5 - .08 = .42 to obtain the reference area. Now find the z score such that an area of .42 falls between the mean and that score. The positive value is z = 1.41 ◆

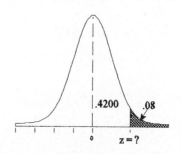

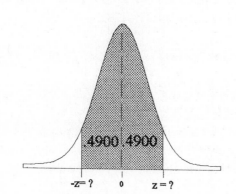

19. We have to find a z value so that the area between the negative z and the positive z is .98. Since the table only references half of the curve, we will do the same. Thus we want to find the z score so that the area between the mean and that z score is .4900 (half of .98). The closest area value in the table is .4901. The corresponding z score is 2.33. Therefore 98% of the curve lies between the z scores of -2.33 and 2.33 ◆

21. $\mu = 85.$ $\sigma = 25$
x = the milligrams of glucose per deciliter of blood.

$z - \dfrac{60-85}{25} - -1$

a) P(x >60)
converting to a z interval we get P(z > -1) = .3413 +.5 = .8413 ◆

$z - \dfrac{110-85}{25} - 1$

b) P(x < 110) = P(z < 1)
.5 + .3413 = .8413◆

c) Use the z-scores found in parts a and b
P(60 >x> 110) = P(-1< z<1) = 3413 + .3413 = .6826 ◆

$z - \dfrac{140-85}{25} - 2.2$

d) P(x > 140) = P z >2.2) = .5 - .4861 = .0139 (about 1%) ◆

166

25. $\mu = 68$ lb.; $\sigma = 12$ lb.

$z \cdot \dfrac{50 - 68}{12} \cdot -1.5$

a) $P(x < 50) = P (z < -1.5) = .5 - .4332 = .0668 \blacklozenge.$

$z \cdot \dfrac{80 - 68}{12} \cdot 1$

b) $P(x > 80) = P(z > 1) = .5 - .3413 = .1587 \blacklozenge$

c)Use parts a and b to solve. $P(50 < x < 80) = P(-1.5 < z < 1) = .4332 + .3413 = .7745 \blacklozenge$

29. $\mu = 5$ pounds . ; $\sigma = 1.6$ pounds   x= weight gain for student.

$z \cdot \dfrac{2 - 5}{1.6} \cdot -1.88$ and $z \cdot \dfrac{6 - 5}{1.6} \cdot .63$ a) $P(2 < x < 6) = P (-1.88 < z < .63)$
$= .4699 + .2357 = .7056 \blacklozenge$

$z \cdot \dfrac{1 - 5}{1.6} \cdot -2.5$

b) $P(x \le 1) = P(z \le -2.5) = .5 - .4938 = .0062 \blacklozenge$

$z \cdot \dfrac{10 - 5}{1.6} \cdot 3.13$

c) $P(x \ge 10) = P(z \ge 3.13) = .5 - .4991 = .0009 \blacklozenge$

31. $\mu = 45$ months and $\sigma = 8$ months

$z \cdot \dfrac{36 - 45}{8} \cdot -1.13$

a) Find the probability that x is less than 36 months.
After finding the z-score of -1.13, find $P(z < -1.13) = .5 - .3708 = .1292 \blacklozenge$

b) Find the value of x representing the length of time a battery lasts so that 10% or fewer will have died. We must first determine the standard normal z score so that. 10% of the curve is to the left of it (leaving 90% to the right). This can only be true if z is on the left side of the mean. This is equivalent to finding the value of z such that 40% of the area under the curve falls between the mean and that z score. We look within the *area* portion (center) of the standard normal table and see that an area of .3997 is the closest to .4000. The z score which corresponds to this area on the left side of the curve is -1.28.

We now must use the formula $\mathbf{x = \mu + z\sigma}$ to compute the equivalent x value.
$x = 45 + (-1.28)(8) = 34.74$ months.

Thus if we guarantee the batteries for a period of 34 months we are assured that we will not have to replace more than 10% of them. $\blacklozenge$

35. $\mu = 90$ mo. ; $\sigma = 3.7$ mo.

We must first find the standard z score such that 99% of the curve is to the right of it and 1% to the left. We do this by first determining that 49% must be between that score and the mean (since 50% is to the left of the mean). Looking in the area portion of the table for the closest value to .4900, we find .4901. The z score on the left side of the curve which corresponds to this is -2.33. We now convert this to the x value
$x = 90 + (-2.33)(3.7) = 82.38$. The company should insure the satellite for 82 months.

$z = \dfrac{84-90}{3.7} = -1.62$ b) $P(x < 84) = P(z < -1.62) = .5 - .4474 = .0526$ ♦

37.   For a, b and c: $\mu = 8000$ and $\sigma = 500$

$z = \dfrac{7200-8000}{500} = -1.6$

a) $P(x < 7200) = P(z < -1.6) = .5 - .4452 = .0548$

$z = \dfrac{8900-8000}{500} = 1.8$

b) $P(x > 8900) = P(z > 1.8 = .5 - .4641 = .0359$ ♦

c) $P(7200 < x < 8900) = P(-1.6 < z < 1.8) = .4452 + .4641 = .9093$ ♦

For parts d, e and f use $\mu = 228$ minutes. (3 hours and 48 minutes = 180 minutes + 48 minutes = 228 minutes) and $\sigma = 52$ min.

d) Reference is Area of .4000. (.5000 area for the left side + .4000 area beyond the mean gives area of .9000. The closest listed area is .3997 which corresponds to a z score of 1.28.
1.28 is the z-score that corresponds to this area value.
Converting from z to x, $x = 228 + 1.28(52) = 294.56$ minutes (4.9 hours) ♦

e) Use $.5 - .15 = .3500$ as the reference area. This corresponds to a z-score of -1.04. Converting to an x value we get $x = 228 + (-1.04)(52) = 173.94$ minutes. (2.9 hours) ♦

f) Since Friday is a weekday when many people are at work and Saturday is a weekend day when many are off, the arrival time patterns for these days might be expected to be different. ♦

Answers to Thinking About Statistics

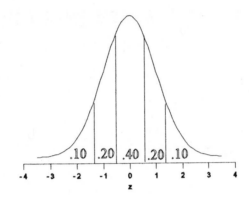

Construct a standard normal distribution curve.
The top 10% (reference area .4000) corresponds to a z score of 1.28.
The top 30% (reference area .2000) corresponds to a z score of .52
The bottom 30% (reference area .2000) corresponds to a z score of -.52
The bottom 10 % (reference area .4000) corresponds to a z score of -1.28.

Using the formula $x = \mu + z \cdot \sigma$ we convert each z score into an x score and round off..
$x = 70 + 7(\mathbf{1.28}) = 78.96 \approx 79$
$x = 70 + 7(\mathbf{.52}) = 73.64 \approx 74$
$x = 70 + 7(\mathbf{-.52}) = 66.36 \approx 66$
$x = 70 + 7(\mathbf{-1.28}) = 61.04 \approx 61$

Use 79, 74, 66 and 61 for the "cut-off" scores that determine the grades A, B, C and D.

A	79 or above
B	74 -78
C	66 -73
D	61 -65
F	60 and below.

Chapter 7

INTRODUCTION TO SAMPLING DISTRIBUTIONS

Section 7.1
Sampling Distributions

Review

I.   Important definitions
      A.   A *population* is the set of ALL measurements, counts or responses which are of interest to the researcher. Because there are often limitations in resources of time and/or money, frequently we are unable to obtain **every possible** member of the population.
      B.   A *sample* is a subset of the population.
            1.   We use information obtained from a sample to make inferences about a population.
            2.   For a given population, there are infinitely many samples.

II.   Numerical information obtained from a population is called a *parameter*.
      A.   Examples of population parameters:
            1.   Population mean = μ.
            2.   Population standard deviation = σ.
            3.   Population value in a binomial experiment of the probability of success for one trial = p (some texts use π).
      B.   A population parameter such as μ is a single fixed number (it does not change). However, most of the time we are unable to determine it directly since we can not obtain all the possible counts or measures.

III.   Numerical information obtained from a sample is called a ***statistic***.
    A.   Examples of sample statistics:
        1.   Sample mean = $\bar{x}$.
        2.   Sample standard deviation = s.
        3.   Sample value for probability of success in a binomial trial is obtained by dividing the number of successes by the total number of trials $\hat{p}= \dfrac{r}{n}$.
            ($\hat{p}$ is read as "p hat".)
    B.   Sample statistics are used to make inferences about population parameters.
        1.   Statistics are used to *estimate the value of a parameter*.
        2.   Statistics are used to *make decisions about the value of a parameter*.
        3.   If we were somehow able to produce an infinite number of samples of the same size, compute each sample mean and then observe the resulting distribution, we would be examining what is called the sampling distribution. When we are interested in investigating a population mean, we must know about the sampling distribution for sample means of a given sample size.

Problem Solving Warm-Up

In the study of Statistics we often use a process called simulation to replicate a statistical experiment. Working through the following simulation problem will help you understand the process of studying sampling distributions. We will use the table of random numbers.

The table of random numbers consists of the digits 0,1,2,3,4,5,6,7,8,and 9 appearing (in theory) with equal frequency. Therefore, each digit has a probability of $\dfrac{1}{10}$ or .10 of appearing

in any place in the table. This is an example of a *uniform* distribution which we studied earlier. A histogram for the distribution of digits looks like the one shown on the right.

We can use a statistical calculator or use the formulas for the mean and standard deviation of a probability distribution to compute the mean of this *population* as 4.5 and the standard deviation as 2.87.
For the *population* of digits: $\mu = 4.5$ and $\sigma = 2.87$

As stated earlier, there are an infinite number of samples for this population of digits. Form 25 of these samples, each sample containing 10 digits. Compute $\bar{x}$, the mean for each sample. Choose a random spot to start on random digit table. Fill in your results below.

Sample 1 _____ $\bar{x}$ = _____

Sample 2 _____ $\bar{x}$ = _____

Sample 3 _____ $\bar{x}$ = _____

Sample 4 _____ $\bar{x}$ = _____

Sample 5 _____ $\bar{x}$ = _____

Sample 6 _____ $\bar{x}$ = _____

Sample 7 _____ $\bar{x}$ = _____

Sample 8 _____ $\bar{x}$ = _____

Sample 9 _____ $\bar{x}$ = _____

Sample 10 _____ $\bar{x}$ = _____

Sample 11 _____ $\bar{x}$ = _____

Sample 12 _____ $\bar{x}$ = _____

Sample 13 _____ $\bar{x}$ = _____

Sample 14 _____ $\bar{x}$ = _____

Sample 15 _____ $\bar{x}$ = _____

Sample 16 _____ $\bar{x}$ = _____

Sample 17 _____ $\bar{x}$ = _____

Sample 18 _____ $\bar{x}$ = _____

Sample 19 _____ $\bar{x}$ = _____

Sample 20 _____ $\bar{x}$ = _____

Sample 21 _____ $\bar{x}$ = _____

Sample 22 _____ $\bar{x}$ = _____

Sample 23 _____ $\bar{x}$ = _____

Sample 24 _____ $\bar{x}$ = _____

Sample 25 _____ $\bar{x}$ = _____

For example, the following chart represents 25 random samples (each having 10 members) taken from the set of digits

Sample#	Sample members = x										$\overline{x}$
Sample 1	8	4	7	4	0	8	7	5	3	0	4.6
Sample 2	7	0	8	7	4	8	3	8	4	3	5.2
Sample 3	8	2	6	2	2	2	5	3	3	9	4.2
Sample 4	7	9	7	0	2	8	1	9	7	2	5.2
Sample 5	4	9	7	3	7	7	4	6	9	3	5.9
Sample 6	8	7	6	3	4	5	6	6	1	3	4.9
Sample 7	8	6	2	0	3	1	7	5	8	8	4.8
Sample 8	7	0	5	9	0	8	2	8	1	2	4.2
Sample 9	6	2	0	9	4	2	7	2	1	0	3.3
Sample10	1	4	0	2	4	6	5	1	8	0	3.1
Sample11	7	8	9	4	3	1	3	9	1	8	5.3
Sample12	4	2	0	7	3	1	1	4	6	9	3.7
Sample13	2	1	5	2	8	0	8	2	8	9	4.5
Sample14	3	3	2	5	0	4	3	9	8	4	4.1
Sample15	7	6	4	5	7	1	6	0	3	4	4.3
Sample16	0	2	0	4	2	4	2	6	8	2	3.0
Sample17	9	7	0	4	7	0	9	0	4	4	4.4
Sample18	3	9	0	0	5	8	8	8	7	8	5.6
Sample19	8	0	6	3	4	7	5	0	6	8	4.7
Sample20	0	2	8	7	1	3	4	9	9	2	4.5
Sample21	5	0	2	6	6	9	0	3	3	4	3.8
Sample22	1	3	0	4	0	4	3	7	2	2	2.6
Sample23	9	2	9	1	3	8	4	1	0	3	4.0
Sample24	8	3	0	0	8	0	0	1	0	6	2.6
Sample25	1	8	6	5	1	3	5	9	2	2	4.2

For each sample shown, the sample mean has been computed.
For example, the first sample is: 8   4   7   4   0   8   7   5   3   0   and its mean is 4.6.

We'll focus on the distribution of the 25 sample means from the generated samples. In a later section we'll see how this relates to the distribution of all samples means when the sample size is n.

1.   Examine the approximate shape of the distribution of sample means by constructing a histogram with 7 classes. Compare this to the probability distribution of digits, which is a *uniform* distribution.

2.   Compute the mean of the 25 sample means.

3.   Investigate the spread of the sample means and contrast this to the spread of the population of individual digits.

Sample Solution

The following represents the solutions to the three given problems as worked out using the given samples. If you have formed your own 25 samples, and for each calculated a sample mean, your answers will differ slightly.

1. A histogram of the values in the $\overline{x}$ column is shown below. The histogram looks somewhat symmetric but with more samples and more classes, it would be even more symmetric. In fact, *it would greatly resemble a normal distribution.* Compare the $\overline{x}$ probability distribution to the one for the population distribution shown underneath it.

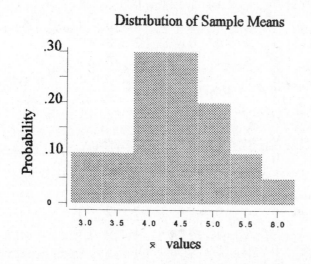

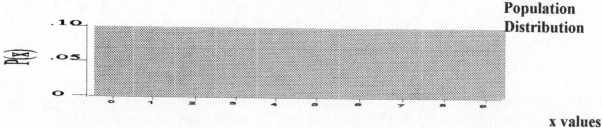

2.   The mean of the 25 means (4.6, 5.2, 5.2, 4.2 etc.) is computed by taking the sum of the sample means the number of means. 106.7/25 = 4.2680. This is close to the mean of the population of digits (0,1,2,...9).

3.   The range of the sample means is from a high of 5.9 to a low of 2.6.

5.9 - 2.6 = 3.3. Contrast this to the fact that the digits themselves have a high of 9 and a low of 0 with a range of 10. In order to get a sample with a mean of 0, we would of course need all 10 digits to be 0. This is highly improbable. Similarly, a sample with all nines would be equally unlikely.

Notice that although the individual digits are spread uniformly from 0 to 9, the sample means are only spread from 2.7 to 5.9. Moreover, they are "bunched up" in the center of the distribution.

Thinking About Statistics

What is the probability that when we randomly choose 10 digits for a sample of the digits (as we did in the Problem Solving Warm-Up), we get a *sample mean* of 0? What is the probability that the *sample mean* will be 9?

Selected Solutions Section 7.1

1.   The population is the set of all measures, counts or responses that are of interest to the researcher. Examples are:
      - The average daily balance of all accounts in a large bank.
      - The I.Q. scores of all high school age people in Michigan.
      - The number of times a person in the United States changes his or her career in a lifetime.

3.   A population parameter is a numerical description of the population. Examples are:
      - The population mean μ.
      - The population standard deviation σ.
      - In a binomial experiment, the probability of success on one trial p.

5.   In statistical inference, we draw conclusions from information we have about samples, to make decisions about the population parameters.

7.   By constructing a graph, we can picture the shape of the distribution to see, for example, if it is symmetric, uniform or skewed.

9.   Knowledge of the appropriate sampling distributions helps us make inferences about population parameters with a high level of certainty.

Answer to Thinking About Statistics

The probability of getting a 0 for the first member of the sample is .10. The probability of getting a 0 for the second member of the sample is also .10. In fact, the probability of getting a 0 on each of the 10 digits for our sample is .10. Therefore, (since each digit is independent of every other) the probability of getting 0 on the first AND 0 on the second AND 0 on the third...and 0 on the tenth is found by *multiplying*

$$(.10)(.10)(.10)(.10)(.10)(.10)(.10)(.10)(.10)(.10) = (.10)^{10} = .0000000001.$$

There is 1 chance in *10 billion* that we would get a sample of all 0's and thus get a sample with a mean of 0. A sample of all 9's would have the same probability. Samples with extreme means are highly unlikely. *We expect to get sample means which are close to the mean of the population, although usually not exactly equal to it.*

Section 7.2
The Central Limit Theorem

Review

The **Central Limit Theorem** is of extreme importance in statistical inference. It tells us what to expect in the *distribution of sample means*. This is referred to as a **sampling distribution.**

I.   *Case 1:* When the variable x which is used to represent individual members of a population is **normally distributed** (i.e. symmetric, mound shaped etc.):
For a random sample of *any* size n the following statements about the distribution of $\bar{x}$ the sample mean are true:
A.   The distribution of $\bar{x}$ is *normal.*
B.   The mean of the distribution of sample means is μ. The grand mean is the same value as the mean of the population.

$$\mu_{\bar{x}} = \mu_x$$

C.   The standard deviation of the distribution of sample means is called the **standard error of the mean** and is smaller than the distribution of x by a factor of $\sqrt{n}$.

$$\sigma_{\bar{x}} = \frac{\sigma_x}{\sqrt{n}}$$

Distribution of x values

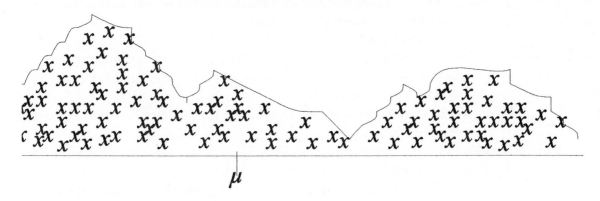

μ

Distribution of x̄

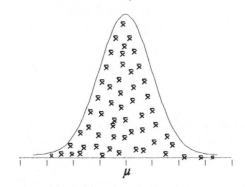

μ

II.   *Case II:* When the variable x comes from any type of distribution, ***no matter how unusual:*** For a random sample which has 30 or more members the following statements about the distribution of sample means are true:

    A.   The distribution of $\bar{x}$ is *normal.*

    B.   The mean of all possible sample means equals the mean of the population. $\mu_{\bar{x}} = \mu_x$

    C.   The standard deviation of the distribution of sample means is smaller than the distribution of x by a factor of $\sqrt{n}$. $\sigma_{\bar{x}} = \dfrac{\sigma_x}{\sqrt{n}}$

III.   How the **Central Limit Theorem** is used

    A.   A given population has fixed parameters μ and σ.

    B.   For each population, however, there are infinitely many samples of size n which can be taken. Each of these samples has a sample mean x̄. ***The x̄ statistic varies from sample to sample.***

C.   The Central Limit Theorem tells us what to expect about sample means.

D.   If x is normally distributed for any size sample, *or* if the sample size is 30 or more, the *sample means are normally distributed.*

    1.   When working with any normal distribution, we have to know the mean of the distribution and the standard deviation. The Central Limit Theorem relates the mean and standard deviation of the original variable x to the mean and standard deviation of x̄.

    2.   When working with normal distribution probabilities, we must convert all values to z-scores.

E.   The Central Limit Theorem is used to investigate the *probability of a sample mean being in a given interval.*

F.   Since we will be working with normal distributions, the x̄ values in the given intervals must be converted to z scores. There are 3 formulas, all of which are equivalent, which may be used to convert from an x̄ value to a z score.

    1.   The deviation of x̄ value from the mean is divided by the standard deviation of the distribution $\sigma_{\bar{x}}$ To use this version, first compute $\sigma_{\bar{x}}$ by dividing σ (the given population standard deviation) by $\sqrt{n}$. Then substitute.

$$z = \frac{\bar{x} - \mu}{\sigma_{\bar{x}}}$$

    2.   In this version directly substitute the fraction $\dfrac{\sigma}{\sqrt{n}}$ for $\sigma_{\bar{x}}$ in the denominator.

$$z = \frac{\bar{x} - \mu}{\dfrac{\sigma}{\sqrt{n}}}$$

    3.   The third version is often the easiest to compute. We will use this one in the solutions to follow. Notice that if you use the rules (invert the denominator and multiply) for complex fractions on the second version of this formula you will get the third.

$$z = \frac{(\bar{x} - \mu)}{\sigma}\sqrt{n}$$

IV.   To find the probability that a *sample mean* is within a given interval.

A.   First check to see if the distribution of x (from which the sample mean was taken) is either a normal distribution, or, if not, the sample size is 30 or more.

B.   Convert each endpoint to a standard normal z score using any one of three formulas given above. Rewrite the problem with the z score interval.

C.   Sketch a standard normal distribution curve and shade the area you wish to compute.

D.   Use the table for standard normal probability distribution to calculate the area (hence probability).

Problem Solving Warm-Up

Suppose it is known that the time spent by customers in MacBurger's fast food restaurant is normally distributed with a mean of 24 minutes and a standard deviation of 6 minutes.
Before starting the problem, it is a good idea to list and label the given information.
$$\mu = 24 \qquad\qquad \sigma = 6$$

a) Find the probability that an individual customer will spend more than 25 minutes in the restaurant.

P(x _____)

z = _____

P(z _____)

a) Note that since we are only investigating the probability of an individual value, we do not need the Central Limit Theorem. The question translates to
P(x > 25)
We convert this to a z interval by using
$$z = \frac{25 - 24}{6} \cdot \frac{1}{6} = .17$$

P(x > 25) = P(z > .17) = .5 - .0675 = .4325.

b) Find the probability that a random sample of 36 customers will have a mean more than 25 minutes.

P($\bar{x}$ _____)

z = _____

P(z _____)

_____

b) The key to the question lies in the fact that we are interested in the probability of a *sample mean* with n = 36.
The problem translates in symbols to
P($\bar{x}$ > 25)

We convert this to a z interval using the formula for sample means:
$$z = \frac{(\bar{x} - \mu) \cdot \sqrt{n}}{\sigma}$$

substituting, we get:
$$z = \frac{(25 - 24) \cdot \sqrt{36}}{6} = 1$$

P($\bar{x}$ > 25) = P(z > 1) = .5 - .3413 = .1577.

c) Find the probability that a random sample of 100 customers will have a mean of more than 25 minutes.

P($\bar{x}$ _____)

z= _____

P(z _____)

_____ _____

c) We want to find the probability of a *sample mean with n = 100*
being in an interval. We convert the problem of
P($\bar{x}$ > 25) into a z interval

$$ z = \frac{(25-24)\cdot\sqrt{100}}{6} = 1.67 $$

P(z > 1.67) = .5 - .4525 = .0475.
Note that as the sample size increases the probability of a sample mean being greater than 25 decreases. The larger the sample, the greater the probability is that the value of the sample mean will be **closer** to 24 (the population mean).

d) Find the probability that in a random sample of 100 there will be a mean between 23.5 and 25.5.

P($\bar{x}$)

z_L = _____
z_R = _____

P(z   )

_____

d) First symbolize the problem:
P(23.5 < $\bar{x}$ < 25.5)
Next convert each endpoint for $\bar{x}$ to a z score.

$$ z_L = \frac{(23.5-24)\cdot\sqrt{100}}{6} = -.83 $$

$$ z_R = \frac{(25.5-24)\cdot\sqrt{100}}{6} = 2.5 $$

Translate into z interval.

P(-.83 < z < 2.5) =.2967 +.4938 =.7905

Thinking About Statistics

Examine the effect of the increase of the sample size on the value of the z score. Let the population mean = 100 and the population standard deviation =15 (as in an I.Q. test). From a random sample of size n, find the probability that the sample mean will be greater than 108. We will increase the size of the sample as we look to answer P($\bar{x}$ > 108). Fill in the table that follows.(μ = 100 and σ= 15)

n	z score for $\bar{x}$ = 108	P($\bar{x}$ > 108)
1		
5		
25		
30		
35		
50		

What seems to happen as n increases?

Selected Solutions

1. $\mu = 15$ $\sigma = 14$

a)   n = 49: Since sample size is at least 30, we know the distribution of $\bar{x}$ will be normal with

$\mu_{\bar{x}} = \mu = 15$ ♦ and $\sigma_{\bar{x}} = \dfrac{14}{\sqrt{49}} = \dfrac{14}{7} = 2$ ♦.

When $\bar{x} = 15$,   z = 0 (since $\mu = 15$)
When $\bar{x} = 17$,

$z = \dfrac{(17-15)}{14} \sqrt{49} = \dfrac{2}{14} \sqrt{49} = 1$

$P(15 \le \bar{x} \le 17) = P(0 \le z \le 1) = .3413$ ♦

b)   n = 64: Since the sample size is at least 30, we know the distribution of $\bar{x}$ will be normal with $\mu_{\bar{x}} = \mu = 15$ ♦ and $\sigma_{\bar{x}} = \dfrac{14}{\sqrt{64}} = \dfrac{14}{8} = 1.75$ ♦

When $\bar{x} = 15$, z = 0
When $\bar{x} = 17$, $z = \dfrac{(17-15)}{14} \sqrt{64} = 1.14$

$P(15 \le \bar{x} \le 17) = P(0 \le z \le 1.14) = .3729$ ♦

c)   In part a the standard deviation for the distribution of $\bar{x}$ is 2 whereas in part b it is 1.75. In a larger sample, there is **less variability** from $\mu_{\bar{x}}$ therefore an increase in the sample size increases the probability of a value of the sample mean being close to the population mean.

5. $\mu = 6.4$ $\sigma = 1.5$ x = interval between check in times.
Since the number of check-in intervals (sample size) is at least 30, we know the distribution of $\bar{x}$ is normal. We now convert each of the endpoints to z scores.

a)   For $\bar{x} = 6$
       For $\bar{x} = 7$ $P(6 \le \bar{x} \le 7) = P(-1.69 \le z \le$ $z = \dfrac{(6-6.4) \cdot \sqrt{40}}{1.5} = -1.69$
       $2.53) = .4545 + .4943 = .9488$
       $\blacklozenge$ $z = \dfrac{(7-6.4) \cdot \sqrt{40}}{1.5} = 2.53$

b)   For $\bar{x} = 6$ $z = \dfrac{(6-6.4) \cdot \sqrt{80}}{1.5} = -2.38$

       For $\bar{x} = 7$ $z = \dfrac{(7-6.4) \cdot \sqrt{80}}{1.5} = 3.58$

       $P(6 \le \bar{x} \le 7) = P(-2.38 \le z \le 3.58) = .4913 + .49997 = .99127 \blacklozenge$

c)   In two check out rounds, the probability that the average interval between check in times falls between 6 and 7 is extremely high. If Arthur's mean check in time interval is greater than 7, he probably is going too slowly. If it is less than 6 he is probably going too fast.

9.   a) (for one VCR) $z_L = \dfrac{70-80}{19} = -.53$ and $z_R = \dfrac{70-80}{19} = .53$

$P(-.53 < z < .53) = .2019 + .2019 = .4038 \blacklozenge$

       b) (for 10 VCR's) $z_L = \dfrac{70-80}{19}\sqrt{10} = -1.66$ and $z_R = \dfrac{70-80}{19}\sqrt{10} = 1.66$
note that the z score has
increased by a factor of $\sqrt{n}$ $P(-1.66 < z < 1.66) = .4515 + .4515 = .9030 \blacklozenge$

       c) When the sample size is at least 30 and the distribution is more or less symmetric, we can say the distribution of $\bar{x}$ is normal. With a sufficiently large sample, the mean of the $\bar{x}$ distribution should be 80 and the standard error of the mean (the standard deviation of the sampling distribution) should be $\dfrac{19}{\sqrt{n}}$.

       d) For 30 VCR's, $z_L = \dfrac{70-80}{19}\sqrt{30} = -2.88$ and $z_R = \dfrac{70-80}{19}\sqrt{30} = 2.88$

$P(-2.88 < z < 2.88) = .4980 +$

$.4980 = .9960$ ♦

e) As the sample size increases there is a higher probability that the sample mean ill be closer to the population mean. As n increases the variability in the sample mean decreases.

13. $\mu = 63.0$ kg and $\sigma = 7.1$ kg.
      a) for a single doe weighing 54 kg.: $z = \dfrac{54-63}{7.1} = -1.27$

$P(x < 54) = P(z < -1.27) = .5 - .3980 = .1020$ (about 10%) ♦

b) For 2200 doe the expected number of undernourished is $2200(.1020) = 224.4$ doe.
c) For n = 50

$z = \dfrac{60-63}{7.1}\sqrt{50} = -2.99$

$P(\overline{x} < 60) = P(z < -2.99)$
$= .5 - .4986 = .0014$ ♦

$z = \dfrac{64.2-63}{7.1}\sqrt{50} = 1.20$ d) $P(\overline{x} < 64.2) = P(z < 1.20) = .5 + .3849 = .8849$ ♦
The population does not appear undernourished. With an average weight for 50 doe of 64.2 kg.

16. $\mu = 68"$ $\sigma = 3"$ n = 1 (probability of *an* 18 yr. old man means a sample size of one.)

Since the distribution of heights of 18 year old men is given as normally distributed, the sample mean distribution (even if the sample only consists of 1 member) will be a normal distribution.

a) $P(67 < \overline{x} < 69) = P(-.33 < z < .33) = .1293 + .1293 = .2586$ ♦

b) $P(67 < \overline{x} < 69) = P(-1 < z < 1) = .3413 + .3413 = .6826$ ♦

c)   The larger the sample, the smaller the standard deviation will be and the less spread out the sample means. With a larger sample, there is a higher probability that a sample mean will be close to the population mean.

17.   a) We are asked to find the probability the total checkout time for the next 30 customers is less than 90 minutes. w = the total checkout time so we are asked to find $P(w < 90)$.

b) $\overline{x} = \sum x_i./30$ and. $\sum x = w$. Using substitution, $\overline{x} = w/30 < 90/30 = 3$. So $P(w < 90)$ is equivalent to $P(\overline{x} < 3)$.

c) Since the distribution of x is mound shaped, the distribution of $\overline{x}$ is approximately normal.

The mean of the $\bar{x}$ distribution is 2.4 minutes and the standard deviation is $\sigma_{\bar{x}} = \dfrac{.6}{\sqrt{30}} = .1095$ ♦

d) Finding the z score, $z = \dfrac{3-2.4}{.1095} = 5.48$. Since P $(z < 5.48)$ is almost 1, we are

virtually guaranteed that the total waiting time w for 30 customers is less than 90 minutes.

21. a) When a distribution is more or less mound shaped (as shown in a histogram) a sample of 30 or more is necessary to claim that the sampling distribution of $\bar{x}$ is approximately normal.

b) If the original distribution of x is normal, then any size sample (even n = 1) will produce a normal sampling distribution.

Answers to Thinking About Statistics

$$\mu = 100 \qquad \sigma = 15$$

n	z score for $\bar{x} = 108$	P($\bar{x} > 108$)
1	.53	.2981
5	1.19	.1170
25	2.67	.0038
30	2.92	.0018
35	3.15	.0008
50	3.77	.00003

Notice that as the sample size increases, the z scores for the sample mean of 108 increase. This places them further away from the mean of a standard normal distribution making them more improbable.

Although almost 30% (29.81%) of the population would have an I.Q. of more than 108, in a sample of 50 randomly selected individuals there would be about 3 chances in 100,000 for the *mean* of a sample of this size to be greater than 108.

Section 7.3

Normal Approximation to the Binomial Distribution

Review

I.   Characteristics of a binomial experiment
    A.   The same action is repeated
        1.   Conditions for repetition must be identical.
        2.   One trial must be independent of all others. (The results of one trial cannot affect another.)
        3.   The number of trials is n.
    B.   A binomial experiment must have 2 outcomes
        1.   Success (which is defined in the problem)
        2.   Failure (all outcomes except those defined as success.)
    C.   On an individual trial
        1. $P(success) = p$
        2. $P(failure) = q$
        3. $q = 1 - p$ (They are complementary events)
    D.   The number of trials that are successful is denoted r where $r \le n$.

II.   Properties of the **Binomial Distribution**
    A.   The mean is $\mathbf{\mu = np}$.

    B.   The standard deviation is $\sigma = \sqrt{npq}$.

    C.   When p = .5 then q = .5 and the curve is perfectly symmetric about the mean.
    D.   As n, the number of trials, gets larger the histogram is symmetric regardless of the value of p.
    E.   *When both the values np and nq are greater than 5, the binomial histogram closely resembles a normal distribution curve.*
        1.   For experiments with p=.5 q=.5 we only need 11 trials to make this condition true: .5(11) > 5 and .5(11) > 5
        2.   As the value of p gets further from .5 we need more trials to insure the symmetry. For example, if p =.1 then q=.9. We need at least 51 trials for the binomial histogram to resemble the normal distribution. In this way both (.1)(51) > 5 as well as (.9)(51) > 5
    F.   Using a normal distribution curve in place of the binomial histogram will enable us to compute binomial probabilities which

1.   Are not on the binomial table (For example: if n > 20)
2.   Are too tedious to compute with the binomial formula.

COMPARISON OF BINOMIAL AND NORMAL DISTRIBUTIONS

	Binomial	Normal
variable used	r (counts the number of successes)	x (a measurement variable)
type of variable	discrete (takes on only whole number values)	continuous (takes on every value in an interval)
graph	histogram with n+1 bars one each for r=0, r=1, r=2...r=n.	a bell shaped curve
To answer a probability question concerning the probability of the variable being in a specified interval.	Add the areas within the appropriate bars.	Convert to z scores and use the standard normal probability table to compute the appropriate areas.

Let us examine a probability question which we are able to answer in two ways. The conditions of the problem are such that

1) we can use the binomial tables since we will use n = 20 and
2) since np > 5 and nq > 5 we will be able to use a normal curve approximation.

Problem

Suppose you are taking a true-false test and have no idea about any of the answers. It goes without saying that this is not a test in Statistics! There are 20 questions. What is the probability that you will guess between 14 and 16 (including 14 and 16) correctly.

Using Binomial Probabilities

n = 20 p =.5 and q =.5

P(14 ≤ r ≤16) MEANS P(r=14 OR r=15 OR r=16

Using the Normal Distribution Probabilities

In order to use the standard normal probability distribution, we must know the mean and the standard deviation of the distribution which will enable use to convert x values into

We will now look up the areas on the binomial table for n=20, p = .5

P(14 ≤r ≤16) = .037 +.015 + .005 = .057.

standard z score.

The mean can be computed by μ =np=(20)(.5) =10 and the standard deviation by $\sigma = \sqrt{npq} = \sqrt{20)\,(.5)\,(.5)} = \sqrt{5} = 2.24\,\sigma$ Comparing the horizontal scales for the r variable and the x variable, we realize that the bar over r = 14, actually extends on a continuous number line from 13.5 to 14.5. For r = 15 the continuous interval extends from 14.5 to 15.5 and for r = 16 from 15.5 to 16.5. Since x is a continuous variable, we must adjust from the r interval of P(14 ≤r ≤16) to the continuous x interval of 13.5 < x< 16.5. This is called a *correction for continuity* and it is done by subtracting .5 from any left- hand endpoint and adding .5 to any right- hand

$$z = \frac{13.5\text{-}10}{2.24} = 1.56$$

$$z = \frac{16.5\text{-}10}{2.24} = 2.90$$

endpoint of the r interval.

We now convert the x interval into a z interval. Thus P(14 ≤r ≤16) = P(13.5 <x <16.5)
= P(1.56 < z < 2.90) = .4981 - .4406 = .0575 which is very close to .057 as computed with the binomial tables.

Why does this work?

The total area within the rectangles of a binomial histogram has approximately the same area as that under a normal probability curve. The graphic illustrates why you must add .5 to a right hand endpoint and subtract .5 from a left.

III.   Steps to take to solve a binomial probability question with a normal distribution curve

A.   Check to see that both np > 5 and nq > 5

B.   Express the problem with an r interval. Determine the left and right-hand endpoints for this interval.

C.   Convert the r interval to a continuous x interval by subtracting .5 from the left- hand endpoint and adding .5 to the right-hand one. This is called the correction for continuity.

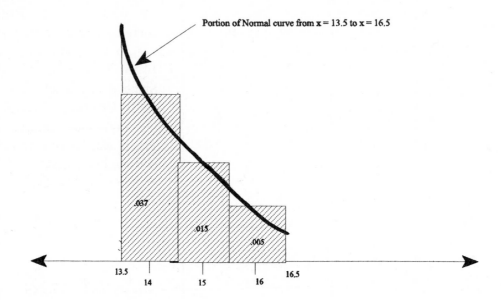

Portion of Normal curve from x = 13.5 to x = 16.5

D.   Using the binomial formulas μ =np and $\sigma = \sqrt{npq}$ compute the mean and the standard deviation for the distribution.

E.   Use the formula $z = \dfrac{x - \mu}{\sigma}$

for each endpoint to convert the interval into a standard normal z score interval.

F.   Use the standard normal distribution table to calculate the probability.

r interval ⇒ x interval ⇒ z interval

Thinking About Statistics

An alternate method for computing binomial probabilities using the normal curve approximation is to use the following formulas for z scores.

For the left endpoint of an interval use $z = \dfrac{r - .5 - np}{\sqrt{npq}}$ and for the right endpoint $z = \dfrac{r + .5 - np}{\sqrt{npq}}$.

Explain why this method will give you an equivalent answer to the one discussed in your text.

Problem Solving Warm-Up

Now we will try a problem for which
a)   The binomial tables do not exist and
b)   We definitely would not want to use a formula to calculate the area for *each rectangle* involved.

Solution

It has been shown that 60% of leukemia patients who are given a bone marrow transplant which is completely compatible will survive. If 500 patients are given a transplant next year, find the probability that at least 275 of them will survive.

1.   This is a binomial experiment, however our tables do not include 500 trials.

np= _____

nq= _____

P(r   )

P(x   )

P(z   )
_____

We test np = .6(500) and nq = .4(500) and see that they are both over 5. This means we can use the normal distribution curve as an approximation for the binomial probabilities. First we state the problem in terms of the discrete variable r

$P(r \geq 275)$. The left hand endpoint is 275 and there is no right hand endpoint.
Converting to a continuous variable, x interval we restate the problem

$P(x \geq 274.5)$.
Since we are working with a normal distribution we must find the mean and the standard deviation. This is done by using the binomial formulas
$\mu = 500(.6) = 300$ and
$\sigma = \sqrt{500(.6)(.4)} = \sqrt{20} = 10.95$.
We must now convert to a z interval so we convert the endpoint of 274.5
into a z score.

$$z = \frac{274.5 - 300}{10.95} = -2.32$$

$P(z > -2.33) = .5 + .4901 = .9901$

There is a slightly better than 99% chance that at least 275 patients out of the 500 will survive the transplant.

2.   Assume we have a binomial experiment with 200 trials. Express each of the following statements as an r interval inequality. Then convert into an equivalent x interval inequality for a continuous number line.

a)   More than 150 successes

a) $r > 50$ This is a strictly greater than statement $r = 151, 152, 153 ... 200$
The left hand endpoint is 151 and there is no right hand endpoint. Subtracting .5 from the left endpoint we get $x > 151.5$.

b)   At least 120 successes

b) At least means 120 or more so we write $r \geq 120$. Listing the r values we have $r = 120, 121, 122 ... 200$. The left hand endpoint is 120 and there is no right hand endpoint. The equivalent x interval is $x \geq 119.5$.

c)   Less than 95 successes

c) $r < 95$ means $r = 0, 1, 2, ... 94$. There is no left hand endpoint and the right hand endpoint is 94. Converting the right hand endpoint to an x interval by adding .5 we get $x < 94.5$.

d)   75 or fewer successes

d) $r \leq 75$ which means $r = 0, 1, 2, ... 75$. Since 75 is the right hand endpoint, we add .5 to get $x \leq 75.5$.

e)   Between 75 and 150 successes

e) In these problems *between* means "including the endpoints." The r interval is $75 \leq r \leq 150$. Subtracting .5 from the left and adding .5 to the right we get the x interval of
$74.4 \leq x \leq 150.5$

Selected Solutions Section 7.3

1.   This is a binomial experiment with n = 50 p = .64 and q = .36.

First test the conditions that allow us to use a normal curve approximation.
np = 50(.64) = 32 >5   and nq = 50 (.36) = 18 >5
Calculate the mean and the standard deviation for the distribution using formulas from Chapter 5.

$$\mu = np = 50(.64) = 32 \quad and \quad \sigma = \sqrt{npq} = \sqrt{50(.64)(.36)} = \sqrt{11.52} = 3.39$$

Next convert the r interval into an x interval and then into the standard z interval.

a)   P(r < 25) This means r = 0, 1, 2, ...24.
We add .5 to 24, the right hand endpoint to get the x interval   P(x < 24.5)

Calculate the z score $z = \dfrac{24.5 - 32}{3.39} = -2.21$

Convert to a z interval to get   P(z< -2.21) = .5 - .4864 = .0136 ♦

b)   P(r >35) This means r = 36,37,38 ...50.
Subtract .5 from the left hand endpoint to express with an x interval
          P(x > 35.5)

Calculate the z score: $z = \dfrac{35.5 - 32}{3.39} = 1.03$

Finally, P(z > 1.03) = .5 - .3485 = .1515 ♦

c)   P(30≤ r ≤ 45) = P(29.5 ≤x ≤ 45.5)
Converting each endpoint to a z score
we get P(-.74 ≤ z ≤3.98) = .2704 +.49997 = .77037 ♦

5.   This is a binomial experiment with n= 753 p = .035 and q = .965

Testing the conditions for a normal approximation to the binomial, we compute np = 753(.035) = 26.355   and 753(.965) = 752.965. Both are greater than 5.

We can calculate the mean and the standard deviation as μ = 26.355 and $\sigma = \sqrt{25.43} = 5.04$ for the distribution.

a)   P(r ≥ 15) means r = 15,16,17...753.
Subtracting .5 from the left endpoint, we get the statement for the x interval
P(x ≥ 14.5)
Then computing the z score $z = \dfrac{14.5-26.355}{5.04} = -2.35$

Finally, P(z ≥ -2.35) = .5 + .4906 = .9906 ◆

b)   P(r ≥ 30) means r = 30,31,32...753
P(x ≥ 29.5)
Finally, P(z ≥.62) = .5 -.2324 = .2676 ◆

c)   P(25 ≤ r ≤ 35) means r= 25,26,27...35.
P(24.5 ≤ x ≤ 35.5)
Finally, P(-.37 ≤ z ≤ 1.81) = .6902 ◆

d)   P(r > 40) means r = 41,42,42...753
P(x > 40.5)
Finally P(z > 2.80) = .5 -.4974 = .0026. ◆

9.   a) The probability r is more than 280 corresponds to the probability r is 281 or 282 or 283...420. Since 281 is the left end value, subtract .5 from it to get the following equivalence. P(r > 280) is the same as P(x > 280.5). Using the normal approximation for the binomial, convert the value of x = 280.5 into a z score. This requires computing the mean as $\mu = np = .70(430) = 301$ and $\sigma = \sqrt{npq} = \sqrt{430\,(.70)\,(.30)} = \sqrt{90.3} = 9.50$.

$z = \dfrac{280.5-301}{9.50} = -2.16$ P(z > -2.16) = .5 + .4846 = 9846 ◆

$z = \dfrac{319.5-301}{9.50} = 1.95$

b) At least 320 means r = 320 or 321 or 322.... Subtracting .5 from the left end point we see that P(r ≥ 320) = P(x ≥ 319.5). = P(z >1.95) = .5 - .4744 = .0256. ◆

$z = \dfrac{279.5-301}{9.50} = -2.26$

$z = \dfrac{220.5-301}{9.50} = 2.05$

c) Between 280 and 320 means 280, 281, ...320. Adjusting the endpoints we get the x interval of 2.79 < x < 320.5. (Recall that in the binomial chapter the phrase "between" included the endpoints.)

P(-2.26 < z < 2.05) = .4881 + .4798 = .9679 ♦

d) 430(.70) =301 and 430(.30) = 129. Since both are greater than 5 we can use a normal approximation to the binomial distribution areas. The binomial histogram will resemble the normal distribution curve when both np>5 and nq>5. ♦

13.   A binomial experiment with p = .80 q = .20 and n = 100

Check the conditions np = 100(.80) = 80 >5 and nq = 100(.20) =20>5.
This enables us to use the normal distribution approximation.

Now calculate $\mu = np = 80$ and $\sigma = \sqrt{npq} = \sqrt{100(.80)(.20)} = \sqrt{16} = 4$

a)   P(r≥ 85) = P(x≥ 84.5) Since the center of the left most bar is labeled 85, subtract .5.

Convert to a z interval using $\mu = 80$, $\sigma = 4$ and x = 84.5
P(z ≥ 1.13) = .5 - .3708 = .1292 ♦

b)   P(r≤68) = P(x ≤ 68.5) Since the right most bar is labeled 68 add .5 to form the right boundary of the normal distribution.

Convert to a z interval
P(z≤-2.88) = .5 - .4980 =.0020 ♦

c)   P(69 ≤ r ≤ 84) = P(68.5 ≤ x ≤ 84.5)

Of course we could solve this by using the z score interval P(-2.88 ≤ z≤ 1.13).
However, it is simpler to notice that parts a) and b) of this problem form the complement to part c. We add the answers to parts a and b and subtract from 1 to get:

.1292 + .0020 = .1312 = total area **not** in specified interval.
Subtract from 1 to find the area which <u>is</u> in the interval.   1 -.1312 = .8688 ♦

Chapter 8

ESTIMATION

Section 8.1
Estimating μ with Large Samples

Review

Although we are often unable to obtain the exact value of a population parameter such as μ we can use techniques of statistical inference to get a reliable *estimate* for it.

I.   Important Concepts
        A.   ***Point Estimate***
                1.   A single number used as a "best guess."
                2.   For example, we use x̄, a *sample* mean as our "best guess" for μ, the *population* mean.
        B.   ***Error of Estimate***
                1.   The distance between the point estimate and the population parameter.
                2.   The value of the point estimate x̄ is known but the population parameter μ is unknown (which is why we are estimating it).
                3.   We symbolize the error of estimate as E.
                4. $\bar{x} - \mu = \pm E$ *or* $E = \left| \bar{x} - \mu \right|$. We use the absolute value notation since we are only concerned with the magnitude of the difference.
                5.   We will be computing the *maximal error tolerance* for this error.
        C.   ***Confidence Interval***
                1.   The probability that our unknown μ is ***exactly*** equal to the point estimate x̄ is virtually zero.
                2.   To make a more reliable estimate, we form an interval around our point estimate of x̄.

3. The level of confidence, denoted c, gives us the level of reliability with which we make our estimate.
4. The level of confidence is usually set at .90, .95 or .99.
5. For a level of confidence of c = .90, we form an interval of values such that we can be 90% sure that the actual value of μ is within that interval. Similarly when we set c = .95, we are 95% sure that μ is between the boundaries of this interval.

II. For estimations of μ using large samples (n≥ 30) or if σ is known.

    A. The Central Limit Theorem from chapter 7 tells us that if our sample size is over 30, our *sample* means will be:

        1. Normally distributed
        2. Have a mean equal to the population mean. (Which in this case is unknown.)
        3. Have a standard deviation which is the population standard deviation divided by the square root of n. Although the population standard deviation σ may also be unknown, ***in a "large" sample, the sample standard deviation s is almost equal to the population standard deviation σ*** $If\ n \geq 30$, $\sigma \approx s$.

    B. With an estimate using a large sample, we can therefore rely on normal distribution probabilities. We will use z scores.

        1. For any normal distribution, and in particular, the distribution of sample means with sample size 30 or more, we can use the following facts.
            a. 80% of the population will fall between z = ± 1.28
            b. 90% of the population will fall between z = ± 1.645.
            c. 95% of the population will fall between z = ± 1.96.
            d. 99% of the population will fall between z = ± 2.58.
        2. When converting sample means into standard z scores we used $z = \dfrac{(\bar{x}-\mu)\cdot\sqrt{n}}{\sigma}$
        3. If we substitute ±E for $\bar{x}$ - μ, we get: $z = \dfrac{\pm E \cdot \sqrt{n}}{\sigma}$
        4. Multiplying both sides by σ and dividing by $\sqrt{n}$ we get $\quad E = \pm z \cdot \dfrac{\sigma}{\sqrt{n}}$
        5. Use the above formula to calculate the maximal error tolerance for the error of estimate.

III. Steps to find the confidence interval with a large sample.

    A. From the given information, check to see that n≥ 30.
    B. Determine the point estimate $\bar{x}$, the *sample* mean. This will be the center point of the interval.
    C. Determine the level of confidence. Use the appropriate z score.
        1. z_{80} = 1.28
        2. $z_{.90}$= 1.645
        3. $z_{.95}$= 1.96

4. $z_{.99} = 2.58$

D.   Determine the maximal error tolerance for the error of estimate. $E = z_c \cdot \dfrac{\sigma}{\sqrt{n}}$

E.   Find the left-hand boundary of the interval by subtracting $\bar{x}$ - E

F.   Find the right-hand boundary of the interval by $\bar{x}$ + E.

G.   The confidence interval consists of all points in the interval between $\bar{x}$ -E and $\bar{x}$ + E.

H.   Make a probability statement such as : We are 90% sure that the population mean μ falls between $\bar{x}$ -E and $\bar{x}$ + E.

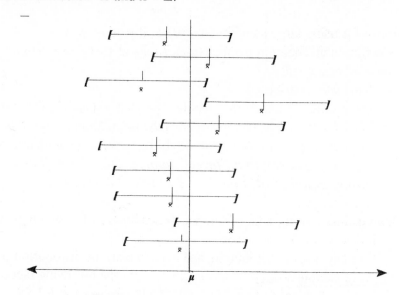

The graphic above illustrates the 90% confidence interval concept. At the bottom the true value of μ, the population mean is marked. Above it are shown 10 different confidence intervals obtained from drawing 10 samples. Note that 9 out of 10 span the population mean. The 4th one from the top does not. If we form a 90% confidence interval there is a .90 probability it will span the population mean.

Problem Solving Warm-Up

1. As part of a study concerning the effect of physical attractiveness on mental health, a psychologist rated 231 subjects on a scale of 1 to 5 (with 1 being highly unattractive and 5 being highly attractive) for attractiveness. The sample mean was 3.94 and the sample standard deviation .75.

a)   Construct a 90% confidence interval for the population mean μ.

Fill in the blanks with the given information.

n = _____

$\bar{x}$ = _____

s = _____

c = _____

z_c = _____

The point estimate = _____

The maximal value for the error of estimate is E = _____

The left-hand endpoint to the interval is _____

The right-hand endpoint of the interval is _____

Probability statement about your c o n f i d e n c e   i n t e r v a l :
_____
_____

b)   Form a 95% confidence interval for the population mean.

The point estimate is _____

E = _____

Solution

Sample size is n = 231
Use the large sample formulas.

The sample statistic is $\bar{x}$ = 3.94

From the sample. For large samples this is close enough to use in place of σ in the formula. s = .75 ≈ σ

c = .90 This gives the level of reliability of your estimation. For a large sample , we use a normal distribution and convert to a z score of ± 1.645

We are asked to *estimate* μ, the **population mean**. The *point* estimate is $\bar{x}$ =3.94 the sample mean.

$$E = \pm z_\sigma \cdot \frac{\sigma}{\sqrt{n}}$$

$$E = \pm 1.645 \left(\frac{.75}{\sqrt{231}} \right) = .08$$

The left-hand endpoint of the interval is:
$\bar{x}$ - E = 3.94 - .08 = 3.86

The right-hand endpoint of the interval is:
$\bar{x}$ + E = 3.94 + .08 = 4.02

Confidence interval: We are 90% sure that μ is between 3.86 and 4.02.

The *point* estimate is $\bar{x}$ =3.94 the sample mean.

$$E = \pm 1.96 \frac{.75}{\sqrt{231}} = .10$$

The	left-hand	endpoint	is	$\bar{x} - E = 3.94 - .10 = 3.84$

The	right-hand	endpoint	is	$\bar{x} + E = 3.94 + .10 = 4.04$

Probability statement about your confidence interval:_____

We are 95% sure that μ, the population mean is between 3.84 and 4.04

Thinking About Statistics

1. What effect does increasing the level of confidence have on the length of the confidence interval?

2. What effect does increasing the sample size and leaving every other number the same have on the length of the confidence interval?

3. What effect does a larger standard deviation have on the length of the confidence interval?

Selected Solutions Section 8.1

1. <u>Given information</u>

   $n = 35$

   $\bar{x} = 146.5$ calories

   $s = 12.7$ calories

   $c = 80\%$

   <u>Interpretation</u>

   Sample size is large since it is greater than 30. Therefore, we'll use the large sample formulas.

   Your *sample statistic*

   From the sample. For large samples this is close enough to use in place of σ in the formula.

   The level of reliability of your estimation. For a large sample, we use a normal distribution and convert to a z score of ± 1.28.

We are asked to *estimate* μ, the **population mean**.
The *point* estimate is x̄ = 146.5 , the sample mean.

The maximal value for the error of estimate is: $E = \pm z_\sigma \cdot \frac{\sigma}{\sqrt{n}} = \pm 1.28 \left(\frac{12.7}{\sqrt{35}}\right) = \pm 2.7478$

The left-hand endpoint of the interval is x̄ - E =
146.5 -.2.7478 = 143.7522
The right-hand endpoint of the interval is x̄ +E = 146.5 +.2.7478 = 149.2478

Confidence interval: We are 80% sure that μ is between 143.75 and 149.25 ♦
The length of the interval is 149.25 - 143.75 = 5.50 ♦

c)   The maximal value for the error of estimate is $E = \pm z_\sigma \cdot \frac{\sigma}{\sqrt{n}} = \pm 1.645 \left(\frac{12.7}{\sqrt{35}}\right) = \pm 3.5313$

The left-hand endpoint of the interval is x̄ - E = 146.5 -3.5313 = 142.9687
The right-hand endpoint of the interval is x̄ +E = 146.5 +3.5313 = 150.0313

Confidence interval: We are 90% sure that μ is between 142.97 and 150.03 ♦
The length of the interval is 150.03 - 142.97 = 7.06 ♦

d)   The maximal value for the error of estimate is $E = \pm z_\sigma \cdot \frac{\sigma}{\sqrt{n}} = \pm 2.58 \left(\frac{12.7}{\sqrt{35}}\right) = \pm 5.5387$

The left-hand endpoint of the interval is x̄ - E = 146.5 -5.5387 = 140.9613
The right-hand endpoint of the interval is x̄ +E = 146.5 +5.5387 = 152.0387

Confidence interval: We are 99% sure that μ is between 140.96 and 152.04 ♦
The length of the interval is 152.04 - 140.96 = 11.08♦

e)   *As the level of confidence increase, the lengths of the confidence intervals also increase.*

5.   n = 40   Sample size is large n≥30. Use the large sample formulas.
      x̄ = 51.16° F   Your *sample statistic*
      s = 3.04° F   From the sample. For large samples this is close enough to use in place of σ in the formula.

      b)= 90%   This gives the level of reliability of your estimation. For a large sample, we use a normal distribution and convert to a z score of ± 1.645

We are asked to *estimate* μ, the **population mean**. The *point* estimate is x̄ = 51.16 the sample mean.

The maximal value for the error of estimate is $E = \pm z_\sigma \cdot \frac{\sigma}{\sqrt{n}} = \pm 1.645 \left(\frac{3.04}{\sqrt{40}}\right) = .7907$

The left-hand endpoint of the interval is x̄ - E = 51.16 - .7907 = 50.3693
The right-hand endpoint of the interval is x̄ + E =51.16 + .7907 = 51.9507

Confidence interval: We are 90% sure that μ is between 50.37 and 51.95 ♦

c)   The maximal value for the error of estimate
       is

$$E = \pm z_\sigma \cdot \frac{\sigma}{\sqrt{n}} = \pm 2.58 \left(\frac{3.04}{\sqrt{40}}\right) = 1.2401$$

The left-hand endpoint of the interval is x̄ - E = 51.16 - 1.2401 = 49.9199
The right-hand endpoint of the interval is x̄ + E =51.16 + 1.2401 = 52.4001

Confidence interval: We are 99% sure that μ is between 49.92° and 52.40°.

d)   Since you are 99% sure the January mean is between 49.92° and 52.40°, the claim is highly
       improbable based on the given information. (There's a 1% chance that the temperature falls
       outside the confidence interval boundaries so there is only a ½% or .005 chance that the
       temperature is higher than the upper boundary of 52.40°.)

9.   n = 38   Sample size is greater than 30. Use the large sample formulas.
       x̄ = 2.5 minutes   Your *sample statistic*
       s = .7 minutes   From the sample. For large samples this is close enough to use in
                           place of σ in the formula.
a)   c = .90   For a large sample , we use a normal distribution and convert to a z
                           score of ± 1.645

We are asked to *estimate* μ, the **population mean**.
The *point* estimate is x̄ = 2.5, the sample mean.
The maximal value for the error of estimate is

$$E = \pm z_\sigma \cdot \frac{\sigma}{\sqrt{n}} = \pm 1.645 \left(\frac{.7}{\sqrt{38}}\right) = .1868$$

The left-hand endpoint of the interval is x̄ - E = 2.5 - .1868 = 2.3132
The right-hand endpoint of the interval is x̄ + E =2.5 + .1868 = 2.6868

Confidence interval: We are 90% sure that μ is between 2.31 and 2.69 ♦
The length of the interval is .38

b)   The *point* estimate is x̄ = 15.2, the sample mean.
       The maximal value for the error of estimate is

$$E = \pm z_\sigma \cdot \frac{\sigma}{\sqrt{n}} = \pm 1.645 \left(\frac{4.8}{\sqrt{38}}\right) = 1.2809$$

The left-hand endpoint of the interval is x̄ - E = 15.2 - 1.2809 = 13.9191

The right-hand endpoint of the interval is $\bar{x} + E = 15.2 + 1.2809 = 16.4809$

Confidence interval: We are 90% sure that μ is between 13.92 and 16.48 ◆
The length of the interval is 2.56 ◆

c)   The *point* estimate is $\bar{x} = 25.7$, the sample mean.
    The maximal value for the error of estimate is

    $$E = \pm z_\sigma \cdot \frac{\sigma}{\sqrt{n}} = \pm 1.645\left(\frac{8.3}{\sqrt{38}}\right) = 2.2149$$

The left-hand endpoint of the interval is $\bar{x} - E = 25.7 - 2.2149 = 23.4851$
The right-hand endpoint of the interval is $\bar{x} + E = 25.7 + 2.2149 = 27.9149$

Confidence interval: We are 90% sure that μ is between 23.49 and 27.91 ◆
The length of the interval is 4.42 ◆

d)   As the standard deviation increases, the lengths of the confidence intervals increase for the same level of confidence. In the formula for E, you multiply by the standard deviation. A higher value for σ would produce a higher value for E.

13.   n = 36   Sample size is 36 therefore, use the large sample formulas.
    $\bar{x} = 16,000$ cars   Your *sample statistic*
    s = 2400 cars   From the sample. For large samples this is close enough to use in place of σ in the formula.

    c = .90,.

We are asked to *estimate* μ, the **population mean**.
The *point* estimate is $\bar{x} = 16.000$ taken from the **sample** mean.
The error of estimate is

$$E = \pm z_\sigma \cdot \frac{\sigma}{\sqrt{n}} = \pm 1.645\frac{2400}{\sqrt{36}} = 658$$

16000- 658 = 15342 and 16000+658 = 16658. We are 90% sure the mean number of cars falls between 15342 and 16658. ◆

17.   n = 40   Sample size is 40; therefore
                use the large sample formulas.
    $\bar{x} = 55.98$ Your *sample statistic*
    s = 10.73   From the sample. For large samples this is close enough to use in place of σ in the formula.
    c = 99%   z= 2.58

We are asked to *estimate* μ, the **population mean**.
The *point* estimate is x̄ = 55.98 the sample mean.
The maximal value for the error of estimate is

$$E = \pm z_\sigma \cdot \frac{\sigma}{\sqrt{n}} = 2.58\frac{10.73}{\sqrt{40}} = 4.38$$

The left-hand endpoint of the interval is x̄ - E = 55.98 - 4.38 = 51.60
The right-hand endpoint of the interval is x̄ + E =55.98 + 4.38 = 60.36

Confidence interval: We are 99% sure that μ is between $51.60 and $60.36

b)   Since the <u>Denver Post</u> figure of $62.50 is not within the confidence interval, there is reason to suspect that the figure in the <u>Post</u> is too high.

Answers to Thinking About Statistics

1.   When we increase the level of confidence (leaving every other number the same) the length of the confidence interval increases. Examining the formula for E, we can see that when the confidence interval increases, the z score increases.
Mathematically, we multiply the same standard error = $\frac{\sigma}{\sqrt{n}}$ by a z score.

Notice as the level of confidence increases, the corresponding z scores increase. Since we are multiplying by a larger value for a larger level of confidence, our E will be larger and hence the interval will widen. Intuitively, it makes sense to think that you will have a better chance of hitting a larger target . However, a larger "target" means a less precise estimate.

2.   When we increase the size of the sample (leaving all the other numbers the same) the length of the confidence interval *decreases*. Mathematically, this occurs because we *divide* by the square root of the sample size to get E. Dividing by a larger number gives a smaller quotient. *A larger sample gives a more precise estimate.*

3.   When the standard deviation is larger, the value of E is larger , thus making the confidence interval larger. A larger standard deviation indicates more variability and less consistency. Thus we need a wider interval for the same level of accuracy when we have a larger standard deviation.

Section 8.2
Estimating μ with Small Samples
Review

In the last section we looked at estimating the value of μ the mean of a population when we were able to work with a large sample (at least 30). There are times when a large sample does not exist for the study we are doing or it is just not feasible to obtain one. We will now look at forming a confidence interval to estimate μ when we have to work with a small sample.

Small Sample Estimation of μ Compared to Large

	Use Large Sample	Use Small Sample
number in sample	$n \geq 30$ or σ known	$n < 30$ and σ unknown
distribution of $\bar{x}$	Normal dist.	Student's t dist.
variable used	z	t
formula for variable	$z = \dfrac{(\bar{x}-\mu)\sqrt{n}}{\sigma}$	$t = \dfrac{(\bar{x}-\mu)\sqrt{n}}{s}$
population standard deviation	In a large sample, s is close enough to σ. We use s as a substitute for σ in the formula for E. We can also use large sample formulas if σ is known even though our sample size may be less than 30.	The value of σ is unknown. We must use s in the formula instead.
Maximal value for the Error of Estimate	$E = z_c \dfrac{\sigma}{\sqrt{n}}$	$E = t_c \dfrac{s}{\sqrt{n}}$

| Assumption about the population distribution of x | None; the population can have any shaped distribution. | The population of x should be close to normal (symmetric and mound shaped). |

I.   Student's t distributions

    A.   A family of distributions where there is a different curve for 1 degree of freedom, 2 degrees of freedom, 3 degrees of freedom, etc.

    B.   The t curves are mound shaped and symmetric about t=0 (the mean) but have thicker tails than the standard normal distribution curve.

    C.   As the number of degrees of freedom (d.f.) increase, the tails get thinner. If there are more than 30 d.f. we can use the z values from the standard normal curve in place of the t values.

    D.   How to read the Student's t distribution table

        1.   t values are listed for each of 30 different curves according to the number of degrees of freedom.

        2.   For each value of d.f. there are four t values, one each for levels of confidence of c = .90, .95, .98 and .99.

        3.   Read across the row on top listing c, the level of confidence. For the time being you can ignore the rows labeled α' and α''.

        4.   Read down the column marked d.f. to locate the appropriate number. For these estimation problems, we will use d.f.=n-1.

        5.   The intersecting cell gives the positive t value.

For example: Your sample has 15 values. Find the appropriate t value you will need to form a confidence interval at the 95% level of confidence.

d.f.\c	.90	.95	.98	.99
α'	---	---	---	---
α''	---	---	---	---
1		↓		
2		↓		
.				
.				
14	→ → → →	2.145		
.				
.				
30				

Read across the c row until you get to c = .95

When n = 15, use d.f.= n-1 = 14. Read down the d.f. column until you get to 14. The value in the intersecting cell is t = 2.145.

Interpretation: 95% of the area under the t distribution curve with 14 degrees of freedom lies between t = ± 2.145.

II.   Steps to find the confidence interval with a small sample.
   A.   Use when n < 30 and population is normally distributed if σ is unknown. If σ is known you may use large sample formulas.
   B.   Determine the point estimate x̄. This will be the center point of your interval.
   C.   Determine the level of confidence.
   D.   Determine the degrees of freedom by computing (n-1) and read the appropriate t score from the Student's t distribution table.

   E.   Determine the maximal error tolerance for the error of estimate. $E = t_c \cdot \frac{s}{\sqrt{n}}$
   F.   Find the left-hand boundary of the interval by subtracting E from x̄.
   G.   Find the right-hand boundary of the interval by adding E to x̄.
   H.   The confidence interval consists of all points in the interval between x̄ - E and x̄ + E.
   I.   Make a probability statement such as : We are 90% sure that the population mean μ falls between x̄ -E and x̄ + E.

III.   Differences from large sample estimations.
   J.   Original population (x distribution) must be close to normal for a small sample.
   K.   For E = the error of estimate (small sample) use $E = \frac{t_c \cdot s}{\sqrt{n}}$

Problem Solving Warm-Up

1.   Suppose we decide to do a study of our own concerning physical attractiveness and mental health. (Assume the variable rating physical attractiveness is normally distributed.) We rate 15 subjects for attractiveness (on the scale of 1 to 5) with the resulting sample mean of 3.94 and the standard deviation .75.

a)   Construct a 95% confidence interval
       for the population mean μ.
       Fill in the blanks with
       Given information   *Solution*

       n = _____   Sample size is n = 15 so we can use small sample formulas since the distribution of x is normal.

$\overline{x} =$ _____

The sample statistic is $\overline{x} = 3.94$

$s =$ _____

The sample standard deviation $= .75$

$c =$ _____

$c = .95$ This gives the level of accuracy for the estimation. For a small sample , we use the Student t distribution with 14 d.f. and determine $t = 2.145$

point est.= _____

We are asked to *estimate* μ, the **population mean**.
The *point* estimate is $\overline{x} = 3.94$ the sample mean.
The error of estimate is

$E =$ _____

$$E = \pm t_\sigma \cdot \frac{s}{\sqrt{n}}$$

$$E = \pm 2.145 \left(\frac{.75}{\sqrt{15}}\right) = .415$$

The left-hand endpoint of the interval is:
$\overline{x} - E = 3.94 - .415 = 3.525$

The right-hand endpoint of the interval is:
$\overline{x} + E = 3.94 + .415 = 4.355$

Answer: _____
_____

Confidence interval: We are 95% sure that μ is between 3.525 and 4.355.

b) Form a 99% confidence interval for the population mean.

b) With a 99% confidence interval using a small sample we use a t score of ± 2.977 when calculating E, the maximal error tolerance.
The *point* estimate is $\overline{x} = 3.94$ the sample mean.
The error of estimate is

Point est.= _____

E = _____

$$E = \pm t_c \cdot \frac{s}{\sqrt{n}} = \pm 2.977 \left(\frac{.75}{\sqrt{15}}\right) = .58$$

The left-hand endpoint of the interval is:
$\bar{x} - E = 3.94 - .58 = 3.36$

The right-hand endpoint of the interval is:
$\bar{x} + E = 3.94 + .58 = 4.52$

Answer: _____
_____

Confidence interval: We are 99% sure that μ is between 3.36 and 4.52.

Thinking About Statistics

When determining the appropriate value of t to use, we discussed the fact that we had to examine the Student t curve which had the number of "degrees of freedom" which corresponded to the problem. For these problems it was n-1.

The following example should help give you an idea about the concept of "degrees of freedom."

Suppose in your course you will have 5 equally weighted tests and you have decided that you want a B average. This implies that you will need a mean of 79.6 for your 5 tests.

On the first test, you are "free" to get any grade, and still (in theory) be able to have a mean of 79.6. You are also "free" to get any grade on the second, third and fourth test and still have a possibility of a 79.6 mean. For the last test, you no longer have the "freedom" to get whatever grade you want. Thus you could freely determine 4 test grades out of 5 once the mean is pre-determined.

Suppose your first four grades were 73, 68, 81, and 87. What grade would you need on your fifth test to get a mean of 79.6?

Selected Solutions Section 8.2

1.   n= 18 so there are 18 - 1 = 17 d.f. Looking under the value of c = .95, the value of t = 2.110. This means that in the student t curve which has 17 degrees of freedom, 95% of the area falls between t = ± 2.110. ♦

5.   To make this estimate, we must compute the sample mean and sample standard deviation. $\bar{x}$ = 1272 years and s = 37 years (remember to use the formula which divides by n-1.

   n = 9   Sample size is n=9
                            The distribution is normal so we can use the small sample formulas.
   $\bar{x}$ = 1272   The mean of the *sample*
   s = 37   The sample standard deviation
   c = .90   The t-value with 8 d.f. is 1.860.

   We are asked to *estimate* μ, the **population mean**.

   The *point* estimate is $\bar{x}$ =1272 the sample mean.

   The error of estimate is

$$E = \pm t_c \cdot \frac{s}{\sqrt{n}} = 1.860 \frac{37}{\sqrt{9}} = 22.94$$

   The left-hand endpoint of the interval is $\bar{x}$ - E = 1272 -22.94 = 1249.06
   The right-hand endpoint of the interval is $\bar{x}$ + E =1272 +22.94 = 1294.94

   Confidence interval: We are 90% sure that μ is between 1249.06 and 1294.94 ◆

9.   n = 10   Sample size is 10. The distribution is normal so we can use the small sample
                          formulas.
   $\bar{x}$ = 15.5   The mean of the sample. *sample statistic*
   s = 3.56   The sample standard deviation.
   c = .95   For a small sample , we use a Student's t distribution. The t score with 9d.f.
                          =2.262

   We are asked to *estimate* μ, the **population mean**.

   The *point* estimate is $\bar{x}$ = 15.5 the sample mean.

   The maximal value for the error of estimate is $E = \pm t_c \cdot \frac{s}{\sqrt{n}} = 2.262 \frac{3.56}{\sqrt{10}} = 2.5465$

   The left-hand endpoint of the interval is $\bar{x}$ - E =
   15.5 - 2.5465= 12.9535
   The right-hand endpoint of the interval is $\bar{x}$ + E =15.5 + 2.5465= 18.0650

   Confidence interval: We are 95 % sure that μ is between 12.95 and 18.07 ◆

c)   A PE ratio is below average since it falls below the lower limit for the 95% confidence
       interval. This might be a bargain stock!

13.   n = 18   Sample size is 18. The distribution is normal so we can use the small
                                 sample formulas.
   $\bar{x}$ = 6.7 days   The mean of the sample. *sample statistic*
   s = .5 days   The sample standard deviation.
   c = 90%   For a small sample , we use a Student's t distribution. The t score with
                            17 d.f. is 1.740.

We are asked to *estimate* μ, the **population mean**.
The *point* estimate is x̄ =6.7 the sample mean.
The error of estimate is

$$E = \pm t_c \cdot \frac{s}{\sqrt{n}} = 1.740 \frac{.5}{\sqrt{18}} = .2051$$

The left-hand endpoint of the interval is x̄ - E = 6.7 - .2051 = 6.4949
The right-hand endpoint of the interval is x̄ + E = 6.7 + ..2051 = 6.9051

Confidence interval: We are 90% sure that μ is between 6.49 and 6.91 days ♦

17.   n = 8   Sample size is 8
                            The distribution is normal so we can use the small sample formulas.
         x̄ = 12.35   The mean of the sample. *Sample statistic*
         s = 2.25   The sample standard deviation.
         c = 90%   For a small sample , we use a Student's t distribution. The t score for
                            7 d.f. is 1.895.
We are asked to *estimate* μ, the **population mean**.
The *point* estimate is x̄ = 12.35 the sample mean.
The maximal value for the error of estimate is

$$E = \pm t_c \cdot \frac{s}{\sqrt{n}} = 18.95 \frac{2.25}{\sqrt{8}} = 1.5075$$

The left-hand endpoint of the interval is x̄ - E = 12.35 - 1.5075 = 10.84
The right-hand endpoint of the interval is x̄ + E =12.35 + 1.5075 = 13.86

Confidence interval: We are 90% sure that μ is between $10.84 and $13.86.♦

Answers to Thinking About Statistics

In order to get the mean of 5 scores to equal 79.5, the sum of the five scores has to be 5(79.6) = 398.
Your first four test scores of 73, 68, 81 and 87 add up to 309 points. Therefore, you will need 398 -
309 = 89 points on your last test to get a B average.
When a mean is fixed at a certain value, the first n-1 scores have the "freedom" to be any value. The
last score, however, will be pre-determined.

Section 8.3
Estimating p in the Binomial Distribution
<u>Review</u>

I.   Estimating p in the binomial distribution
- A.   p= the population proportion , percentage or probability of success on a single trial of a binomial experiment.
- B.   We use $\hat{p} = \frac{r}{n}$ as a point estimate for p.
  - 1.   r= the number of successes in the sample.
  - 2.   n= the number trials in the sample.
- C.   When both np and nq are greater than 5, the binomial histogram is shaped approximately like the normal distribution curve with a mean $\mu = np$ and standard deviation $\sqrt{npq}$. This means that once we standardize , we will be working with z scores.
- D.   The sampling distribution of $\hat{p}$ is normal with a mean of μ and a standard error of σ
  $$= \sqrt{\frac{pq}{n}}$$
- E.   E = the error of estimate is $|\hat{p} - p|$
- F.   The maximal value for the Error of Estimate is given by $E = z_\alpha \sqrt{\frac{(\hat{p})(1-\hat{p})}{n}}$
- G.   For the given level of confidence, use the appropriate z score.
  - 1. $z_{80} = 1.28$
  - 2. $z_{.90} = 1.645$
  - 3. $z_{.95} = 1.96$
  - 4. $z_{.99} = 2.58$

II.   Steps to form the confidence interval for p in a binomial experiment.
- A.   Check to see that both np and nq are greater than 5.
- B.   Identify r and n from the sample and calculate $\hat{p} = \frac{r}{n}$ to use as your point estimate for p.
- C.   Calculate $1 - \frac{r}{n}$ which is the point estimate for q.
- D.   Calculate the maximal value for the error of estimate = E.
- E.   Use $\hat{p} - E$ as the left boundary for the interval.
- F.   Use $\hat{p} + E$ as the right boundary for the interval.
- G.   Make a probability statement such as: We are 90% sure that p is between $\hat{p} - E$ and $\hat{p} + E$.

Problem Solving Warm-Up

A study of recent graduates of Studymore University indicated that out of 1527 graduates, 1038 had changed their major at least once while enrolled. Form a 95% confidence interval for the proportion of students at Studymore who change their major at least once.

This is a binomial experiment where "success" is defined as "students changes major at least once while enrolled." We are asked to form a confidence interval for p, the proportion of successes.

Fill in with the given information.

$r =$ _____

$n =$ _____

point estimate for p= _____

point estimate for q= _____

$c =$ _____

Solution

The number of "successes" is 1038.

The number of trials is 1527.

The point estimate for p is $\hat{p}$= r/n = 1038/1527 = .68

The point estimate for q is $1-\hat{p} = 1-.68 = .32$

c = .95. Since we will be using a normal distribution, we will use z = 1.96.

We are asked to *estimate* p, the proportion of successes in the **population.**
The *point* estimate for p is $\hat{p} = \frac{r}{n} = .68$.
The maximal value for the error of estimate is

$$E = \pm z_c \sqrt{\frac{(\hat{p})(1-\hat{p})}{n}} = 1.96\sqrt{\frac{(.68)(.32)}{1527}} = .02$$

The left-hand endpoint of the interval is: $\hat{p} - E = .68 - .02 = .66$.

The right-hand endpoint of the interval is: $\hat{p} + E = .68 + .02 = .70$

Confidence interval:

We are 95% sure that the population proportion p is between .66 and .70.

Thinking About Statistics

We have looked at ways of estimating a population parameter such as μ or p.
The overall method is similar, no matter which type of situation you are in.

1.   List the similarities among the methods of estimating.
2.   Fill in the table that follows below to emphasize the differences among the three situations.

	large sample estimate of μ	small sample estimate of μ	binomial estimate of p
conditions for use			
point estimate			
formula for maximal error of estimate			

Selected Solutions Section 8.3

1.   a) r = 62   n = 39   The point estimate for p is $\hat{p} = \frac{r}{n} = \frac{39}{62} = .629$ ◆
        b) c = .95

$$E = \pm z_\alpha \sqrt{\frac{(\hat{p})(1-\hat{p})}{n}} = 1.96 \sqrt{\frac{(.629)(.571)}{62}} = .1202$$

$\hat{p} - E = .5088$ and $\hat{p} + E = .7493$. We are 95% sure that the population proportion of professional actors who are extroverts is between .5088 and .7493. (50.88% and 74.93%) ◆

c)   np = 62(.629) = 38.998 and nq = 62(.371) = 23.002 so np and nq are each greater than 5. This is an important consideration since we base our estimation on the normal approximation to the binomial distribution. This approximation is only close when the conditions np>5 and nq>5 are both satisfied.◆

5.   a) r = 518   n = 421   The point estimate for p is $\hat{p} = \frac{r}{n} = \frac{421}{518} = .8187$ ◆
        b) c = .99

$$E = \pm z_\alpha \sqrt{\frac{(\hat{p})(1-\hat{p})}{n}} = 2.58 \sqrt{\frac{(.8127)(.1873)}{518}} = .0442$$

$\hat{p} - E = .7685$ and $\hat{p} + E = .8570$. We are 99% sure that the population proportion of blue spruce trees that survive replanting is between .7685 and .8570 (76.85% and 85.70%) ◆

c)   np = 518(.8127) =420.98 and nq = 518(.1873) = 97.02 so np and nq are each greater than 5. This is an important consideration since we base our estimation on the normal approximation to the binomial distribution. ◆

9.   a) r = 1.927   n = 2,503   The point estimate for p is $\hat{p} = \frac{r}{n} = \frac{1927}{2503} = .7699$ ♦
        b) c = .90

$$E = \pm z_\alpha \sqrt{\frac{(\hat{p})(1-\hat{p})}{n}} = 1.645 \sqrt{\frac{(.7699)(.2301)}{2503}} = .0138$$

$\hat{p} - E = .7560$

and $\hat{p} + E = .7837$. We are 95% sure that the population proportion is between .7560 and .7837. (75.60% and 78.37%) Since np = 1927 and nq =576 are both greater than 5, the use of the normal distribution in approximating the binomial is justified since the sampling distribution is normal.♦

13.   a)   r = 36   and n = 51 so the point estimate is $\hat{p} = r/n = 36/51 = .7059$. The maximal value for the error of estimate is $E = \sqrt{\frac{(.7059)(.2941)}{51}} = .1050$

$\hat{p} - E = .6009$ and $\hat{p} + E = .8108$. We are 90% sure the population proportion of economic forecasters who overestimate is between .6009 and .8108. ♦

b)   r = 9   and n = 51 so the point estimate is $\hat{p} = r/n = 9/51 = .1765$ The maximal value for the error of estimate is $E = \sqrt{\frac{(.1765)(.8235)}{51}} = .0878$

$\hat{p} - E = .0887$ and $\hat{p} + E = .2643$. We are 90% sure the population proportion of economic forecasters who are close to the actual rate is between .0887 and .2643. ♦

c)   r = 6   and n = 51 so the point estimate is $\hat{p} = r/n = 6/51 = .1176$. The maximal value for the error of estimate is $E = \sqrt{\frac{(.1176)(.8824)}{51}} = .0742$

$\hat{p} - E = .0434$ and $\hat{p} + E = .1919$. We are 90% sure the population proportion of economic forecasters who overestimate is between .0434 and .1919. ♦

d)   In a, np = 36 and nq = 15, for part b np = 9 and nq = 42 and finally for c np = 6 and nq = 45. Since the conditions np >5 and nq >5 are met for all three parts, the normal approximation to the binomial is justified.

17.   The point estimate is $\hat{p} = r/n = 590/100 = .59$. The maximal value for the error of estimate is

$E = 2.58 \sqrt{\frac{(.59)(.41)}{1000}} = .0401$. $\hat{p} - E = .5499$ and $\hat{p} + E = .6301$. We are 99% sure the population proportion is between 55% and 63%.

21.   The point estimate is $\hat{p} = 19\%$ and the margin of sampling error = E = 3%.

$\hat{p}$ - E = 19% -3% = 16% and $\hat{p}$ + E = 19% + 3% = 22%. The 95% confidence interval is from 16% to 22%.

Answers to Thinking About Statistics

1.   For each of the three methods discussed in forming a confidence interval, the basic ingredients were essentially the same.
   - In each we were estimating an unknown *population parameter* using a known *sample statistic.*
   - In each we needed a point estimate which we obtained from a sample.
   - In each we also computed a maximal value for E the error of estimate.
   - The left-hand boundary for each was obtained by POINT ESTIMATE - E.
   - The right-hand boundary from POINT ESTIMATE + E.
   - Each confidence interval had a length of 2E and had the point estimate at its center.

2.   Differences among estimates

	large sample estimate of μ	small sample estimate of μ	binomial estimate of p
conditions for use	$n \geq 30$ or σ known	distribution of x should be nearly normal	$np > 5$ and $nq > 5$
point estimate	$\bar{x}$	$\bar{x}$	$\hat{p} = r/n$
formula for maximal value for error of estimate	$E = z_c \dfrac{\sigma}{\sqrt{n}}$	$E = t_c \dfrac{\sigma}{\sqrt{n}}$ use n-1 d.f.	$E = z_c \sqrt{\dfrac{\hat{p}(1-\hat{p})}{n}}$

Section 8.4
Choosing the Sample Size

Review

We have seen earlier that for a given level of confidence, we can achieve a higher degree of accuracy by increasing the size of the sample.

I.   Determining the sample size for a large sample estimate of μ.

    A.   If we obtain a sample with $n \geq 30$ and compute its mean $\bar{x}$ and its standard deviation s, we can compute the maximal error tolerance by $E = z_c \cdot \dfrac{\sigma}{\sqrt{n}}$.

    B.   When this error tolerance E is too large for our needs we may need to get a bigger sample. The question is how large a sample is necessary in order to keep E within given limits.

    C.   Solving the equation above for n, the sample size, we get $\quad n = (\dfrac{z_c \sigma}{E})^2$

    D.   Thus if we use s as a preliminary estimate for σ (or σ is known), we determine how large our sample should be by following the steps below:

        1.   Obtain the appropriate z score value for the given level of confidence.

        2.   Multiply this by the value of s which we will use in place of σ. (Or by the known value of σ.)

        3.   Divide by the given allowable tolerance E.

        4.   Square the result.

        5.   Since the result may not be a whole number, round your result *up* to the next whole number. This will be the minimum number of values that you will need for your sample in order to be within E units of the population mean μ for the given level of confidence.

II.   Determining the sample size for an estimate of p in a binomial experiment.

    A.   If we can obtain a preliminary sample, we can use $\hat{p} = \dfrac{r}{n}$ as our estimate for p and $(1 - \hat{p})$ as our estimate for q. We obtain a maximal value for error tolerance E by using the formula: $\quad E = z_c \sqrt{\dfrac{\hat{p}(1-\hat{p})}{n}}$

    B.   Solving for n we get $n = \hat{p}(1-\hat{p})(\dfrac{z_c}{n})^2$

    C.   If we do not have a preliminary sample from which to get preliminary estimates for p and q, we can determine a minimum sample size by using the fact that in a binomial experiment, pq = p(1-p) is always less than .25.

D.   Without a preliminary estimate, you will usually need to obtain a larger sample than with one.   *Use* $n \geq .25 \left(\frac{z_c}{E}\right)^2 \geq \hat{p}(1-\hat{p}) \left(\frac{z_c}{E}\right)^2$

Problem Solving Warm-Up

1.   In Section 8.1 we discussed a study on physical attractiveness and found a confidence interval for the population mean of a rating which was done on a scale of 1 to 5 where 231 subjects were rated for attractiveness. In the sample we used the mean was 3.94 and the standard deviation .75.

When we constructed the 95% confidence interval. we found the value of E to be .10. Suppose we are asked to form a 95% confidence interval so that we are within E = .05 of the population mean μ. How large should our sample size be? How many more will we have to add to our preliminary study?

Fill in the blanks with the information given.

What is the unknown? _____

Write the formula needed to find it.

_____

The necessary information is:

c = _____

z_c = _____

σ = _____

E = _____

Substitute in the formula and find a minimum value for n.

n ≥ _____

round up to n≥   _____

Solution

The unknown is n, the sample size.

$$n = \left(\frac{z_c \cdot \sigma}{E}\right)^2$$

c = .95

$z_{.95}$ = 1.96

$\sigma \approx s = .75$ from the preliminary study.

E = .05

$$n \geq \left(\frac{1.96 \cdot .77}{.05}\right)^2$$

n ≥ 864.36

Rounding up to the next whole number we find that the minimum sample size is 865.

216

How many MORE? _____   Since we have already obtained results from our preliminary sample of 231, we will need 634 *more* for our sample.

2.   We wish to do a survey of students at Studymore University to determine a 90% confidence interval for the proportion of students who change their major at least once while enrolled. We need to be within .01 of the true proportion.
If no preliminary study is available, how large should we make our sample?

Fill in the blanks with the information given.   *Solution*

What is the unknown? _____

Write the formula needed to find it.   The unknown is n, the sample size.

_____

$$n = .25 \left(\frac{z_c}{E} \right)^2$$

The necessary information is:

c = _____   c = .90

z_c = _____ $z_{.90} = 1.645$

E = _____   E = .01

Substitute in the formula and find n.

$$n \geq .25 \left(\frac{1.645}{.01} \right)^2 .25 (1.645)^2$$

n ≥ _____

$$n \geq 6765.0624$$

round up to n≥ _____   The minimum number for our sample is 6766.

3.   Suppose we do a preliminary study for our estimation of p, the proportion of students at Studymore University who change their majors and find that out of 1527 in the study, 1038 changed their majors at least once while at Studymore. How many *more* would we need for our sample in order to be within .01 of the true proportion?

Fill in the blanks with the information given.   *Solution*

What is the unknown? _____   The unknown is n, the sample size.

Write the formula needed to find it.

$$n = p \cdot q \left(\frac{z_c}{E} \right)^2$$

_____

The necessary information is:

c = _____

z_c = _____

preliminary est. for p = _____
preliminary est. for q = _____

E =

Substitute in the formula and find n.

n≥ _____

round up n≥ _____

c = .90

$z_{.90}$ = 1.645

estimate of p = 1038/1527 = .68
estimate of q = 1 - .68 = .32

E = .01

$$n \geq (.68)(.32) \left(\frac{1.645}{.01} \right)^2$$

n ≥ 5888.3101
The minimum number for our sample with a preliminary estimate for p is 5889. We will need 5889 - 1527 = 4362 *more* in our sample to be within .01 of p.

Thinking About Statistics

1.   If everything else remains the same, what is the effect of an increase of c, the level of confidence on the sample size?

2.   If everything else remains the same what is the effect of a larger σ on the necessary sample size?

3.   If everything else remains the same, what is the effect of making our requirement for E, the error of estimate, smaller?

4.   We stated earlier that in a binomial experiment the value of p·q is always less than or equal to .25. This can be proved in several ways, including the use of Calculus. Convince yourself (without a **proof) that the value of p·q will never be greater than .25. Fill in the following table of values to do so.**

p	0	.10	.20	.30	.40	.50	.60	.70	.80	.90	1	*
q												
p·q												

* Fill in any appropriate value for p. Remember that it must be between 0 and 1.

Selected Solutions Section 8.4

1. i) We are going to estimate population mean μ. We are asked How many 50 meter square would be included in the sample, so we'll use the following formula. $n \geq (\frac{z_c \cdot \sigma}{E})^2$

The information given for the problem is c = .95 $\sigma \approx s = 44$
E = 10 saplings (The clue is we want to be *within* 10 saplings for the estimate)
Use $z_{.95} = 1.96$

$$n \geq (\frac{(1.96)(44)}{10})^2 = (8.624)^2 = 74.37$$

We should use at least 75 plots. ♦

5. We are estimating a population mean μ. We are asked <u>How many *more* basketball players should included in the sample.</u>

$$n \geq (\frac{z_c \cdot \sigma}{E})^2 = (\frac{1.645(26.58)}{4})^2 = (10.93)^2 = 119.48$$

Since we need to use at least 120 players and we've already used 56, we need 120 - 56 = 64 more. ♦

9. We are estimating a population mean μ. Use the formula:

$$n \geq (\frac{z_c \cdot \sigma}{E})^2 = (\frac{2.58(1.75)}{.5})^2 = (9.03)^2 = 81.54$$

We'll need at least 82 readings for our sample. Since we have already done 30 readings, we'll need 52 more. ♦

11.   We are asked to estimate p, the population <u>proportion. If *no preliminary sample* is taken, how large a sample is necessary?</u>

$$n \geq .25 \left(\frac{z_c}{E}\right)^2$$

c = .85   E = .06 (*clue* within a distance of .06 from p) $z_{.85}$ = 1.44

$$n \geq .25 \left(\frac{1.44}{.06}\right)^2 = 144 \;\blacklozenge$$

b)   <u>With a preliminary study of 58 trees, how many *more* trees?</u>

c = .85   E = .06

$\hat{p}$ = r/n = 19/58 = .33 preliminary estimate for p.

1- $\hat{p}$ = 1 - .33 = .67 = preliminary estimate for q.

$z_{.85}$ = 1.44

$$n \geq (.33)(.67)\left(\frac{1.44}{.06}\right)^2 = 127.35$$

The minimum number needed is 128. Since there were 58 in the preliminary sample, 70 *more* are needed. ♦

13.   We are estimating a population proportion

a   <u>If *no preliminary sample* is taken, how large a sample is necessary?</u>

$$n \geq .25 \left(\frac{z_c}{E}\right)^2 = .25 \left(\frac{2.58}{.01}\right)^2 = .25(66564) = 16,641$$

With no preliminary sample we need at least 16,642 voters in our sample. ♦

b)   <u>With a preliminary value of $\hat{p}$ = .67, how large a sample is needed?</u> $n = .67)(1-.67)\left(\frac{2.58}{.01}\right)^2 = 14717.30$

We need at least 14,718 in the sample. ♦

17.   We are estimating p, the population proportion. With no preliminary study we need $n \geq .25 \left(\frac{1.645}{.1}\right)^2 = 67.67$. We need at least 68 Cheyenne truck owners. ♦

b) Using $\hat{p}$ = .24 for a preliminary estimate, we'll need at least $(.24)(.76)\left(\frac{1.645}{.1}\right)^2 = 49.36$. .We need at least 50 in the sample. ♦

Answers to Thinking About Statistics

1.   Increasing the level of confidence will increase the number necessary for your sample.

2.   When σ is larger, you will need a larger sample for the same degree of reliability.

3.   If the value of E, the maximal error tolerance is *decreased* the sample size should be increased.

p	0	.10	.20	.30	.40	.50	.60	.70	.80	.90	1	p
q	1	.90	.80	.70	.60	.50	.40	.30	.20	.10	0	1-p
p·q	0	.09	.16	.21	.24	.25	.24	.21	.16	.09	0	$p-p^2$

No matter what value you chose for p , as long as it is between 0 and 1, its product with q which is 1-p will never exceed .25. The value of pq is equal to .25 when both p and q are .5.
If you have the resources to get a preliminary sample you will need a smaller sample (for the same degree of accuracy) than if you do not have the resources and can not get one. The sample size with a preliminary sample and without a preliminary sample will be the same only when p = q = .5.

Section 8.5

Estimating μ_1 - μ_2 and p_1 -p_2

Review

In the first 3 sections of this chapter we looked at estimating the value of a population parameter for one single population. Now we look at confidence intervals that are used to estimate the *difference* between the values of a parameter value of one population and the parameter value of a second population.

I.   Ways of sampling from two populations to estimate the difference. (For example to estimate the difference between the mean of one population and the mean of a second.)
        A.   Dependent samples

1.   Members in the first population are randomly selected and paired with corresponding members of a second population on a one-to-one basis. The value of a random variable x_1 is determined for each member in the first population and the corresponding measure x_2 is determined for its partner in the second population. Then, for each pairing, the difference $x_1 - x_2$ in the measured value is computed.

        a.   Before and after measurements are common.

        b.   Measures from identical twin studies.

2.   Problems involving inferences about the difference for populations when we work with dependent samples will be examined in Chapter 9.

B.   Independent samples

    1.   Members in population 1 are randomly selected.

    2.   Members from population 2 are randomly selected.

    3.   There is no pairing between samples.

II.   Forming a confidence interval for the difference in population means $\mu_1 - \mu_2$ using large (each over 30) independent samples.

A.   A sample is taken from population 1 and the mean $\overline{x}_1$ and the standard deviation s_1 are computed. A sample is also taken from population 2 and the mean $\overline{x}_2$ and standard deviation s_2 are computed. The difference between the sample means $\overline{x}_1 - \overline{x}_2$ is used as a point estimate for the difference in population means.

B.   Sampling distribution of $\overline{x}_1 - \overline{x}_2$ (large samples)

    1.   If we could repeat the sampling process an infinite number of times and compute the difference between the sample means we would get a distribution of differences that is:

        a.   Normal

        b.   The mean of the sampling distribution $= \mu_1 - \mu_2$.

        c.   The standard error $= \sqrt{\dfrac{\sigma_1^2}{n_1} + \dfrac{\sigma_2^2}{n_2}}$

C.   Confidence interval for estimating $\mu_1 - \mu_2$ (large samples)

    1.   Point estimate is $\overline{x}_1 - \overline{x}_2$

    2.   The maximal value for the error of estimate is: $E = z_c \sqrt{\dfrac{\sigma_1^2}{n_1} + \dfrac{\sigma_2^2}{n_2}}$

        a. σ_1 and σ_2 are estimated by s_1 and s_2.

    3.   The left endpoint is $(\overline{x}_1 - \overline{x}_2) - E$.

    4.   The right endpoint is $(\overline{x}_1 - \overline{x}_2) + E$.

III.   Forming a confidence interval for the difference in population means $\mu_1 - \mu_2$ using small (at least one is under 30) independent samples.

A.   Necessary assumptions

1. Parent populations are approximately normal (symmetric and mound shaped).
2. Standard deviations (and variances) for the two populations are approximately equal.

B. A sample is taken from population 1 and the mean $\overline{x}_1$ and the standard deviation s_1 are computed. A sample is also taken from population 2 and the mean $\overline{x}_2$ and standard deviation s_2 are computed. The difference between the sample means $\overline{x}_1 - \overline{x}_2$ is used as a point estimate for the difference in population means.

C. An estimate for the common (since they are assumed to be equal) population standard deviation is made using a <u>pooled variance.</u> (The term pooled refers to the fact that values from both samples are used for the estimate.)

    1. The pooled variance is: $s^2 = \dfrac{(n_1-1)\, s_1^2 + (n_2-1)\, s_2^2}{n_1 + n_2 - 2}$

    2. The pooled standard deviation is then $s = \sqrt{s^2} = \sqrt{\dfrac{(n_1-1)\, s_1^2 + (n_2-1)\, s_2^2}{n_1 + n_2 - 2}}$

D. Sampling distribution of $\overline{x}_1 - \overline{x}_2$ (small samples)

    1. If we could repeat the sampling process an infinite number of times and compute the difference between the sample means we would get a distribution of differences that is:

      a. A Student t-distribution with $n_1 + n_2 - 2$ degrees of freedom.

      b. The mean of the sampling distribution $= \mu_1 - \mu_2$

      c. The standard error is: $s = \sqrt{s^2} = \sqrt{\dfrac{(n_1-1)\, s_1^2 + (n_2-1)\, s_2^2}{n_1 + n_2 - 2}}$

      d. The maximal value for the error of estimate is given by

$$E = t_c s \sqrt{\dfrac{1}{n_1} + \dfrac{1}{n_2}}$$

      e. The left endpoint is $(\overline{x}_1 - \overline{x}_2) - E$.

      f. The right endpoint is $(\overline{x}_1 - \overline{x}_2) + E$.

IV. Confidence intervals for estimating $\boldsymbol{p_1 - p_2}$, *the difference in population proportions.*

A. A binomial experiment is performed on a sample taken from population 1. $n_1 =$ the size of this sample and r_1 is the number of "successes" for this sample. An estimate for the population proportion of successes is then made by computing $\hat{p}_1 = \dfrac{r_1}{n_1}$. The binomial experiment is also performed in population 2. $n_2 =$ the number in this sample and r_2 is the number of "successes". The estimate for the population proportion of successes is then $\hat{p}_2 = \dfrac{r_2}{n_2}$. The point estimate for the difference in proportions is $\hat{p}_1 - \hat{p}_2$.

B. Sampling distribution of $\hat{p}_1 - \hat{p}_2$

1. If we could repeat the sampling process an infinite number of times and compute the difference between the sample proportions we would get a distribution of differences that is:
    a. Normal (provided $n_1 p_1$, $n_1 q_1$, $n_2 p_2$ and $n_2 p_2$ are all greater than 5.)
    b. The mean of the sampling distribution $= p_1 - p_2$.
    c. The standard deviation is approximately $\sigma = \sqrt{\dfrac{\hat{p}_1 \hat{q}_1}{n_1} + \dfrac{\hat{p}_2 \hat{q}_2}{n_2}}$
    d. The maximum value for the error of estimate is $E = z_c \sqrt{\dfrac{\hat{p}_1 \hat{q}_1}{n_1} + \dfrac{\hat{p}_2 \hat{q}_2}{n_2}}$.
    e. The left endpoint is $(\hat{p}_1 - \hat{p}_2) - E$.
    f. The right endpoint is $(\hat{p}_1 - \hat{p}_2) + E$.

V. General conclusions
    A. If the confidence intervals for the difference in population means $\mu_1 - \mu_2$ or the difference in proportions $p_1 - p_2$ contains only negative values (such as an interval from -2.5 to -1.7) we can be confident (at c%) that the parameter for the first population is less than the parameter for the second.
    B. If the confidence interval for the difference contains only positive values,(such as an interval from 1.7 to 2.5 to) we are c% confident that the parameter in population 1is greater than that of population 2.
    C. If the confidence interval contains both positive and negative values,(such as an interval from -2.5 to 1.7) we cannot conclude one population has greater values for its parameter than the other. It is possible if we shorten the interval we will find all positive or all negative values.

Problem Solving Warm-Up

1. The student services department at a large university conducted a study to determine the difference in study hours between student athletes and students who were not athletes. A random sample of 46 student athletes produced a mean equal to $\overline{x}_1 = 19.79$ hours studied per week and a standard deviation of $s_1 = 4.9$ hours. A second random sample of 93 non-athletes produced a mean equal to $\overline{x}_2 = 22.41$ hours per week and a standard deviation equal to $s_2 = 5.8$ hours. Form a 90% confidence interval for $\mu_1 - \mu_2$ the difference in study time for the two populations.

Identify the type of problem.

This problem calls for the formation of confidence interval for the difference in population means using large samples.

_____

$n_1 =$ $\overline{x}_1 =$ $s_1 =$

$n_2 =$ $\overline{x}_2 =$ $s_2 =$

$n_1 = 46$ $\overline{x}_1 = 19.79$ $s_1 = 4.9$

$n_2 = 93$ $\overline{x}_2 = 22.41$ $s_2 = 5.8$

The point estimate is

$$\overline{x}_1 - \overline{x}_2 = 19.79 - 22.41 = -2.62$$

The maximal value for the error of estimate is:

$$E = z_c \sqrt{\frac{\sigma_1^2}{n_1} + \frac{\sigma_2^2}{n_2}}$$

$$E = 1.645 \sqrt{\frac{(4.9)^2}{46} + \frac{(5.8)^2}{93}} = 1.645 \sqrt{.8837}$$

$$= 1.645 (.9400) = 1.5464$$

The left endpoint is

The right endpoint is -

Statement on confidence interval

$$-2.62 - 1.5464 = -4.1164$$

$$-2.62 + 1.5464 = -1.0736$$

Interpretation of interval

We are 90% sure the difference in the mean number of hours is between -4.17 and -1.07.

We are 90% sure the difference in population means is negative. This means we are 90% sure $\mu_1 < \mu_2$ meaning that student athletes study less time than non-athletes.

2. A personnel manager suspects a difference in the mean length of work time lost due to sickness for male and female employees. For the first group, she randomly samples 15 males and finds the mean number of sick days in the past year was $\overline{x}_1 = 12.8$ days with a standard deviation of $s_1 = 7.9$. A second random sample of 12 females produced a mean of $\overline{x}_2 = 10.4$ sick days with a standard deviation of $s_2 = 8.1$ days. Calculate a 95% confidence interval for $\mu_1 - \mu_2$. (Assume both populations are normally distributed and that they have equal standard deviations.

Identify the type of problem.

This problem calls for the formation of confidence interval for the difference in population means using small samples.

$n_1 =$	$\overline{x}_1 =$	$s_1 =$
$n_2 =$	$\overline{x}_2 =$	$s_2 =$

$n_1 = 15$	$\overline{x}_1 = 12.8$	$s_1 = 7.9$
$n_2 = 12$	$\overline{x}_2 = 10.4$	$s_2 = 8.1$

The point estimate is

$$\overline{x}_1 - \overline{x}_2 = 12.8 - 10.4 = 1.6$$

What is the sampling distribution?

The sampling distribution is the t distribution with 15 +12-2=25 df. $t_{95} = 2.060$.

The estimate for the common value for the standard deviations of the populations is:

$$s = \sqrt{s^2} = \sqrt{\frac{(n_1-1)\,s_1^2 + (n_2-1)\,s_2^2}{n_1+n_2-2}}$$

$$= \sqrt{\frac{(15-1)\,(7.9)^2 + (12-1)\,(8.1)^2}{25}}$$

$$= \sqrt{\frac{14\,(7.9)^2) + 11\,(8.1)^2}{25}} = \sqrt{63.818} = 7.99$$

The maximal value for the error of estimate is:

$$E = t_c s \sqrt{\frac{1}{n_1} + \frac{1}{n_2}} = 2.060\,(7.99)\sqrt{\frac{1}{15} + \frac{1}{12}}$$

$$= 2.060(7.99)(.3873) = 6.3747$$

The left endpoint is

$$1.6 - 6.3747 = -4.7747$$

The right endpoint is

$$1.6 + 6.3747 = 7.9747$$

Statement on confidence interval

We are 95% sure the difference in the number of sick days in the two population means is -4.77 and 7.97

Interpretation of interval

The confidence interval contains both positive and negative values. We can not conclude either type has higher number of sick days

3. Two types of knee reconstruction surgical procedures were performed. Procedure A was performed on a random sample of $n_1 = 37$ patients. Two years later, the operation was successful for

$r_1 = 29$ of these patients. Procedure B was performed on $n_2 = 43$ patients. Out of these, $r_2 = 32$ were successful after two years. Form a 99% confidence interval for the difference in success rates for the two types of surgeries.

Identify the type of problem.

_____

_____

$n_1 = $ $r_1 = $ $\hat{p}_1 = $ $\hat{q}_1 = $
$n_2 = $ $r_2 = $ $\hat{p}_2 = $ $\hat{q}_2 = $

Check the necessary assumptions:

The point estimate is

_____

The maximal value for the error of estimate is:

The left endpoint is

_____

The right endpoint is

_____

Statement on confidence interval

_____

_____

Interpretation of interval

_____

_____

This problem calls for the formation of confidence interval for the difference in population proportions.

$n_1 = 37$ $r_1 = 29$ $\hat{p}_1 = .7838$ $\hat{q}_1 = .2162$
$n_2 = 43$ $r_2 = 32$ $\hat{p}_2 = .7442$ $\hat{q}_2 = .2558$

$n_1\hat{p}_1 = 29$, $n_2\hat{p}_2 = 32$, $n_1\hat{q}_1 = 8$ $n_2\hat{q}_2 = 11$
Since all these are greater than 5, we use a normal approximation to the binomial.

$\hat{p}_1 - \hat{p}_2 = .7838 - .7442 = .0396$

$$E = z_c\sqrt{\frac{\hat{p}_1\hat{q}_1}{n_1} + \frac{\hat{p}_2\hat{q}_2}{n_2}} = $$

$$= 2.58\sqrt{\frac{(.7838)(.2162)}{37} + \frac{(.7442)(.2558)}{43}}$$

$$= 2.58\sqrt{.0090} = \sim 2.58(.0949) \sim = \sim .2449$$

$.0396 - .2449 = -.2053$

$.0396 + .2449 = .2845$

We are 99% sure the difference in the proportion of successful surgeries for the two techniques is between -.21 and .28

The confidence interval contains both positive and negative values. We can not conclude either type of surgery has a higher rate of success.

Thinking about Statistics

Compare the techniques used in this section with those used in sections 8-1, 8-2 and 8-3. What is the basic difference between the problems (no pun intended)? What are the similarities?

Selected Solutions Section 8.5

1.   The confidence interval is for the difference of population means. Since $n_1 = 9$ and $n_2 = 10$, use the small sample technique. The point estimate for the difference is $\overline{x}_1 - \overline{x}_2 = 91.00 - 61.5 = 29.5$.

The sampling distribution is the t distribution with 9+10-2=17 df. $t_{95} = 2.110$. The estimate for the standard error is:

$$s = \sqrt{s^2} = \sqrt{\frac{(n_1-1)\,s_1^2 + (n_2-1)\,s_2^2}{n_1+n_2-2}}$$

$$= \sqrt{\frac{(9-1)(33.92)^2 + (10-1)(34.03)^2}{9+10-2}} = \sqrt{\frac{8(33.92)^2) + 9(34.03)^2}{17}}$$

$$= \sqrt{1154.5235} = 33.9783$$

The maximal value for the error of estimate is given by $\quad E = t_c s \sqrt{\dfrac{1}{n_1} + \dfrac{1}{n_2}} = 2.110\,(33.9783)\sqrt{\dfrac{1}{9} + \dfrac{1}{10}}$

$$= 2.110\,(33.9783)\sqrt{.2111} = 2.110\,(33.9783)(.4595) = 32.94$$

The left endpoint is 29.5 - 32.94 = -3.44 and the right endpoint is 29.5 + 32.94 = 62.44. We are 95% sure the difference in population means of start up costs of sporting goods business and travel agent business is between -3.44 and 62.44. ◆

c)   The confidence interval contains both positive and negative values. We can not conclude either type has higher starting costs at this level confidence.

5. Difference in the population proportions between married couples with two or more personality preferences in common and those with no personality preferences in common.

population 1

$r_1 = 289$ $n_1 = 375$

$\hat{p}_1 = \frac{289}{375} = .7707$ and

$\hat{q}_1 = 1 - .7707 = .2293$

Check conditions:

$n_1\hat{p}_1 = 289$ and $n_1\hat{q}_1 = 86$

population 2

$r_2 = 23$ $n_2 = 571$

$\hat{p}_2 = \frac{23}{571} = .0403$ and

$\hat{q}_2 = 1 - .0403 = .9597$

Check conditions:

$n_2\hat{p}_2 = 23$ and $n_2\hat{q}_2 = 548$

Since all are greater than 5, we can use the normal approximation to the binomial distribution

The point estimate for the difference in population proportions is $\hat{p}_1 - \hat{p}_2 = .7707 - .0403 = .7304$.

The maximal value for the error of estimate is $E = z_c\sqrt{\dfrac{\hat{p}_1\hat{q}_1}{n_1} + \dfrac{\hat{p}_2\hat{q}_2}{n_2}} =$

$$E = 2.58\sqrt{\frac{(.7707)(.2293)}{375} + \frac{(.0403)(.9597)}{571}} = 2.58\sqrt{.000539} = 2.58(.0232) = .0599$$

The left endpoint is $.7304 - .0599 = .6705$ and the right endpoint is $.7304 + .0599 = .7903$. We are 99% sure the difference in proportions is between 67% and 79%.

c. Since the confidence interval contains only positive differences there is a 99% probability that there is a higher proportion of married couples with 2 or more personality traits in common than there is married couples with no traits in common.

9. This problem calls for the formation of confidence interval for the difference in population means using large samples.

$n_1 = 51$ $\overline{x}_1 = 74.04$ $s_1 = 17.19$

$n_2 = 36$ $\overline{x}_2 = 94.53$ $s_2 = 19.66$

The point estimate is $\overline{x}_1 - \overline{x}_2 = 74.04 - 94.53 = -20.49$.

The maximal value for the error of estimate is $E = z_c\sqrt{\dfrac{\sigma_1^2}{n_1} + \dfrac{\sigma_2^2}{n_2}}$

$$E = 1.96\sqrt{\frac{(17.19)^2}{51} + \frac{(19.66)^2}{36}} = 1.96\sqrt{16.5306} = 1.96(4.0658) = 7.9689$$

The left endpoint is -20.49 -7.9689 = - 28.4589 and the right endpoint is -20.49 +7.9689 = -12.5211.

We are 95% sure the difference in the mean weight of the bucks in the Cache la Poudre Region and the Mesa Verde Region is between -28.46 and -12.52 kg. ◆

c.   All values for this confidence interval are negative which indicates that we can be 95% certain that the bucks in Mesa Verde weigh more on the average than those in the Cache la Poudre region. ◆

13.   This problem calls for the formation of confidence interval for the difference in population means using large samples.

$$\text{Males:} \quad n_1 = 47 \quad \overline{x}_1 = 483.43 \quad s_1 = 126.62$$
$$\text{Females} \quad n_2 = 51 \quad \overline{x}_2 = 414.43 \quad s_2 = 105.99$$

The point estimate is $\overline{x}_1 - \overline{x}_2 = 483.43 - 414.43 = 69$

The maximal value for the error of estimate is $E = z_c \sqrt{\dfrac{\sigma_1^2}{n_1} + \dfrac{\sigma_2^2}{n_2}}$

$$E = 1.645 \sqrt{\frac{(126.62)^2}{47} + \frac{(105.99)^2}{51}} = 1.645\sqrt{561.3918} = 1.645(23.69) = 38.9762$$

The left endpoint is 69 - 38.98 = 30.02 and the right endpoint is 69 + 38.98 = 107.98. We are 90% sure the difference in premiums between males and females age 45 is from $30.02 and $107.98. ◆

c.   Since the confidence interval for the difference contains only positive values we can conclude that males in the 45 year age group probably pay more in premiums than females in the same age category. ◆

Answers to Thinking About Statistics

The problems in section 8-4 involve finding a confidence interval for the difference between the parameter value in two populations. In the first three sections of this chapter, we were finding a confidence interval for a single value.

In all cases, however, a point estimate must be determined. Then a value for the maximal error of estimate is found. For the left hand value of the interval, subtract this error value from the point estimate and for the right hand endpoint add the error of estimate to the point estimate.

The length of the confidence interval is always twice the value of the error of estimate.

Chapter 9

HYPOTHESIS TESTING

Section 9.1
Introduction to Hypothesis Testing

Review

Along with estimation, hypothesis testing is an important technique of statistical inference. In both cases we use sample statistics to make decisions about population parameters.

I.   *Hypothesis:* A theory, guess or assumption. In Statistics we make hypotheses about unknown population parameters or about differences in population parameters. In a statistical test we will always formulate *two* hypotheses, the null and the alternate.

    A.   The **null hypothesis,** denoted H_0 is an assumption that is set up primarily for the purpose of seeing whether it can be rejected.

        1.   In many hypothesis tests the null hypothesis is a claim that the value of the population parameter is equal to some fixed number.

        2.   The claim is everything is good or as it should be.

        3.   It contains the = symbol in its statement.

    B.   The **alternate hypothesis**, denoted H_1 is a contradiction to the null hypothesis. When we reject the null hypothesis, we choose the alternate hypothesis.

        1.   It can claim the parameter being tested is *greater than* the value in H_0.

        2.   It can claim the parameter being tested is *less than* the value in H_0

        3.   It can claim the parameter being tested is *not equal to* the value in H_0

II.   Logical development of a hypothesis test

    A.   We assume the null hypothesis is true. This means that we will know the behavior of the sampling distribution for our sample statistic. (For example, it could be normally distributed, come from a t distribution or from other distributions that we will study later.)

B.   We form a random sample and compute appropriate sample statistics. We also determine the sample test statistic. For tests of μ, this is $\overline{x}$.

C.   We standardize our sample statistic within the known distribution. This might mean, for example, converting a value of $\overline{x}$ to a standardized z value.

D.   Based on probabilities, we either reject the null hypothesis or fail to reject it.

    1.   If there is enough statistical evidence,(i.e. the standard value is highly improbable based on the assumption that H_0 is true) we decide to **reject the null hypothesis.** (We are in effect choosing the alternative hypothesis as being more probable.)

    2.   We could also **fail to reject H_0** if there is not enough evidence to reject it. This does not mean that we accept the null hypothesis without a shadow of a doubt, only that we must fail to reject it.

III.   *Level of Significance*

A.   <u>Ideally</u>, when the null hypothesis is true, we will fail to reject. And when the null hypothesis is false the decision will be to reject it.

B.   As you learned in previous chapters, variation is natural from one sample to another. It is entirely possible that a test is performed with no statistical errors but there is an error in the decision. (In real life, innocent people are sent to jail and guilty ones are set free.)

C.   The chart below should help distinguish between different types of unavoidable errors made in hypothesis testing.

DECISION MADE

	Fail to reject H_0	Reject H_0
H_0 is really true	correct decision	*Type I error*
H_0 is really false	*Type II error*	correct decision

    1.   A Type I error is made when the null hypothesis is really true but you decide to reject it.

    2.   A Type II error is made when the null hypothesis is really false but you fail to reject it.

D.   Either type of error is always possible, but we like to keep the probability of making these errors very small.

    1.   The probability of making a type I error is denoted α (lower case Greek letter alpha) and is called the *level of significance* of a hypothesis test.

        a.   We generally set the level of significance to be .01 or .05.

    b.   At the 1% level of significance, we take a risk that 1% of the time we will reject a null hypothesis when it is actually true.

    c.   At the 5% level of significance, we take a risk that 5% of the time we will reject a null hypothesis when it is actually true.

2.   The probability of making a type II error is denoted β (lower case Greek letter beta) and $1-\beta$ is called the *power* of a hypothesis test.

    a.   When we increase the level of significance we decrease β.

    b.   This concept is dealt with in more advanced courses.

    c.   The following chart summarizes the probabilities of making various decisions.

DECISION MADE

	Fail to reject H_0	Reject H_0
H_0 is really true	probability = $1 - \alpha$	probability = α
H_0 is really false	probability = β	probability = $1-\beta$

IV.   *Critical values of a hypothesis test*

    A.   Based on the assumption that H_0 is true you make the decision to reject it if your sample evidence indicates there is a low probability it is true.

    B.   Based on the assumption that H_0 is true you fail to reject it if there is not enough sample evidence to reject it.

    C.   The **critical region(s)** are the region(s) under the distribution curve that are in the "tails" (outer regions) where the null hypothesis is the least probable. These regions have a total area that is equal to the level of significance. The alternate hypothesis will determine the location of the critical region(s).

        1.   When the alternate hypothesis contains a statement claiming the parameter is *greater* than the value in the null hypothesis, the critical region is in the *right* tail of the sampling distribution.

        2.   When the alternate hypothesis contains a statement claiming the parameter is *less* than the value in the null hypothesis, the critical region is in the *left* tail of the sampling distribution.

        3.   When the alternate hypothesis contains a statement that claims the parameter is not equal to the value in the null hypothesis, the critical regions are found in both tails of the sampling distribution. The area in each of the two tails is equal to half of the level of significance.

D.   The **critical value(s)** are the values that separate the critical rejection region from the rest of the curve. In the sections which follow we will develop formulas for critical values. These formulas will be based on H_0, H_1, α and the sampling distribution.

E.   When a sample statistic falls in a critical region, we reject the null hypothesis. If the sample statistic does not fall in a critical region, we fail to reject H_0.

F.   The concept of a critical value can be made more clear by the following example:

    1.   You wish to test a coin to see if it is fair. Your null hypothesis then is the coin is fair. Your alternate is that the coin is not fair (it is 'loaded'). You decide that you will toss this coin 100 times and then make the decision as to whether it is fair or not. Start by assuming H_0 that the coin is, in fact fair.

    2.   If on 100 tosses, you get 50 heads and 50 tails, everyone would agree the coin is fair.

    3.   Suppose you got 48 heads and 52 tails. You would probably conclude that this is just due to your sample of tosses and would to fail to reject the null hypothesis that the coin as fair.

    4.   Suppose you get 45 heads and 55 tails? 40 heads and 60 tails? 30 heads and 70 tails? The decision of whether or not the coin is fair is not obvious. It is always **possible** that the coin is fair, but is it *probable?*

    5.   Before you start your coin tosses, you must decide on guidelines with which to make your decision. Suppose you decide (before you toss the coin) that if you get fewer than 41 heads or more than 59 heads you will reject the hypothesis that the coin is fair. Otherwise, you will say it is fair. Thus if you then toss the coin 100 times and get 61 heads you will say it is not fair. If you get 58 heads, however, you will choose the hypothesis that it is fair.

Number of heads in 100 tosses

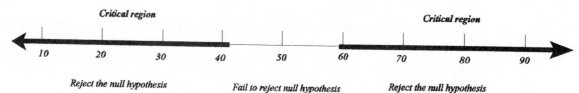

    6.   Your critical values are 41 and 59

        a.   You have 2 critical (rejection) regions. One consists of all numbers less than 41, the other all numbers more than 59

        b.   For the region between (or including) 41 to 59 you would fail to reject the null hypothesis that the coin is fair.

V.   Concluding the test

    A.   Decide to reject H_0 if your sample statistic falls in the improbable critical (rejection) region, beyond the critical values.

234

B.   Otherwise fail to reject H_0

Problem Solving Warm-Up

Flakey Cereal is sold in boxes which are marked net contents 18 oz. Formulate a pair of null and alternate hypotheses for each situation below.

1.   As a consumer, we believe that the contents of the box is less than 18 oz.

Circle two hypotheses from given choices. Select one as the null hypothesis and the other as the alternative hypothesis.

- a) $\mu \neq 18$
- b) $\mu > 18$
- c) $\mu = 18$
- d) $\mu < 18$

$H_0 : \mu = 18$
The null hypothesis always contains the statement of equality. It says things are as they should be.

$H_1 : \mu < 18$
The claim is there is less than 18 oz.

2.   You are head of production at Flakey Cereal. You claim that the boxes are filled with more than 18 oz.

Circle two hypotheses from given choices. Select one as the null hypothesis and the other as the alternative hypothesis.

- a) $\mu \neq 18$
- b) $\mu > 18$
- c) $\mu = 18$
- d) $\mu < 18$

$H_0 : \mu = 18$
The null hypothesis always contains the statement of equality. It says things are as they should be.

$H_1 : \mu > 18$
The claim is that there is more than 18 oz.

3.   You are working for a company specializing in quality control. You are hired to see whether Flakey Cereal boxes contain 18 oz.

Circle two hypotheses from given choices. Select one as the null hypothesis and the other as the alternative hypothesis.

a) $\mu \neq 18$
b) $\mu > 18$
c) $\mu = 18$
d) $\mu < 18$

$H_0 : \mu = 18$
The null hypothesis always contains the statement of equality. It says things are as they should be.

$H_1 : \mu \neq 18$
When we do not know whether a mean is more or less than a number we use the $\neq$ inequality.

Thinking About Statistics

The first step in setting up a hypothesis test is formulating the pair of hypotheses. Remember that hypotheses are about unknown population parameters. It does not matter which of the two hypotheses you set up first. The important point is that the null hypothesis contains the statement of equality it is the one that is assumed to be true and is usually set up with the purpose of rejecting it.. The following examples will serve as practice for setting up hypotheses. Underline key words before you begin.

1.   Over a period of time it has been found that the average number of cavities a child has per year is .36. Freshdent Company has developed a new toothpaste. Test the claim that children who use Freshdent toothpaste have better yearly checkups.

2.   The average time that Sam Quick has been running a mile is 4.3 minutes. He has been working under a new training program to get into better condition. Test the claim that after his new training program Sam quick is running faster than he did before.

3   A major car manufacturer has come out with a new sports model XJJ. The advertisements claim the car will get 32 miles per gallon of gas. Assuming that the company does not underestimate, test the claim that the XJJ model gets 32 miles per gallon.

4.   Americom Corporation manufactures parts for satellites. A particular gear is designed to be 3" in diameter. Set up the hypotheses to test the claim that the diameter of the gears is different from 3".

Selected Solutions

1. a) A statistical hypothesis is a guess or theory or assumption about one or more population parameters. ♦

    b) A null hypothesis is the assumption that everything is as it should be, and there is nothing wrong. The null hypothesis is set up to see whether it can be rejected. It contains the equality statement.♦

    c) An alternate hypothesis is the theory we will choose if we reject the null hypothesis.

    d) A type I error occurs when the null hypothesis is actually true, but on the basis of evidence from sample statistics it is rejected. ♦
    A type II error occurs when the null hypothesis is actually false and there is not enough evidence to reject it. ♦

    e) The level of significance of a test is the probability of making a type I error. We usually set α at .01 or .05 thus keeping this probability low. The power of a test is the probability $(1-\beta)$ of correctly rejecting a null hypothesis. When α is increased, β will decrease. β can be decreased by taking a larger sample. ♦

    f) For the test of this section, hen the hypotheses involve the population parameter μ. the sample statistic is $\overline{x}$. If the sample size is 30 or more (or if the population is normal) then the sampling distribution is normal. In other sections we will see if the sample size is under 30 and the population is normal, we will use a t-distribution with a(n-1) degrees of freedom. ♦

    g) A critical region is an interval of values which, assuming the null hypothesis is true, would *probably* NOT be sample values. Thus if our sample value falls in a critical region, we will reject the null hypothesis. Otherwise, we will fail to reject the null hypothesis. A critical value is a number that separates the critical (rejection) region from the rest of the distribution. ♦

    g) In all tests, we set up a pair of hypotheses such that when one is true the other will be false. We select α a level of significance. We determine a critical region by computing a critical value. We will reject H_0 if the sample statistic falls in the critical region. Otherwise, we will fail to reject it. ♦

    h) When the test statistic falls in a critical region of the sampling distribution, we reject the null hypothesis. If the test statistic doe not fall in a critical region, we fail to reject the null hypothesis. This does not mean we accept the null hypothesis as absolutely true, only that we do not have enough evidence to say it is false. ♦

3. If we fail to reject the null hypothesis, we have not proven it is true beyond all doubt. Only that we do not have enough evidence to reject it. ♦

5. H_0 : The defendant is innocent (everything is good-nothing is wrong)
    H_1 : The defendant is guilty ♦

b)   The jury finds a defendant innocent when there is not enough evidence to find him or her guilty. ♦

c)   When a defendant is found guilty it means that the evidence was strong enough to say that the probability of his or her innocence was very low. ♦

d)   The working hypothesis is always the null hypothesis. ♦

e)   In both cases the null hypothesis is assumed to be true. Then the evidence is looked at. The decision to fail to reject (find innocent) or to reject (find guilty) is made based on the probability of obtaining the specific evidence based on the assumption the null hypothesis is true. ♦

f)   In a good statistical test, human behavior or personality will not affect the decision. However in a court of law there are factors present such as the ability of the attorneys to convince the jury. ♦

9.   a) $H_0 : \mu = 8.7$. H_1, the alternate would be $\mu \neq 8.7$ ♦

b) $H_1 : \mu > 8.7$ H_0 would still be $\mu = 8.7$ ♦

c) $H_1 : \mu < 8.7$ H_0 would still be $\mu = 8.7$ ♦

d)   For part b, the critical region would be to the right of the mean. It is on this side that the alternate hypothesis would have a higher probability of being true. In part c the critical region would be on the eft side of the mean, since the alternate hypothesis would have a higher probability of being true. ♦

e)   We need a level o significance (the probability of rejecting the null hypothesis when it in fact, true. We also need to collect a test statistic and determine the sampling distribution to use. We would the have to compute the critical value(s) and finally determine whether out test statistic is in the critical region or not. If it is in a critical region, will reject H_0. Otherwise, we will fail to reject it. ♦

Answers to Thinking About Statistics

1.   <u>Test the claim that children who use Freshdent toothpaste have better yearly checkups.</u>
Better yearly checkups → fewer cavities.
Let μ represent the average number of cavities a child has per year.
One of the hypotheses is $\mu < .36$
The contradiction to this is $\mu = .36$.

Let $H_0 : \mu = .36$ (the claim with the = sign)
       $H_1 : \mu < .36$

2.   <u>Test the claim that after his new training program Sam quick is running faster than he did before.</u>

runs faster → runs in *less* time.

Let μ represent Sam Quick's average time to run a mile.

One of the hypotheses is μ < 4.3

The contradiction to this is μ = 4.3.

Let H_0 : μ = 4.3 (the claim with the = sign)
          H_1 : μ < 4.3

3.   <u>Assuming that the company does not underestimate, test the claim that the XJJ model gets 32 miles per gallon.</u>

Let μ represent the average miles per gallon for an XJJ model car.

One of the hypotheses is μ = 32.

Does not underestimate → manufacturer may overestimate. If someone overestimates, the belief is the mileage is less than claimed.

The other hypothesis is μ < 32.

Let H_0 : μ = 32 (the claim with the = sign)
          H_1 : μ < 32

4.   <u>Set up the hypotheses to test the claim that the diameter of the gears is different from 3".</u>

Different from → is not equal to.

Let μ represent the diameter of the gear.

One of the hypotheses is μ ≠ 3.

The other is μ = 3.

Let H_0 : μ =3
          H_1 : μ ≠3

Regardless of which hypothesis you are trying to prove (or to disprove), the null hypothesis always contains the = symbol.

Use the ≠ version for the alternative hypothesis when the phrasing of the problem does not indicate a direction. Look for key phrases like "different from", "change from" and "not equal to."

When using > or < in the alternate hypothesis look from comparative phrases or words such as greater than, more than, slower than, better than or does not overestimate. Be sure to translate them properly.

Section 9.2
Tests Involving the Mean μ

Review

In this section we will examine the structure of one particular type of hypothesis test, a large sample test of μ the population mean. Other tests, which will be discussed in later sections will involve very similar steps.

I.   When we are testing the value of a population mean, the null hypothesis will always be **H_0: μ = a given value**. It always contains the condition of equality.

   A.   Assuming H_0 is true we should get a sample mean close to the value in the null hypothesis.

   B.   In a test with α = .05, we take a 5% chance of rejecting H_0 when it is in fact true. 5% of the time we will make a type I error (but 95% of the time we will not).

   C.   The choice of alternate hypothesis determines the type of test.

      1. $H_1 : μ >$ some number produces a ***right tail test.***

         a.   Since our alternate hypothesis says μ > some number, we locate a region on the right tail of the curve which contains 5% of the area. In this region, the alternate hypothesis is more likely than the null.

         b.   We can reject H_0 and thus choose H_1 when our sample statistic falls in the right tail. This will be our critical region.

      2. $H_1 : μ <$ some number produces a ***left tail test.***

         a.   In this case the 5% of the time which we will be rejecting a true null hypothesis (a Type I error) will be to the far left of the curve. In this region this alternate hypothesis would be more probable than the null.

         b.   We can reject H_0 and thus choose H_1 when our sample statistic falls in the left tail.

      3. $H_1 : μ ≠$ some number produces a ***two tail test.***

         a.   We do not know which direction our alternate hypothesis is so we divide the 5% critical area into two parts.

         b.   We locate 2.5% in the left tail and 2.5% in the right tail. Our rejection areas fall into two separate regions-those furthest away from the assumed population mean μ.

II.   Steps for a hypothesis test of μ (large sample)

   A.   Formulate a pair of hypothesis about μ, the population mean.

      1. H_0 contains the statement of equality.

        2. H_1 contradicts the null hypothesis.

B.   Determine α the level of significance.

        1.   This is the probability that you will make a type I error (reject H_0 when it is actually true).

        2. α is usually set at .01 or .05.

C.   Gather your sample evidence

        1.   Determine n the sample size; this will tell you whether you can use a large sample test. To use a large sample technique n should be at least 30.

        2.   Determine $\bar{x}$ the sample mean; this will later be used as evidence on your sketch of the sampling distribution for sample means.

        3.   In a few cases the value of σ is known. If it is not, determine s. For a large sample, you can replace this for σ in the critical value formula.

D.   Assume H_0 is true. This means (from the Central Limit Theorem) the distribution of sample means of size n will be normal with a mean equal to the value given in the null hypothesis and a standard deviation equal to $\sigma_{\bar{x}} = \dfrac{\sigma}{\sqrt{n}}$

E.   Determine your critical z value(s) using:

	right tail test	left tail test	two tail test
$\alpha = .01$	z = 2.33	z = -2.33	z = 2.58 and z = -2.58
$\alpha = .05$	z = 1.645	z = -1.645	z = 1.96 and z = - 1.96

F.   Calculate the z test statistic using $z = \dfrac{\bar{x} - \mu_{H_0}}{\dfrac{\sigma}{\sqrt{n}}}$

G.   Make a normal distribution sketch representing the distribution of sample means.

        1.   The mean of this distribution is μ your hypothesized population mean. It corresponds to a value of z = 0.

        2.   Locate the critical z value(s) on your sketch.

        3.   Shade the critical tail region or regions.

        4.   Place your sample z statistic on the sketch.

H.   Make your decision.

        1.   If the z statistic is in the critical region, reject H_0.

        2.   If the z statistic is not in the critical region, fail to reject H_0.

Problem Solving Warm-Up

1. Over a period of time it has been found that the average number of cavities a child has per year is .36. Freshdent Company has developed a new toothpaste. A random sample of 40 children who used Freshdent for a year was taken. The mean number of cavities for the sample was .31 with a standard deviation of .15 cavities. Test the claim at the .05 level of significance that children who use Freshdent toothpaste have better yearly checkups.

A. Formulate the pair of hypotheses.
    H_0 : =_____
    H_1 : =_____

A. Results are from Section 9.1
    H_0 : μ = .36
    H_1 : μ < .36

B. Determine α (level of significance).

    _____

B. α = .05

C. The sample statistics are:
    n = _____
    $\bar{x}$ = _____
    s = _____

C.
    n = 40 (a large sample)
    $\bar{x}$ = .31
    s = .15 (let σ =s)

D. Assume H_0 is true.

D. Assume μ = .36

E. Determine the sampling distribution.

E. The sampling distribution of $\bar{x}$ with n = 40 is a normal distribution with μ = .36 and z = 0.

F. Determine the critical z value

    z = _____

F.   Since this is a left tail test with α=.05,

    z = - 1.645

G. Find the sample test statistic and convert it to a z value.
    = _____

The sample test statistic is $\bar{x}$ = .31. Its z equivalent is:
$$z = \frac{.31 - .36}{\frac{.15}{\sqrt{40}}} = -2.11$$

H. Make a sketch of the sampling distribution. Locate the critical region and place your sample statistic and its z equivalent on the sketch..

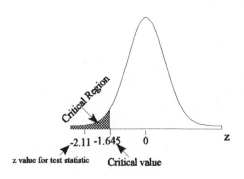

I. Make your decision.

_____

I.   The sample statistic z = - 2.11 falls in the critical region. Therefore we can reject H_0. The test indicates children do better using Freshdent toothpaste.

2.   Americom Corporation manufactures parts for satellites. A particular gear is designed to be 3" in diameter. The quality control officer obtains a random sample of gears and measures their diameters. She obtains a sample of 95 gears and finds that the mean diameter of the sample is 2.89 and the standard deviation is .76. Test the claim at the 1% level of significance that the diameter of the gears is different from 3".

A.   Formulate the pair of hypotheses.
        H_0 : =_____
        H_1 : =_____

A. Results are from Section 9.1
        H_0 : $\mu = 3"$
        H_1 : $\mu \neq 3"$

B.   Determine α (level of significance).

_____

B. $\alpha = .01$

C.   The sample statistics are:
        n = _____
        $\bar{x}$ = _____
        s = _____

C.
n = 95 (a large sample)
        $\bar{x} = 2.89$
        s = .76 (let σ =s)

D.   Assume H_0 is true.

D. Assume $\mu = 3"$

E.   Determine the sampling distribution

The distribution of $\bar{x}$ is normal. (n≥30).

243

F.   Determine the critical z value

z = _____

F.   Since this is a two test with $\alpha = .01$,

z = - 2.58 and z = 2.58

G.   Determine the sample test statistic and compute the z value for it.

= _____

The sample test statistic is = $\overline{x}$ = 2.89. Its z value is:

$$z = \frac{2.89 - 3}{\frac{.76}{\sqrt{95}}} = -1.41$$

H.   Make a sketch of the distribution of sample statistics. Locate the critical value(s), shade the critical region(s) and locate the sample test statistic.

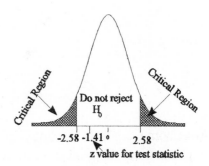

I.   Make your decision.

_____

I.   The sample statistic does not fall in the critical region. We fail to reject H_0. We do not have enough evidence to say the gears are significantly different from 3".

Thinking About Statistics

Suppose you were performing a hypothesis test on Freshdent toothpaste as described above in the Problem Solving Warm-Up section and your sample mean was .38. What differences would this make in your test?

Selected Solutions

1.   Given information is n = 36, $\overline{x}$ = 14.1, s = 3.2 and α = .01
     a) $H_0 : \mu$ = 16.4 feet

$H_1 : \mu < 16.4$ feet ("Does this information indicate the storm is retreating...")
Use a left tail test with $\alpha = .01$

b) The sampling distribution is the normal distribution. The critical z_0 value is -2.33.

d) $z = \dfrac{15.1 - 16.4}{\dfrac{3.2}{\sqrt{36}}} = -2.44$

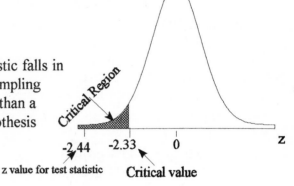

e) Since the z value for the test statistic falls in the critical region of the sampling distribution, reject H_0. There is less than a 1% chance of rejecting the null hypothesis when it is, in fact, true. We choose the hypothesis that the storm is retreating from its severe rating.

5. Given information is $n = 52$, $\overline{x} = \$5.25$, $s = \$1.15$ and $\alpha = .01$

a) $H_0 : \mu = 4.75$ (no problem-her claim is as she stated)
$H_1 : \mu > 4.75$ (average tip is more than \$4.75)
Use a right tail test with $\alpha = .01$

b) The sampling distribution is the normal distribution. The critical z_0 value is 2.33.

d) $z = \dfrac{5.25 - 4.75}{\dfrac{1.15}{\sqrt{52}}} = 3.14$

e) Since the z value for the test statistic falls in the critical region of the sampling distribution, reject H_0. There is less than a 1% chance of rejecting a true null hypothesis. We choose the hypothesis that Maureen's average tip was significantly more than \$4.75. ♦

9. The given information is : $n = 54$, $\overline{x} = \$6.78$, $s = \$1.77$ and $\alpha = .01$.

a) $H_0 : \quad \mu = 7.62$
$H_1 : \quad \mu < 7.62$ (Average daily ownership expenses are less than the national average.)
This is a left tail test at the .01 level of significance. Use a left tail test with $\alpha = .01$

b) The sampling distribution is the normal distribution. The critical z_0 value is -2.33.

d) $z = \dfrac{6.78 - 7.62}{\dfrac{1.77}{\sqrt{54}}} = -3.49$

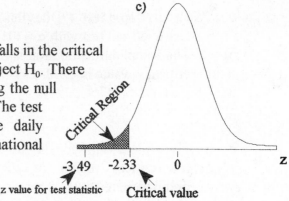

e) Since the z value for the test statistic falls in the critical region of the sampling distribution, reject H_0. There is less than a 1% chance of rejecting the null hypothesis when it is, in fact, true. The test indicates college students' average daily ownership expenses are less than the national average. ♦

13. The given information is n = 36, $\overline{x}$ = 1.51, s = .38 and α = .05.

    a) $H_0 : \mu = 1.43\%$ growth

        $H_1 : \mu \neq 1.43\%$ growth ("Does this indicate the population mean growth rate is different..." Use a two tail test with $\alpha = .05$

    b) The sampling distribution is the normal distribution. The critical z_0 values are -1.96 and 1.96.

    d) $z = \dfrac{1.51 - 1.43}{\frac{.38}{\sqrt{36}}} = 1.26$

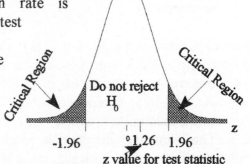

    e) Since the z value for the test statistic does not fall in the critical region of the sampling distribution, do not reject H_0. There is not enough evidence to indicate the population mean rate is different from 1.43%

17. The given information is : n = 45, $\overline{x}$ = \$18.2 thousand s = \$ 4.55thousand, assume α = .05.

    a) $H_0 : \quad \mu = 16.5$

        $H_1 : \quad \mu > 16.5$ Use a left tail test with $\alpha = .05$

    b) The sampling distribution is the normal distribution. The critical z_0 value is -1.645.

    d) $z = \dfrac{18.2 - 16.5}{\frac{4.55}{\sqrt{45}}} = 2.51$

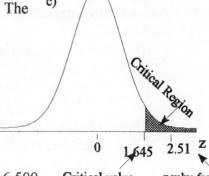

    e) Since the z value for the test statistic falls in the critical region of the sampling distribution, reject H_0. There is less than a 5% chance of rejecting the null hypothesis when it is, in fact, true. It is likely that the mean start up costs are higher than \$16,500.

rejecting the null hypothesis when it is, in fact, true.

Answer to Thinking About Statistics

Your pair of hypothesis would be the same.

$$H_0 : \mu = .36$$
$$H_1 : \mu < .36$$

The alternative hypothesis indicates a left tail test. Your sample statistic $\bar{x} = .38$ is to the *right of .36* and thus could *not* be in the critical region. Therefore you can fail to reject H_0 automatically.

Note that your hypotheses are ***not*** based on the sample mean. They are based on the claim being made. Do not look at the sample mean when formulating your hypothesis. Analyze the claims being made.

Section 9.3
The P Value in Hypothesis Testing

I.   Suppose we conduct a hypothesis test for the mean of a population and our hypotheses are:

$$H_0 : \mu = 54.3$$
$$H_1 : \mu > 54.3$$

II.   Furthermore, when we gather our sample statistics we get:
   - A. $n = 35$
   - B. $\bar{x} = 57.8$
   - C. $s = 9.8$

III.   Critical values
   - A.   If $\alpha = .01$ the critical z value is 2.33 At the .01 level, the critical region consists of all values to the right of $z = 2.33$.
   - B.   If $\alpha = .05$ the critical value is 1.645. At the .05 level, the critical region consists of all values to the right of 1.645.

IV.   Decision
   - A.   The sample test statistic corresponds to a z value of $z = \dfrac{57.8 - 54.3}{\frac{9.8}{\sqrt{35}}} = 2.11$.

B.   At the .01 level, the z value for the test statistic does not fall in the critical region, so we would fail to reject H_0 .

C.   At the .05 level, the z value for the test statistic falls in the critical region to the right we would reject H_0.

V.   Alternate method using a **P value.**

A.   The P value is the smallest level of significance for which the observed sample statistic tells us to reject H_0.

B.   To find the P value, we compute $P(z > 2.11) = .5 - .4826 = .0174$.

C.   We say the P value for this test is .0174.

1.   There is only .0174 of the curve to the right of our test statistic $\bar{x} = 57.85$

2.   There is a probability of .0174 that the null hypothesis is being rejected when it is in fact true. (A type I error)

VI.   Statistical software packages compute the P value when performing a hypothesis test on a computer.

A.   In a right tail test the P value is the area to the right of the test statistic.

B.   In a left tail test the P value is the area to the left of the test statistic.

C.   In a two tail test the P value is the sum of the areas in both. In symmetric distributions, such as the normal curve, the P value is twice the area in the tail bounded by the sample test statistic. Non symmetric distributions will be examined later.

D.   Making a hypothesis test decision using P values.

1.   Convert the test statistic to a standard score appropriate to the sampling distribution. (In this section we've used z scores, but we'll look at other distributions later.)

2.   Determine the P value from a table in the text (or from a calculator or computer program.)

3.   Compare the values of α and P.

a.   Reject H_0 the P value is less than α.

b.   Fail to reject H_0 the P value is greater than α.

Problem Solving Warm-Up

Make a conclusion to reject or fail to reject H_0 at a) the .01 level and at b) the .05 level, based on the given information.

1.   P value = .036   There is .036 area left in the tail beyond the statistic (for a one tail test) At the .01 level we

would fail to reject H_0 since .036>.01. We would reject H_0 at the .05 level.

2.   P value = .005

There is only .005 area beyond our statistic. This would fall in the critical region for both α = .01 and .05. Therefore at α = .01 we reject H_0 as well as for α = .05.

3.   P value = .063

There is .063 area beyond our statistic. For both .05 and .01 we would fail to reject H_0 .

4.   P value = .02

There is .02 area beyond our statistic. We would reject H_0 at the .05 level and fail to reject it at the .01 level.

2.   Over a period of time it has been found that the average number of cavities a child has per year is .36. Freshdent Company has developed a new toothpaste. A random sample of 40 children who used Freshdent for a year was taken. The mean number of cavities for the sample was .31 with a standard deviation of .15 cavities. Use the P value method to test the claim at the .05 level of significance that children who use Freshdent toothpaste have better yearly checkups.

A.   Formulate the pair of hypotheses.
       H_0 : =_____
       H_1 : =_____

A.

       H_0 : μ = .36
       H_1 : μ < .36

B.   Determine α (level of significance).

       _____

B. α = .05

C.   The sample statistics are:
       n = _____
       $\bar{x}$ = _____
       s = _____

C.

       n = 40 (a large sample)
       $\bar{x}$ = .31
       s = .15 (let σ =s)

D.   Assume H_0 is true.

D. Assume μ = .36

E.   Determine the sampling distribution.

E. The sampling distribution of $\bar{x}$ with n = 40 is a normal distribution with μ = .36 and z = 0.

F.   Find the sample test statistic and convert it to a z value.

=   _____

The sample test statistic is $\bar{x} = .31$. Its z equivalent is:

$$z = \frac{.31 - .36}{\frac{.15}{\sqrt{40}}} = -2.11$$

H.   Make a sketch of the sampling distribution. Locate the z value for the sample statistic and calculate the area that falls to the left of this z value.

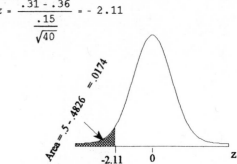

I. Make your decision.

_____

I.   The P value is the smallest level of significance for which we can reject the null hypothesis. This means we reject H_0 for all $\alpha > .0174$. At the .05 level, reject H_0. *(If α were .01 we would fail to reject H_0.)*

2.   Americom Corporation manufactures parts for satellites. A particular gear is designed to be 3" in diameter. The quality control officer obtains a random sample of gears and measures their diameters. She obtains a sample of 95 gears and finds that the mean diameter of the sample is 2.89 and the standard deviation is .76. Use the P value method to test the claim at the 1% level of significance that the diameter of the gears is different from 3".

A.   Formulate the pair of hypotheses.
H_0 : = _____
H_1 : = _____

A.
H_0 : $\mu = 3"$
H_1 : $\mu \neq 3"$

B.   Determine α (level of significance).

_____

B. $\alpha = .01$

C.   The sample statistics are:
n = _____
$\bar{x}$ = _____
s = _____

C.
n = 95 (a large sample)
$\bar{x}$ = 2.89
s = .76 (let σ =s)

D.   Assume H_0 is true.

D. Assume $\mu = 3''$

E.   Determine the sampling distribution

The distribution of $\overline{x}$ is normal. ($n \geq 30$).

F.   Determine the sample test statistic and compute the z value for it.

    = _____

The sample test statistic is = $\overline{x}$ = 2.89. Its z value is:

$$z = \frac{2.89 - 3}{\frac{.76}{\sqrt{95}}} = -1.41$$

H.   Make a sketch of the distribution of sample statistics. Locate the z value for the sample statistic.

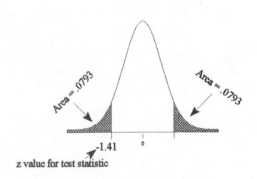

z value for test statistic

I.   Make your decision.

    _____

I.   The area to the left of z = -1.41 = .5 - .4207 = .0793. Since this is a two tail test, the P value is .0793 + .0793 = .1586. The P value is greater than the level of significance, so we fail to reject H_0. We do not have enough evidence to say the gears are significantly different from 3".

Thinking About Statistics

1. Fill in the chart below with the decision to either reject H_0 or fail to reject H_0.

P value	Decision at .01 level	Decision at .05
Greater than .05		
Between .01 and .05		
Less than .01		

2. As the value of z gets further away from 0, what happens to the corresponding P value?

Selected Solutions

1. a)   P = .0312 α = .01. Since P > α, fail to reject H_0. Recall that P is the <u>smallest</u> level of significance for which we can reject H_0. At the .01 level, we would reject H_0 for P values less than or equal to .01.

    b)   P = .0312 α = .05. Since P < α, reject H_0. Now the value of P is less than the level of significance.

5. a)   P = .0262 α = .01. Since P > α, fail to reject H_0.
    b)   P = .0262 α = .05. Since P < α, reject H_0.

9. a) $z = \dfrac{16.8 - 18}{\frac{3.2}{\sqrt{38}}} = -2.31$

    c) Since this is a left tail test (from H_1: μ < 18), the P value is equal to the area to the left of the z value of -2.31. This is .5 - .4896 = .0104.
    d) At α = .05, reject H_0. (Since .0104 < .05)
       At α = .01, fail to reject H_0. (Since .0104 > .01)

13. a) $z = \dfrac{121 - 115}{\frac{19}{\sqrt{50}}} = 2.23$ ◆

    c) Since this is a two tail test (H_1: $\mu \ne$ 115), the P value is the sum of the areas in the two tails for z = 2.23 and z = -2.23. The area in the right tail is .5 - .4901 = .0099. The area in the left tail is also .0099. Adding the two areas together we get .0198. ◆

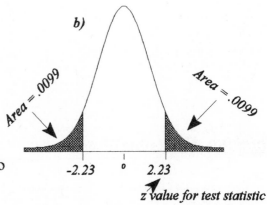

b)

Area = .0099   *Area = .0099*

-2.23   0   2.23

z value for test statistic

d) At the .05 level, reject the null hypothesis since the P value would be less than α. However, at the .01 level, fail to reject the null hypothesis. The lowest level at which the null hypothesis would be rejected in .0198. ♦

Answers to Thinking About Statistics

P value	Decision at .01 level	Decision at .05
Greater than .05	fail to reject H_0	fail to reject H_0
Between .01 and .05	fail to reject H_0	reject H_0
Less than .01	reject H_0	reject H_0

2. As the value of z moves away from 0 (to the right on the positive side and to the left on the negative), there is less area remaining in the corresponding tail. Therefore, the value of P will decrease.
THE CLOSER THE P VALUE IS TO ZERO, THE STRONGER IS THE EVIDENCE TO REJECT H_0. Conversely, when the value of z is close to 0, the P value will be large (closer to 1) and so there will not be enough evidence to reject H_0.

Section 9.4
Tests Involving the mean μ (Small Samples)

Review

When large samples are unavailable, it may be possible to test hypotheses with small samples provided that the populations we are testing are nearly normally distributed. (They have a mound shaped and symmetric distribution.) The techniques discussed in this section should be used when the sample size is less than 30 and the population standard deviation is not known.

I.   Tests of the population mean using a *small sample* are similar to those with a large sample with the following exceptions:
A.   The sampling distribution of $\overline{x}$ is a t-distribution with n-1 degrees of freedom.

B.   The sample test statistic $\overline{x}$ is converted to a t value using $\quad t = \dfrac{\overline{x} - \mu}{\dfrac{s}{\sqrt{n}}}$

C.   In small sample tests, the value of σ is unknown and can *not* be estimated by s. Therefore we use s in the formula.

II.   Steps in performing a t test for the value of a population mean.

A.   Formulate the null and the alternate hypotheses in the same way you would using large sample.

B.   Determine the level of significance, α for the test. Again, this is the probability of rejecting the null hypothesis when it is actually true. (Type I error)

C.   Determine the sampling distribution. This time the sampling distribution of $\overline{x}$ will be a t distribution with n-1 degrees of freedom.

D.   Using the t distribution table to find the critical value(s) t_0.

1.   For a right tail test, read across the row marked α' and under the appropriate level of significance. read the t value on the line corresponding to n-1 d.f.

2.   For a left tail test, read across the row marked α' under the appropriate level of significance. read across the row marked e corresponding to n-1 d.f. Use -t for the critical value.

3.   For a two tail test read across the row marked α'' and under the appropriate level of significance. The critical values will be t and -t.

E.   Determine the sample test statistic $\overline{x}$ and convert it to a t value using $\quad t = \dfrac{\overline{x} - \mu}{\dfrac{s}{\sqrt{n}}}$

F.   Sketch the sampling distribution, place the critical value on it and shade the critical region. Locate the t value equivalent to the test statistic on the sketch.

G.   Make your decision

1.   If the t test statistic is in the critical region, reject H_0.

2.   Otherwise, fail to reject it.

III.   Using the P value technique for a t test

A.   Formulate your null and alternate hypotheses, determine the level of significance and compute the t value for your $\overline{x}$ test statistic.

B.   The t value you compute will usually be located between two given t values on the appropriate d.f. line.

C.   Since t values listed in table 7 are limited, so we will only be able to approximate a P value within an interval of values.

1.   For a one tail test, use P values found in the α' line for the distribution with n-1 d.f..

2.   For two tail tests use P values found in the α'' line for the distribution with n-1 d.f.

D.   Reject H_0 if the P value is less than the level of significance. Otherwise fail to reject the null hypothesis.

E.   Remember t values closer to 0, will have higher P values and t values further from 0 will have lower P values.

Problem Solving Warm Up

The problems for this section are similar to those presented in the Problem Solving Warm Up for tests of the population mean using large samples. Find the similarities and the differences as you answer the following questions.

1.   Over a period of time it has been found that the average number of cavities a child has per year is .36. Sparkledent Company has developed a new toothpaste. A random sample of 12 children who used Sparkledent for a year was taken. The mean number of cavities for the sample was .33 with a standard deviation of .11 cavities. Test the claim at the .05 level of significance that children who use Sparkledent toothpaste have better yearly checkups.
        a) Use the critical value method
        b) Use the P value method

a) The critical value method

A.   Formulate the pair of hypotheses.   A.
        $H_0 : =$ _____ $H_0 : \mu = .36$
        $H_1 : =$ _____ $H_1 : \mu < .36$

B.   Determine α (level of significance).   B. $\alpha = .05$
        _____

C.   The sample statistics are: C.
        $n =$ _____ $n = 12$ (a small sample)
        $\bar{x} =$ _____ $\bar{x} = .33$
        $s =$ _____ $s = .11$

D.   Assume H_0 is true.   D. Assume $\mu = .36$

E.   Determine the sampling distribution.   E. The sampling distribution of $\bar{x}$ with $n = 12$ is a t distribution with 11 degrees of freedom.

F.   Determine the critical t value   F.   Since this is a left tail test with $\alpha' = .05$, t = _____   t = - 1.796

G.   Find the sample test statistic and convert it to a t value.

      = _____

The sample test statistic is $\overline{x}$ = .33. Its t equivalent is:

$$t = \frac{.33 - .36}{\frac{.11}{\sqrt{12}}} = -.94$$

H.   Make a sketch of the sampling distribution. Locate the critical region and place your sample statistic and its t equivalent on the sketch..

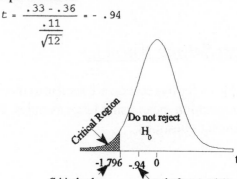

I. Make your decision.

_____

I.   The sample statistic t = - .94 does not fall in the critical region. Therefore we do not reject H_0. There is not enough evidence to claim that children do better using Sparkledent toothpaste.

b) Using the P value technique. Use parts A to E from the critical value method.

Determine the P value for the t statistic.

_____

On the line corresponding to 11 d.f. the value of t = .94 is less than the lowest given t value of 1.214. When t = 1.214, the (one tail) P value is .125. This means a t value of .94 is closer to 0 than the t value of 1.214 and has a higher P value.

The P value for the test statistic is higher than .125. This means P > .125 > .05, and since P > α, fail to reject H_0.

Make your decision

_____

2.   U.S. Parts Corporation manufactures parts for satellites. A particular gear is designed to be 3" in diameter. The quality control officer obtains a random sample of gears and measures their diameters. He obtains a sample of 15 gears and finds that the mean diameter of the

sample is 3.45 and the standard deviation is .61. Test the claim at the 1% level of significance that the diameter of the gears is different from 3".

        a) Use the critical value method
        b) Use the P value method

A.   Formulate the pair of hypotheses.

$H_0 :=$ _____
$H_1 :=$ _____

A.

$H_0 : \mu = 3"$
$H_1 : \mu \neq 3"$

B.   Determine α (level of significance).

_____

B. $\alpha = .01$

C.   The sample statistics are:

$n =$ _____
$\bar{x} =$ _____
$s =$ _____

C.

$n = 15$ (a small sample)
$\bar{x} = 3.51$
$s = .61$

D.   Assume H_0 is true.

D. Assume $\mu = 3"$

E.   Determine the sampling distribution

The sampling distribution of $\bar{x}$ is a t distribution with 14 d.f.

F.   Determine the critical t value

t = _____

F.   Since this is a two test with $\alpha=.01$,

$t = -2.977$ and $z = 2.977$

G.   Determine the sample test statistic and compute the t value for it.

= _____

The sample test statistic is $= \bar{x} = 3.51$. Its t value is:

$$t = \frac{3.51 - 3}{\frac{.61}{\sqrt{15}}} = 3.238$$

H.   Make a sketch of the distribution of sample statistics. Locate the critical value(s), shade the critical region(s) and locate the sample test statistic.

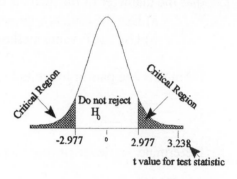

t value for test statistic

I.   Make your decision.

_____

b) Use the P value technique
Parts A to E are the same as in a.

Determine the P value for the t statistic

_____

Make your decision

_____

I.   The sample statistic falls in a critical region. Reject H_0. We choose the hypothesis that the gears are significantly different from 3".

On the 14 d.f. row, the t value of 3.238 is greater than 2.977. Reading up to the α'' line, we can then see that the P value is less than .01.

Reject H_0 at the .01 level.

Thinking About Statistics

1.   In the chapter 7 we worked with the t-distributions for confidence intervals when we could only obtain small samples and did not know σ. We used the entries in the table corresponding to the row headed by c at the top. In hypothesis testing of small samples we also use the t distributions, but this time use the designations of α' and α''.
   a)   Explain why for the same number of degrees of freedom, the entry under c = .90 is the same as that of $\alpha' = .05$.

b)   Explain why the entry under c = .99 is the same as the entry under $\alpha'' = .01$.

Selected Solutions

1.   Answer appears under α' row .05 on the 8 d.f. row t= - 1.860 ♦ (negative t on the left side)

5.   Answer appears under α'' row .05 on the 11 d.f. row. t =± 2.201 ♦

9.   Given information: n = 10, $\overline{x}$ = 90.90, s = 14.18 α = .01
        a) $H_0 : \mu = 85$ $H_1 : \mu \neq 85$
        Use a two tail test with α = .01 ♦
        b)   The sampling distribution is a t distribution with
                10 - 1 =9 d.f. The critical t_0 values are + 3.250
                and -3.250.

d) The test statistic is $\overline{x}$ = 90.90 and the corresponding t value
is $t = \dfrac{90.90 - 85}{\dfrac{14.18}{\sqrt{10}}} = 1.316$

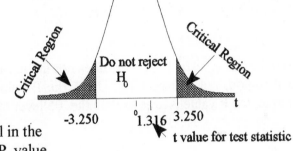

e) On the 9 d.f. row, the t value of 1.316 falls
between t = 1.230 and 1.383. Reading on the
α'' line, this means the P value is between .250
and .200.

f) Since the test statistic t = 1.316 does not fall in the
critical region, fail to reject H_0. Using the P value
technique we see that the P value is not less than the .01 level of
significance, so fail to reject H_0.

13.   Given information: n = 9, $\overline{x}$ = \$133.79 thousand , s =
        \$23.38thousand α = .01
        a) $H_0 : \mu = 155.8$ $H_1 : \mu \neq 155.8$
        Use a two tail test with α = .01 ♦
        b)   The sampling distribution is a t distribution
                with 9 - 1 =8 d.f. The critical t_0 values are +
                3.355 and -3.355.

d) The test statistic is $\overline{x}$ =133.79 and the corresponding t
value is $t = \dfrac{133.79 - 155.8}{\dfrac{23.38}{\sqrt{9}}} = -2.82$

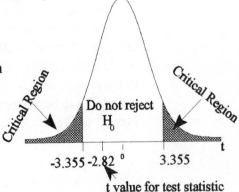

e) For 8 d.f., the t value of -2.82 falls between-2.306 and -2.896 This means the P value is between the corresponding P values found in the α "row. So the P value is less than .05 and greater than.02.

f) Since the test statistic t = 1.316 does not fall in the critical region, fail to reject H_0. Using the P value technique, the P value is greater than the .01 level of significance, so fail to reject H_0.

17. Given information: n = 20, $\overline{x}$ = 74.45, s = 18.09 α = .05

   a) $H_0 : \mu = 77$ $H_1 : \mu < 77$
   Use a left tail test with α = .05 ♦
   b)   The sampling distribution is a t distribution with 20 - 1 =19 d.f. The critical t_0 value is -1.729.

d) The test statistic is $\overline{x}$ = 74.45and the corresponding t value is

$$t = \frac{74.45 - 77}{\frac{18.09}{\sqrt{20}}} = -.6304$$

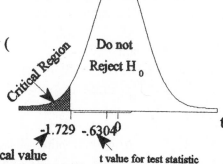

e) For 19 d.f., the t value of -.6304 falls closer to the center (t=0) than the lowest given t value of 1.187. This means t = -.6304 has a *higher* P value than t = 1.187. The P value on the α' row for t = 1.187 is .125. so P > .125 >.05 = α.

f) Since the test statistic t = -.6340 does not fall in the critical region, fail to reject H_0. Using the P value technique, the P value is greater than the .05 level of significance, so fail to reject H_0.

Answers to Thinking About Statistics

1.   a)   In a particular t curve, say with 20 d.f., the value of t for c = .90 is 1.725. This means 90% of the area under the curve falls between t = -1.725 and t= 1.725. Of the 10% of the area remaining, 5% lies in the left tail and 5% in the right. Therefore in a one tail test where α' = .05, 5% of the area under the curve will fall to the right of t =1.725, the same t value as for c = .90.

      b)   In the t curve with 20 d.f. 99% of the curve lies between t = ±2.845. This leaves 1% of the area to be located in both the tails, or .005 in the right tail and .005 in the left. For a 2 tail test with α'' = .01 this is exactly the same area we are locating.

Section 9.5

Tests Involving a Proportion

Review

In the previous sections of this chapter the focus was on conducting hypothesis tests for the value of a population mean. Hypothesis tests can also be conducted for other parameters such as the value of a population proportion for a binomial experiment The general methods for conducting them are similar to the tests conducted for the value of the population mean. The differences will be outlined below.

I.   Test for the value of p, the proportion of successes in the population.
    A.   Formulate your hypotheses
        1. H_0 : p = a value (always between 0 and 1)
        2. H_1 : p < a value OR p> a value OR p ≠ a value depending on the claim
            that contradicts H_0 .
    B.   Determine α the level of significance.
    C.   Determine the sampling distribution for the difference of sample means (independent
        samples.
        1.   The sample statistic is $\hat{p} = \dfrac{r}{n}$ where r =the number of successes in the sample
            n =the number of trials.
        2.   The sampling distribution of $\hat{p}$ is normal, provided np > 5 and nq > 5.
        3.   The mean of the sampling distribution is $\mu = p$ (the hypothesized value for the
            population proportion).
        4.   The standard deviation is of the sampling distribution is $\sigma = \sqrt{\dfrac{pq}{n}}$
            where q = 1-p.
    D.   The critical z_0 values are as follows:

	right tail test	left tail test	two tail test
$\alpha = .01$	z = 2.33	z = -2.33	z = 2.58 and z = -2.58
$\alpha = .05$	z = 1.645	z = -1.645	z = 1.96 and z = - 1.96

E. Convert the sample test statistic to a z value using

$$z = \frac{\hat{p} - p}{\sqrt{\dfrac{pq}{n}}}$$

F. Make a sketch of the sampling distribution placing the critical z value(s) on the sketch. Shade the critical region(s).
G. Place the test statistic z value on the sketch.
H. Make your decision.
   1. Reject H_0 if the test statistic falls in the critical region.
   2. Otherwise fail to reject H_0.

II. The P value method of testing the value of p.
   A. Formulate the hypotheses, determine the level of significance, compute the z value for the test statistic $\hat{p}$.
   B. For a one tail test, use the normal distribution table in your text. Locate the z value and calculate the area falling in the tail beyond it (To do so subtract the table value from .5)
   C. For a two tail test, calculate the area in the tail beyond the test statistic. Since the normal distribution is symmetric, double the area to find the P value.
   D. Make your decision:
      1. Reject the null hypothesis if the P value is less than α.
      2. Fail to reject the null hypothesis if the P value is greater than or equal to α.
      3.

Problem Solving Warm-Up

1. The San Francisco Chronicle reported that of all students who graduated from the eight campuses of the University of California 30% finished their degree requirement within four years. (The remaining 70% took longer than four years to graduate.) Suppose a study was made of a random sample of graduates from Berkeley (part of the U. C. system) where it was found of the 385 graduates questioned that 124 had graduated within four years. Test the claim at the .05 level of significance that 30% of the graduates do so within four years.

   a) Use the critical region technique
   b) Use the P value technique

a) for the critical region technique:

A.   Determine your hypotheses

H_0 :_____

H_1 :_____

A.

$H_0 : p = .30$

$H_1 : p \neq .30$ (two tail test)

B.   Determine α _____

B. $\alpha = .05$

C.   List the given values and calculate the test statistic

r=_____

n=_____

$\hat{p}$=_____

C.

r = 124

n = 385

$\hat{p}$ = 124/385 = .32

D.   What is the sampling distribution?

_____

D.   The sampling distribution is normal with a mean = .30.

E.   Determine the z_0 critical value(s) z_0.

_____

E.

$z_0 = 1.96$ and -1.96

F.   Convert the sample test statistic to z value.

_____

F. $z = \dfrac{.32 - .30}{\sqrt{\dfrac{(.30)(.70)}{385}}} = .86$

G.   Sketch the distribution (normal) and locate the critical values and your z test statistic.

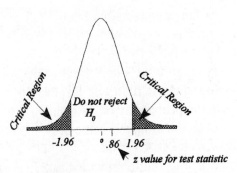

H.   Make your decision

_____

H.   Fail to reject H_0. z = .86 does not fall in the critical region. There is not sufficient evidence to reject the null hypothesis that 30% of the students at U.C. graduate in 4 years.

b)   For the P value technique: Follow the steps A to E from a and form the hypothesis, determine the level of significance and calculate the z value equivalent to the test statistic.

A.   Find the P value

_____

B. The area in the curve that lies to the right of $z = .86$ is $.5 - .3051 = .1949$. Since this is a two tail test, the area for both tails is $.1949 + .1949 = .3898$.

B.   Make the decision.

_____

B. Since $P > \alpha$ fail to reject the null hypothesis.

Selected Solutions Section 9.5

1.   We are given $r = 27$ $n = 39$ so the sample test statistic $\hat{p} = r/n = 31/39 = .795$

a) $H_0 : p = .63,$ $H_1 : p \neq .63$,   Use a two tail test $\alpha = .05$

b) The sampling distribution for $\hat{p}$ is normal since $39(.63)$ and $39(.37)$ are both greater than 5. The critical z_0 values are $+1.96$ and -1.96.

d) $z = \dfrac{.795 - .63}{\sqrt{\dfrac{(.63)(.37)}{39}}} = 2.13$

e) The area remaining in the tail to the right of $z = .78$ is $.5 - .4834 = .0166..$ Since this is a two tail test and the sampling distribution is symmetric we'll find the P value by doubling the area found in the right tail. $P = 2(.0166) = .0332$. For this test, the P value is the probability of obtaining a sample value of $\hat{p}$ that is further away from the assumed value of $p = .63$ than the sample value of $.795$.

f) $P > \alpha$, fail to reject the null hypothesis. The test does not indicate that the population proportion of homeless people in Denver who differ with the statement is significantly different from 63%.

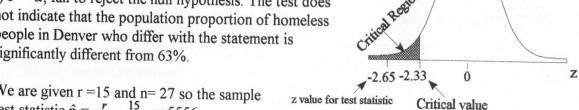

5.   We are given $r = 15$ and $n = 27$ so the sample test statistic $\hat{p} = \dfrac{r}{n} = \dfrac{15}{27} = .5556$

a) $H_0 : p = .77$ and $H_1 : p < .77$, Use a left tail test $\alpha = .01$

b)The sampling distribution for sample proportions $r/n = \hat{p}$ is approximately normal since 27(.77) and 27(.23) are both greater than 5. The critical z_0 value is -2.33

d) $z = \dfrac{.5556 - .77}{\sqrt{\dfrac{(.77)(.23)}{27}}} = -2.65$

e) The area remaining in the tail to the left of z = -2.65 is .5 - 4960= .0040. For this test, we assume that the population proportion is .77. The P value of .0040 is the probability of obtaining a sample value of $\hat{p}$ that is further away from the assumed value of p = .77 than the given sample value of .56.

f) P < α, so reject the null hypothesis. We'll choose the hypothesis that the population proportion is less than .77.

9.   We are given r = 10 and n= 34 so the sample test statistic $\hat{p} = r/n = 10/34 = .2941$

a) H_0 :p = .50, H_1 :p <.50 , Use a left tail test $\alpha = .05$

b) The sampling distribution for $\hat{p}$ is normal since 34(.50) and 34(.50) are both greater than 5. The critical z_0 value is -1.645.

d) $z = \dfrac{.2941 - .53}{\sqrt{\dfrac{(.50)(.50)}{34}}} = -2.40$

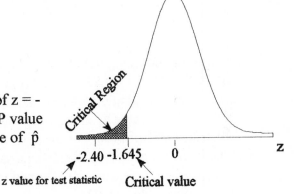

e) The area remaining in the tail to the left of z = -2.40 is .5 - .4918= .0082. For this test, the P value is the probability of obtaining a sample value of $\hat{p}$ that is further away from the assumed value of p = .50 than the given sample value of .29.

f) P <α, so reject the null hypothesis. Choose the hypothesis that says the proportion of female wolves is less than 50%.

13.   We are given r = 490 and n= 1006 so the sample test statistic $\hat{p} = r/n = 490/1006 = .487$

a) H_0 :p = .47, H_1 :p >.47 ,
       Use a right tail test $\alpha = .01$

b) The sampling distribution for $\hat{p}$ is normal since

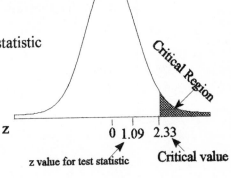

1006(.47) and 1006(.53) are both greater than 5. The critical z_0 value is 2.33

d) $z = \dfrac{.487 - .47}{\sqrt{\dfrac{(.47)(.53)}{1006}}} = 1.09$

e) The area remaining in the tail to the right of $z = 1.09$ is $.5 - .3621 = .1379$. If we assume $p = .47$ then the P value is the probability of obtaining a sample value of $\hat{p}$ that is further away from the assumed value of $p = .47$ than the sample value of .487.

f) $P < \alpha$, so reject the null hypothesis. Choose the hypothesis that the proportion is greater than .47.

17. We are given $r = 323$ and $n = 350$ so the sample test statistic $\hat{p} = r/n = 323/350 = .9229$.

a) $H_0 : p = .94$, $H_1 : p \neq .94$, Use a two tail test $\alpha = .01$

b) The sampling distribution for $\hat{p}$ is normal since 350(.94) and 350(.06) are both greater than 5. The critical z_0 values are +2.58 and -2.58

d) $z = \dfrac{.9229 - .94}{\sqrt{\dfrac{(.94)(.06)}{350}}} = -1.35$

e) The area remaining in the tail to the right of $z = 1.35$ is $.5 - .4115 = .0885$. Since this is a two tail test and the sampling distribution is symmetric we'll find the P value by multiplying this area by 2. $P = 2(.0885) = .1770$. For this test, the P value is the probability of obtaining a sample value of $\hat{p}$ that is further away from the assumed value of $p = .94$ than the given sample value of .92.

Critical Region   Do not reject H_0 Critical Region

-2.58 -1.35   0   2.58

z value for test statistic

f) $P > \alpha$, fail to reject the null hypothesis. There is not enough evidence to reject the null hypothesis that the population proportion is not equal to .94.

Answers to Thinking About Statistics

1.   Each hypothesis test had the following steps in common:

   a.   Formulate a pair of hypotheses -a null and an alternate.
   b.   Decide on a level of significance.
   c.   List and examine your sample statistics. This will often determine the type of test you are performing. Determine your test statistic. (The size of the sample, is σ known are factors for example in choosing a test.)
   d.   Assume the null hypothesis is true, determine the sampling distribution and make a sketch.
   e.   Compute the critical z or t value(s). (In later chapters we'll have others.) Locate the critical region(s) on your sampling distribution graph and shade them.
   f.   Place your sample statistic in appropriate numerical order on your graph.
   g.   If your sample statistic is in the critical region, you will reject H_0 Otherwise, fail to reject H_0.

Section 9.6
Tests Involving Paired Differences (Dependent Samples)

Review

The concepts of dependent and independent samples were discussed in the last chapter while discussing how to estimate the difference between the means of two populations.. In this section we see how to conduct a hypothesis test about the *difference* of two population means when the sampling is done with dependent samples. When testing the difference between two population means, often we can design our study so that we can match or pair each member in the first population to one in the second. This can occur in before/after situations, identical twin studies or any time we can create a one-to-one matching. The advantage in doing this type of test is that we eliminate extraneous or uncontrollable factors in the sample measures and we can concentrate on the differences of the variable being measured.

I.   With dependent samples we use paired difference tests of population means and we test the mean of the population of differences, denoted μ_d.

A. There is a natural pairing between the members of the sample from the first population and those in the second.

B. Obtain a measure of the variable for each member in each of the two samples. Put the measures for the first sample in column I and those for the second in column II.

C. Compute the difference in measures for each pair of values found in columns I and II and put these in column III.

D. Compute the mean of these differences and denote it $\bar{d}$.
    1. Algebraically add the differences.
    2. Divide by the number of pairs.

E. Compute the standard deviation of differences

$$s_d = \sqrt{\frac{\Sigma(d-\bar{d})^2}{n-1}}$$

    1. In column IV compute $d - \bar{d}$ for each row.
    2. In column V square the value from column IV to obtain $(d - \bar{d})^2$.
    3. Add the entries from column V.
    4. Divide this sum by n-1.
    5. Take the square root of the quotient.

II. Steps to perform hypothesis test for the difference of means of two dependent populations.

A. Formulate your hypotheses
    1. $H_0 : \mu_d = 0$
    2. $H_1 : \mu_d < 0$ OR $\mu_d > 0$ OR $\mu_d \neq 0$ depending on whether your claim indicates a left tail, right tail or two tail test.

B. Determine α.

C. Determine the sampling distribution of differences. For dependent samples the sampling distribution is a Student t distribution with n-1 degrees of freedom. (n = the number of pairs.)

D. Determine the critical t value from the table in Appendix II.

E. Sketch the distribution and shade the critical region.

F. Compute the test statistic $\bar{d}$ and s_d.

G. Convert the test statistic to a t value using $\quad t = \dfrac{\bar{d} - \mu_d}{\dfrac{s_d}{\sqrt{n}}}$

    (μ_d is the hypothesized difference which is usually 0)

H. Place the t value of the test statistic on the sampling distribution sketch.

I. Make your decision.
    1. If your test statistic is in the critical region, reject the null hypothesis.
    2. If your test statistic is not in the critical region, fail to reject the null hypothesis.

III. Using P values for Tests of Paired differences

A.   Use the Student t distribution table in Appendix II.
B.   Since areas given in the table are limited, we can only find an interval containing the P value rather than a single number.
C.   For one tailed tests use the values in the row headed by α'. For two tailed tests use those in the α'' row. *(Note that in the t table, the areas have already been doubled for the α'' row values.)*
D.   Reject the null hypothesis if the P value is less than the level of significance. Fail to reject the null hypothesis if the P value is greater than the level of significance.

Problem Solving Warm Up

A course is offered to help prepare for the Scholastic Aptitude Test (SAT). A group of 10 randomly selected students take the SAT before the course. They then take the preparation course and retake the SAT after the course. Test the claim at the .01 level that the preparation course increases your score. Results of the study are given below:

a) Use the critical region technique.   b) Use the P value technique

student	1	2	3	4	5	6	7	8	9	10
before	980	940	1110	1020	1080	1050	920	880	1000	990
after	1050	1030	1130	980	1120	1090	970	950	1070	1030

For the critical value technique:

A.   Formulate the hypotheses
         H_0 :_____
         H_1 :_____

B. $\alpha = $ _____

C.   Determine the sampling distribution
         _____

D.   Find the critical t value(s)

_____

Solution

A. $H_0 : \mu_d = 0$
         $H_1 : \mu_d < 0$

B. $\alpha = .01$

C.   For paired samples, use a t distribution with $10 - 1 = 9$ degrees of freedom.

D.   Look across the α' row and down the .01 column to the line for 9 d.f.. The critical t value is -2.821. (left tail)

E.   Fill in the missing cells to compute $\overline{d}$ and s_d.

I	II	III	IV	V
Before	After	d = B - A	d-$\overline{d}$	(d-$\overline{d}$)²
980	1050			
940	1030			
1110	1130			
1020	980			
1080	1120			
1050	1090			
920	970			
880	950			
1000	1070			
990	1030			

I	II	III	IV	V
Before	After	d = B - A	d-$\bar{d}$	(d-$\bar{d}$)^2
980	1050	-70.00	-25.00	625.00
940	1030	-90.00	-45.00	2,025.00
1110	1130	-20.00	25.00	625.00
1020	980	40.00	85.00	7,225.00
1080	1120	-40.00	5.00	25.00
1050	1090	-40.00	5.00	25.00
920	970	-50.00	-5.00	25.00
880	950	-70.00	-25.00	625.00
1000	1070	-70.00	-25.00	625.00
990	1030	-40.00	5.00	25.00
		-450.00		11,850.00

μ_d = _____

s_d = _____

t = _____

F. Make a sketch of the distribution of differences. Place the assumed mean difference of 0 at the center and locate your critical t value. Shade the critical region. Then locate the t value for the test statistic $\bar{d}$.

The statistics for the sample are: $\bar{d}$ = -450/10 = -45 and

$$s_d = \sqrt{\frac{11850}{9}} = \sqrt{1316}.67 = 36.28$$

The t value is $\dfrac{-45 - 0}{\dfrac{36.28}{\sqrt{10}}}$ = -3.922

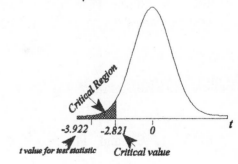

-3.922   -2.821   0

t value for test statistic   Critical value

271

G.   Make your decision about H_0.

G.   The t value for the test statistic -3.922 is in the critical region. We reject H_0. The test scores after the prep course are higher.

b) Using the P value technique

Follow parts A to from the critical region technique.

A.   Find an interval for the P value of the test statistic.

_____

A.   The test statistic t value of -3.922 has a lower P value than -3.250 which is listed in the t table for 9 d.f. The P value for t = -3.250 for a one tail test is .005. This means the P value for t = -3.922 is less than .005.

B.   Make your decision.

_____

B.   Since the P value is less than the level of significance of .01, so reject the null hypothesis.

Thinking About Statistics

1.   In the problem solving warm-up the result of the hypothesis test was that the test scores after the prep course were higher than those before. Does this necessarily mean that the prep course *caused* the scores to be higher?

Selected Solutions Section 9.6

1.   a) $H_0 : \mu_d = 0$ and $H_1 : \mu_d \neq 0$. We'll use a two-tail test at the .01 level of significance.

b) The sampling distribution of differences is a t distribution with 5 - 1 = 4 d.f. The critical t_0 values are ± 4.604.

d) t = $\dfrac{.44-0}{\dfrac{7.2127}{\sqrt{5}}}$ = .137

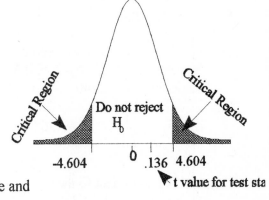

e) The t equivalent to the test statistic t =.137 has a higher P value than the P value for t = 1.344 that is listed in the table. The P value for t = 1.344 is .25. This means the test statistic has a higher P value than .25. There is more than a 25% chance that the null hypothesis would be true and the test statistic would be the one we obtained.

f) Since .25 is higher than the level of significance of .01 we would fail to reject the null hypothesis. Using the critical region technique, we find that the test statistic does not fall in the critical region, so we would fail to reject H₀. At the .01 level there is no significant difference in the number of viewers of CBS and NBC for the days Monday-Friday.

5.   a) $H_0 : \mu_d = 0$ and $H_1 : \mu_d \neq 0$. We'll use a two-tail test at the .05 level of significance.

b) The sampling distribution of differences is a t distribution with 12 - 1 = 11 d.f. The critical t_0 values under $\alpha'' = .05$ are ± 2.201.

d) The differences between corresponding values for Buffalo and Grand Rapids are .7, .1, -1.6, -3.2, -3.3, -3.3, -2.3, -1.7, -.6, -.3, .7 and 1. The value for $\overline{d}$ = -1.15 and the value for s_d = 1.6329.

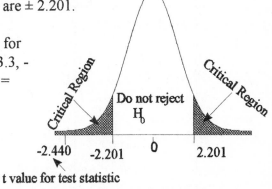

d) t = $\dfrac{-1.15-0}{\dfrac{1.6329}{\sqrt{12}}}$ = -2.440

e) The t equivalent to the test statistic t =-2.440 is between the t values of 2.201 and 2.718 that are listed in the t table for 11 d.f. This means the test statistic has a P value between .02 and .05.

f) Since the P value is less than the .05 level of significance, reject the null hypothesis. There is sufficient evidence to conclude that there is a significant difference in the average temperatures of the two cities. Using the critical region technique, we find that the test statistic falls in the critical region, so we would reject H₀.

9.   a) $H_0 : \mu_d = 0$ and $H_1 : \mu_d \neq 0$. We'll use a two-tail test at the .05 level of significance.

b) The sampling distribution of differences is a t distribution with 5 - 1 = 4 d.f. The critical t_0 values are ± 2.776.

d) The differences between corresponding values for Subarea 1 and Subarea 2 are 6, 3, -6, -3, and 5. The value for $\overline{d} = 1$ and the value for $s_d = 5.2440$

d) $t = \dfrac{1-0}{\dfrac{5.2440}{\sqrt{5}}} = .4264$

Critical Region

Do not reject H_0

Critical Region

-2.776   0 .4264 2.776

t value for test statistic

e) The t equivalent to the test statistic t =.4264 is closer to 0 than the lowest t value given in the 4 d.f. table which is 1.344. This means the P value for the test statistic is greater than the P value given for t = 1.344 which is .250.

f) Since the P value is more than the .05 level of significance, fail to reject the null hypothesis. There is not sufficient evidence to conclude that there is any difference in the number of service ware shards in subarea 1 as compared to subarea 2. Using the critical region technique, we find that the test statistic does not fall in the critical region, so we would fail to reject H_0.

13.   a) $H_0 : \mu_d = 0$ and $H_1 : \mu_d \neq 0$. We'll use a two-tail test at the .05 level of significance.

b) The sampling distribution of differences is a t distribution with 6- 1 = 5d.f. The critical t_0 values are ± 2.967.

d) The differences between corresponding values for Soapstone and Bigyear -8, -3, -20, 1, -12, and -12. The value for $\overline{d} = -9$ and the value for $s_d = 7.4297$.

d) $t = \dfrac{-9-0}{\dfrac{7.4297}{\sqrt{6}}} = -2.967$

Critical Region

Do not reject H_0

Critical Region

-2.967   -2.571   0   2.571

e) The t equivalent to the test statistic t =-2.967 is between the t values of 2.571 and 3.365 that t value for test statistic are listed in the t table for 5 d.f. The corresponding P values are .05 and .02 so the test statistic has a P value between .02 and .05.

f) Since the P value is less than the .05 level of significance, reject the null hypothesis and choose the hypothesis that there is a difference in the wear of the two tire brands. Using the critical region technique, we find that the test statistic falls in the critical region, so we would reject H_0.

would reject H_0.

17.   a) $H_0 : \mu_d = 0$ and $H_1 : \mu_d < 0$. We'll use a left tail test at the .05 level of significance.

b) The sampling distribution of differences is a t distribution with 6 - 1 = 5 d.f. The critical t_0 value is -2.15.

d) The differences between corresponding values for pulse before and pulse after are -16, -7, -8, -11, -17, and -4. The value for $\overline{d}$ = -10.5 and the value for s_d = 5.1672.

$$t = \frac{-10.5 - 0}{\frac{5.1672}{\sqrt{6}}} = -4.977$$

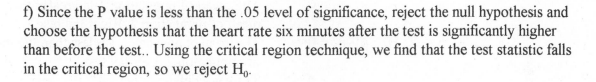

e) The t equivalent to the test statistic t = -4.997 is further away from t = 0 than t = 4.032 the t value found in the last column for the 5 d.f. distribution. Since the P value for t = 4.032 (and also t = -4.032) is .005 for α' (remember this is a one-tail test), the P value for the given test t value of -4.977 must be even lower. (There is less area left in the tail to the left of t = -4.977 than there is area to the left of t = 4.032.)

f) Since the P value is less than the .05 level of significance, reject the null hypothesis and choose the hypothesis that the heart rate six minutes after the test is significantly higher than before the test.. Using the critical region technique, we find that the test statistic falls in the critical region, so we reject H_0.

Answer to Thinking About Statistics

The conclusion of the test was that scores were higher after the prep course than they were before. This may not mean that the higher scores were a result of the prep course. Perhaps the students gained experience in taking the test the first time so that they did better the second time around. Possibly some of the material on the test was covered in their high school courses. There could be dozens of other reasons why they might still have done better without the prep course. An interesting study might be to take a different group of students, give them the SAT a first time and then wait for the same time interval and let them retake the test. Would their improvement be less than that for the students who took the prep course? Note that in order to do this test, you would use the test of sample means for independent samples.

Section 9.7
Tests Involving the Difference of Two Means or Two Proportions (Independent Samples)

Review

In this section we will see how to test the difference between the means of two populations using a) large independent samples and then b) small independent samples. Then we'll see how similar. techniques can be used to test the difference in the proportion of two populations using independent samples.

I.   Steps for a hypothesis test for the difference of the means of two populations (independent large samples).

   A.   Formulate a pair of hypotheses about the differences between the population means.
   1. $H_0 : \mu_1 - \mu_2 = 0$ There is no difference. (Diff. = 0)
   2.   Choose one of the following for the alternate hypothesis:
      a. $H_1 : \mu_1 - \mu_2 > 0$ The mean of population 1 is greater than the mean of population 2. Right tail test.
      b. $H_1 : \mu_1 - \mu_2 < 0$ The mean of population 1 is less than the mean of population 2. Left tail test.
      c. $H_1 : \mu_1 - \mu_2 \neq 0$ There is a difference between the means of the two populations. Two tail test.

   B.   Determine α the level of significance.
   C.   Gather your sample evidence and place it in chart form.
   1.   For each population you will have a sample size , n_1 and n_2. When both your samples are over 30 use formulas for large samples.
   2.   Determine $\bar{x}_1$ and $\bar{x}_2$, the mean of each sample. Your sample statistic will be $\bar{x}_1 - \bar{x}_2$ the <u>difference</u> between the two sample means.
   3.   Determine s_1 and s_2. For a large samples, you can replace them for σ_1 and σ_2 in the critical value formula. (In rare cases σ_1 and σ_2 are known.)
   D.   The sampling distribution for the difference of sample means (large independent samples.
   1.   Normal
   2.   The mean of the distribution is $\mu_1 - \mu_2$. This is 0 when the null hypothesis

276

states that there is no difference.

3. The standard deviation is s $\sqrt{\dfrac{\sigma_1^2}{n_1} + \dfrac{\sigma_2^2}{n_2}}$

4.

E. For the critical values, use the value of z as follows

	right tail test	left tail test	two tail test
$\alpha = .01$	z = 2.33	z = -2.33	z = 2.58 and z = -2.58
$\alpha = .05$	z = 1.645	z = -1.645	z = 1.96 and z = - 1.96

F. Form the sample test statistic of $\overline{x}_1 - \overline{x}_2$ the difference of the sample means and convert to a z score using: $z = \dfrac{(\overline{x}_1 - \overline{x}_2) - (\mu_1 - \mu_2)}{\sqrt{\dfrac{\sigma_1^2}{n_1} + \dfrac{\sigma_2^2}{n_2}}}$.

G. It is easier to first compute the difference in sample means. Note also that the difference in populations means is frequently hypothesized as 0.

H. Make a sketch of the normal distribution curve.
1. Locate the z value(s) for the critical difference(s) on your sketch.
2. Shade the critical tail region or regions.
3. Place your z equivalent to the sample statistic $\overline{x}_1 - \overline{x}_2$ in correct numerical order on your sketch.

I. Make your decision.
1. If your z statistic is in the critical region, reject H_0.
2. If your z statistic is not in the critical region, fail to reject H_0. This will indicate there is not enough evidence to say there is a significant difference.

II. Testing the Difference of Means for Small samples.
A. Tests of the difference of two population means from independent populations based on *small samples* are almost the same as those with large samples with the following exceptions:
1. The distribution of differences of sample means is a t-distribution with $n_1 + n_2 - 2$ degrees of freedom.
2. Assume the two parent populations are normally distributed.
3. Assume that the standard deviations for both these populations are

approximately equal. We can obtain what is called a *pooled estimate for the standard deviation* from the following formula.

$$s = \sqrt{\frac{(s_1)^2(n_1-1)+(s_2)^2(n_2-1)}{n_1+n_2-2}}$$

B.   The t value for the critical difference is found on the Student t table for $n_1 + n_2 - 2$ degrees of freedom.

C.   The t value equivalent to the test statistic is :

$$t = s\sqrt{\frac{1}{n_1}+\frac{1}{n_2}}$$

1.   The value of t is from the table,
2.   The value for s is from the pooled standard deviation $s = \sqrt{\frac{(n_1-1)s_1^2+(n_2-1)s_2^2}{n_1+n_2-2}}$.

3. n_1 and n_2 are the sizes of the two samples.

III.   Tests of the difference between population proportions

A.   Similar to test of the difference between population means except:

1. $H_0 : p_1 - p_2 = 0$ and $H_1 : p_1 - p_2 < 0$ OR $p_1 - p_2 > 0$ OR $p_1 - p_2 \neq 0$.

2.   The sampling distribution for $\hat{p}_1 - \hat{p}_2 = \frac{r_1}{n_1} - \frac{r_2}{n_2}$ is a normal distribution
  a.   mean $\mu = p_1 - p_2$

  b.   standard deviation $\sigma = \sqrt{\frac{p_1 q_1}{n_1} + \frac{p_2 q_2}{n_2}}$

B.   Since we'll test the hypothesis that the two population proportions are equal, we can obtain an estimates for their common value $\hat{p}$ $\hat{p} = \frac{r_1 + r_2}{n_1 + n_2}$ We'll then estimate

the value for $\hat{q}$ with $1 - \hat{p}$.

1.   The z value for the critical difference is determined in the same manner as in the z tests for a single population proportion.

2.   The z value for the test statistic is given by:

$$z = \frac{\hat{p}_1 - \hat{p}_2}{\sqrt{\frac{\hat{p}\hat{q}}{n_1} + \frac{\hat{p}\hat{q}}{n_2}}}$$

$\hat{p}_1 = \frac{r_1}{n_1}$ $\hat{p}_2 = \frac{r_2}{n_2}$ $\hat{p} = \frac{r_1 + r_2}{n_1 + n_2}$ and $\hat{q}$ with $1 - \hat{p}$.

Problem Solving Warm-Up

1.   A study of college freshman was conducted to see whether females do better than males on the Miller Analogy Test. A group of freshman was randomly selected at a large university and given the test. The results were as follows: There were $n_1 = 63$ males in the sample in which the mean $\bar{x}_1 = 51$ and standard deviation $s_1 = 1.2$. There were $n_2 = 45$ females which the mean $\bar{x}_2 = 54$ and the standard deviation $s_2 = 3.1$. Test the claim at the .05 level of significance that females score higher than males on the Miller Analogy Test.

a) Use the critical region approach
b) Use the P value technique

A.   Formulate the pair of hypotheses.
   H_0 : _____
   H_1 : _____

A. $H_0 : \mu_1 - \mu_2 = 0$
   $H_1 : \mu_1 - \mu_2 < 0$ (Male mean - female mean is a negative number.) This will happen when the mean of the males is *lower* than that of the females.

B.   Determine α (level of significance).

   _____

B. $\alpha = .05$

C.   The sample statistics are:
   $n_1 =$_____ $n_2 =$_____
   $\bar{x}_1 =$_____ $\bar{x}_2 =$_____
   $s_1 =$_____ $s_2 =$_____
   TEST STATISTIC =_____

C.   MALES   FEMALES
      $n_1 = 63$ $n_2 = 45$
      $\bar{x}_1 = 51$ $\bar{x}_2 = 54$
      $s_1 = 1.2$ $s_2 = 3.1$
   TEST STATISTIC= 51 -54 = -3

D.   Determine the sampling distribution

D.   The distribution of the differences of sample means is normal since the samples are independent and are both large.

E.   Determine the z value for the critical difference.

   _____

E.   For a left tail test at the .05 level of significance, the critical z value is -1.645.

F.   Make a sketch of the sampling distribution. Shade the critical region.

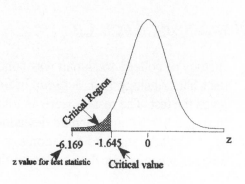

G. Compute the z value for the test statistic.

_____

G. $z = \dfrac{(.51 - .54) - 0}{\sqrt{\dfrac{(1.2)^2}{63} - \dfrac{(3.1)^2}{45}}} = \dfrac{-3}{.4862} = -6.169$

H. Make your decision and interpret it.

_____

H. Since the z value for the test statistic falls in the critical region, reject H_0. Choose the hypothesis that the mean score for males on this test is significantly lower than that for females.

b) Use the P value technique.

A. Calculate a range of P values for the z test statistic computed earlier.

A. The z value of -6.169 is not found on the z table However, it is further away from the mean of z = 0 than z = 5. The P value for z = 5 is .5 - .4999997 = .0000003. (The P value is equal to the area in the left tail for a left tail test.)

B. Make your decision.

B. Since this P value is less than the level of significance reject H_0.

2.   A company executive is interested in the average number of years salespersons have been with the company compared to the average number of years office personnel have been with the company. A random sample of 12 salespersons show the mean number of years with the company is $\overline{x}_1 = 3.2$ with the sample standard deviation $s_1 = .6$. A random sample of 19 office

personnel show the mean number of years with the company is $\bar{x}_2 = 5.6$ with the sample standard deviation .2. Do the data indicate office personnel tend to stay longer. Use $\alpha = .05$.

A. Formulate the pair of hypotheses.

  H_0 : _____

  H_1 : _____

A.

  $H_0 : \mu_1 - \mu_2 = 0$

  $H_1 : \mu_1 - \mu_2 < 0$

B. Determine α (level of significance).

  _____

B. $\alpha = .05$

C. The sample statistics are:

  $n_1 =$ _____ $n_2 =$ _____

  $\bar{x}_1 =$ _____ $\bar{x}_2 =$ _____

  $s_1 =$ _____ $s_2 =$ _____

  TEST STATISTIC = _____

C. SALES   OFFICE

  $n_1 = 12$ $n_2 = 19$

  $\bar{x}_1 = 3.2$ $\bar{x}_2 = 5.6$

  $s_1 = .6$ $s_2 = .2$

  TEST STATISTIC $3.2 - 5.6 = -2.4$

D. Determine the sampling distribution

  _____

D. Since the samples are small, use a t distribution with $12 + 19 - 2 = 29$ d.f.

E. Determine the critical t value.

  _____

E. For the t distribution with 29 d.f. the .05 critical value is 1.699.

F. Calculate the t value for the test statistic.

$$ t = \frac{\bar{x}_1 - \bar{x}_2}{s\sqrt{\frac{1}{n_1} + \frac{1}{n_2}}} $$

$x_1 - x_2 = -2.4$ and s, the pooled standard deviation is given by:

$$ s = \sqrt{\frac{(s_1)^2(n_1 - 1) + (s_2)^2(n_2 - 1)}{n_1 + n_2 - 2}} $$

$$ s = \sqrt{\frac{(.6)^2(11) + (.2)^2(18)}{29}} = .40 $$

$$\sqrt{\frac{1}{12}+\frac{1}{19}} = .37$$

$$\text{So } t = \frac{-2.4}{(.40)(.37)} = 16.216$$

F.   Make a sketch of the distribution of sample statistics. Locate the critical region. Locate the t value for the sample test statistic.

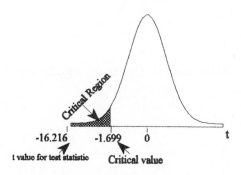

G.   Make your decision.

_____

G.   The t value for the difference of -2.4 falls in the critical region. We reject H_0. The test indicates that office personnel tend to stay longer.

3.   In a New York Times/CBS News survey, 193 of 552 Democrats felt that the government should regulate airline prices. 171 out of 417 Republicans surveyed also felt government should regulate airline prices. Test the claim at the .01 level of significance that there is no difference between the proportion of Democrats and the proportion of Republicans who feel that way.

a) Use the critical region technique.   b) Use the P value technique.

a) The critical region technique

A. H_0 :_____
      H_1 :_____

A. H_0 :$p_1 - p_2 = 0$
      H_1 :$p_2 - p_2 \neq 0$
(Let 1=Dem. and 2=Rep.)

B. $\alpha =$ _____

B. $\alpha = .01$

C.   List the sample statistics
      $\hat{p}_1 = r_1/n_1 =$ _____

C.
      $\hat{p}_1 = r_1/n_1 = .35$

$\hat{p}_{2\,=\,r_2/n_2} =$_____

Test statistic =_____

$\hat{p}_{2\,=\,r_2/n_2} = .41$

Test statistic $= .35 - .41 = -.06$

D.   What is the sampling distribution?

D.   The sampling distribution is normal.

E.   Determine the critical z_0 value(s).

=_____

E.   The critical value(s) are $z = \pm\,2.58$.

F.   Calculate the z value for the test statistic.

F.   Assume $p_1 = -p_2$ (or $p_1 - p_2 = 0$) and calculate the best guess estimate for their common value

calculate $\hat{p} =$ _____

calculate $\hat{q} =$ _____

$$\hat{p} = \frac{r_1 + r_2}{n_1 + n_2} = \frac{364}{969} = .38$$

then $\hat{q} = 1 - .38 = .62$

z = _____

$$z = \frac{-.06}{\sqrt{\frac{(.38)(.62)}{552} + \frac{(.38)(.62)}{417}}} = \frac{-.06}{.0315} = -1.905$$

F.   Sketch your distribution. Shade the critical region. Locate the z value for your test statistic.

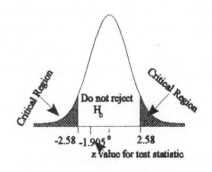

G.   Make your decision.

G.   The z value for the test statistic -.06 does not fall in the critical region. Fail to reject H_0 there is no difference between Republicans and Democrats on this issue.

b) Use the P value technique
Follow steps A to E above and then....

A.   Calculate the P value of the z test statistic.

_____

A.   The area remaining in the left tail beyond z = -1.905 is .5 - .4715 = .0285. Since this is a two tail test, double the area to find the P value. 2(.0295) = .057.

B.   Make your decision.

B.   Fail to reject H_0 since $P > \alpha$.

Thinking About Statistics

The following exercise should help clarify what is meant by the distribution of the differences of sample means for independent samples.

Suppose we are doing a study on the starting salaries of college graduates with business degrees. We wish to determine whether males are offered higher salaries than females. H_0: $\mu_1 - \mu_2 = 0$ (no difference in mean salaries).

We draw a random sample from the population of male graduates and compute the mean starting salary (in thousands). We so the same for the population of female graduates. We are interested in the statistic $d = \bar{x}_1 - \bar{x}_2$. When we perform a test we only obtain one sample from each of the two populations and then compute the difference. There are of course an infinite number of samples which could be drawn from the male population and likewise an infinite number from the female population. The differences between the means of the samples will vary.

Complete the chart that follows by finding the *difference* between sample 1 and sample 2 on each line. What is the average difference?

Male mean $\bar{x}_1$	Female mean $\bar{x}_2$	$\bar{x}_1 - \bar{x}_2$
24	22	
23	26	
19	27	
29	24	
25	21	
30	27	
23	26	

Fill in the following Use the results to do the exercises in your text

Type of Test	Sampling distribution	Formula for z or t Test Statistic
mean of a population large sample		
mean of a population small sample		
population proportion		
difference of two population means independent pop. large samples		
difference of two population means small samples		
difference of two population means dependent populations		
difference between proportions of two samples		

Selected Solutions Section 9.7

When formulating your hypotheses remember that the null hypothesis will contain the condition of equality. **The statement $\mu_1 - \mu_2 = 0$ is equivalent to $\mu_1 = \mu_2$** . The first equation emphasizes that we are testing a *difference* in means (or proportions) and that we are going to assume that the difference is 0. Answers will be given in that form, but you may feel free to answer in the other form.

The statement $\mu_1 - \mu_2 < 0$ is equivalent to $\mu_1 < \mu_2$. The first inequality, however emphasizes that we are hypothesizing a negative (less than zero) difference. Use this formulation of the alternate hypothesis when the claim states the mean of the first population is less than the mean of the second, OR, equivalently, the mean of the second population is greater than that of the first.

The statement $\mu_1 - \mu_2 > 0$ is equivalent to $\mu_1 > \mu_2$. Use this when your claim indicates a positive difference, (i.e. the mean of the first population is greater than the mean of the second.)

1.   a) $H_0 : \mu_1 - \mu_2 = 0$ (or equivalently, $\mu_1 = \mu_2$) and $H_1 : \mu_1 - \mu_2 > 0$
Use a right tail test for the difference in population means with $\alpha = .01$.

<u>10 year old children</u>   <u>35 year old adults</u>
$n_1 = 33$ $n_2 = 32$
$\bar{x}_1 = 2.6$ hours per night $\bar{x}_2 = 1.9$ hours per night
$s_1 = .5$ hours per night $s_2 = .8$ hours per night
   Test statistic is 2.6 - 1.9 = 0.7 hours per night.

b) In this test independent samples are used (there is no pairing) and both samples are
large, so the sampling distribution is a normal distribution. The critical value is $z_0 = 2.33$.

d) The sample test statistic = $\bar{x}_1 - \bar{x}_2 = 2.6 - 1.9 = 0.7$ hours. From
the null hypothesis we assume that $\mu_1 - \mu_2 = 0$. Compute the z value
for the test statistic as:

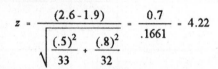

$$z = \frac{(2.6 - 1.9)}{\sqrt{\frac{(.5)^2}{33} + \frac{(.8)^2}{32}}} = \frac{0.7}{.1661} = 4.22$$

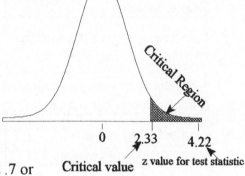

e) The P value for z = 4.22 is less than the P value
for z = 4.0 which is .5 - .49997 = .00003. Assuming
there is no difference in the population means, the
probability of getting a difference between samples that is .7 or
greater is less than .00003. There is less than .00003 area in the
tail to the right of the test statistic.

f) Since the P value is less than α, we reject the null hypothesis. Using the critical region
technique, we reject H_0 since the z value is in the critical region. There is sufficient
evidence to choose the hypothesis that five year old children tend to have significantly
more REM sleep than 50 year old adults.

5.   a) $H_0 : \mu_1 - \mu_2 = 0$ $H_1 : \mu_1 - \mu_2 < 0$

Night workers take more sick leave than day translates to means day minus night is
negative. (left tail test). $\alpha = .05$ ♦

<u>DAY</u>   <u>NIGHT</u>
$n_1 = 38$ $n_2 = 41$
$\bar{x}_1 = 10.6$ $\bar{x}_2 = 12.9$
$s_1 = 3.3$ $s_2 = 4.5$
  TEST STATISTIC = 10.6 - 12.9 = -2.3

b)   In this test independent samples are used (there is no pairing) and both samples are large, so the sampling distribution is a normal distribution. The critical value is $z_0 = -1.645$. ♦

d) The z value that corresponds to the sample statistic is:

$$z = \frac{10.6 - 12.9}{\sqrt{\frac{(3.3)^2}{38} + \frac{(4.5)^2}{41}}} = \frac{-2.3}{.8834} = -2.60$$ ♦

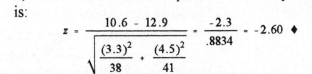

e)   The P value corresponding to z = -2.60 for a one tail test is .5 - .4953 = .0047. If the population means are equal, there is less than a .0047 probability that there would be a z value equivalent of - 2.60 for the difference in sample means. ♦

z value for test statistic   Critical value

f) Since the P value is less than the level of significance, we reject H_0 .The z value for the test statistic falls in the critical region. The test indicates that night workers take more sick time than day workers. ♦

9.   a) $H_0 : \mu_1 - \mu_2 = 0$ $H_1 : \mu_1 - \mu_2 \neq 0$. Use a two tail test with a .05 level of significance. ♦

Region 1	Region 2
$n_1 = 16$	$n_2 = 15$
$\bar{x}_1 = 4.75$	$\bar{x}_2 = 3.93$
$s_1 = 2.82$	$s_2 = 2.43$

TEST STATISTIC = 47.75 - 3.93 = .82

b) Use a t distribution with 16 +15 -2 = 29 d.f. The critical t_0 values are ± 2.045. ♦

d) Compute the pooled estimate for the common standard deviation:

$$s = \sqrt{\frac{(16-1)2.82^2 + (15\ 1)2.43^2}{29}} = \sqrt{6.96395} = 2.6389$$

$$t = \frac{4.75 - 3.93}{2.6389\sqrt{\frac{1}{16} + \frac{1}{15}}} = \frac{.82}{(2.6389)(.3594)} = .865$$

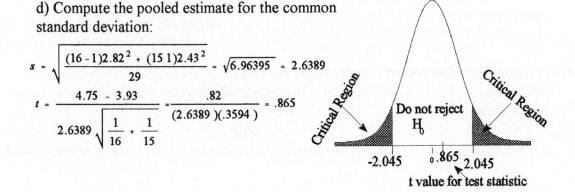

Do not reject H_0

-2.045   0 .865 2.045

t value for test statistic

287

e) The t value of .865 is closer to t = 0 than t = 1.174 found in the 29 d.f. t table. This means that t = .865 has a *higher P* value than does t = 1.174 which has a P value of .250.

f) The t test value does not fall in the critical region, so fail to reject the null hypothesis. Since the P value for the test is higher than .250, we do not have sufficient evidence to reject the null hypothesis at the .05 level (P > α, fail to reject H_0.). There is no significant difference in the mean number of cases of fox rabies between the two regions.

13.   a) $H_0 : \mu_1 - \mu_2 = 0$ $H_1 : \mu_1 - \mu_2 < 0$. Use a left tail test with a .05 level of significance. ◆

Before	With new generator
$n_1 = 10$	$n_2 = 12$
$\bar{x}_1 = 7.2°$ F	$\bar{x}_2 = 10.8°$ F
$s_1 = 2.7°$ F	$s_2 = 2.5°$ F

TEST STATISTIC = 7.2 - 10.8 = -3.6

b) Since the samples are small, use a t distribution with 10.+12 -2 = 20 d.f. The critical t_0 value is -1.725. ◆

d) Compute the pooled estimate for the common standard deviation:

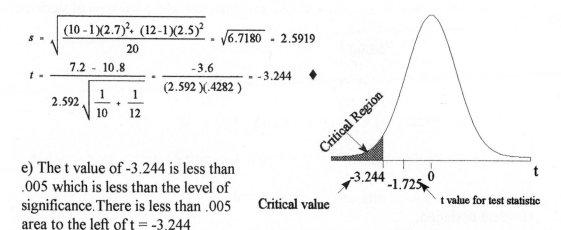

$$ s = \sqrt{\frac{(10-1)(2.7)^2 + (12-1)(2.5)^2}{20}} = \sqrt{6.7180} = 2.5919 $$

$$ t = \frac{7.2 - 10.8}{2.592\sqrt{\frac{1}{10} + \frac{1}{12}}} = \frac{-3.6}{(2.592)(.4282)} = -3.244 \quad ◆ $$

Critical Region

-3.244 -1.725 0   t

Critical value   t value for test statistic

e) The t value of -3.244 is less than .005 which is less than the level of significance. There is less than .005 area to the left of t = -3.244

f) Reject the null hypothesis.(P < α.) Also the t value for the test statistic falls in the critical region. The test indicates that water temperature significantly increases with the new generator.◆

17.   a) $H_0 : p_1 - p_2 = 0$ $H_1 : p_1 - p_2 \neq 0$. Use a two tail test with a .05 level of significance. ◆

$$\underline{1975} \qquad\qquad \underline{1991}$$

$$n_1 = 1484 \qquad\qquad n_2 = 1013$$

$$r_1 = 534 \qquad\qquad r_2 = 324$$

$$\hat{p}_1 = .3598 \qquad\qquad \hat{p}_2 = .3198$$

TEST STATISTIC = .3598 - .3198 = .04

b) Since $n_1\hat{p}$, $n_2\hat{p}$, $n_1\hat{q}$ and $n_2\hat{q}$ are all more than 5, we can use a normal curve approximation to the binomial distribution. The critical z_0 values are ± 1.96. ♦

We are assuming that the proportions for the two populations are equal (i.e. that the null hypothesis is true.) To get an estimate for their common value, use

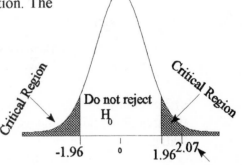

$$\hat{p} = \frac{534 + 324}{1484 + 1013} = .3436 \ .$$

Then $\hat{q} = 1 - .3436 = .6564$.

$$z = \frac{.3598 - .3198}{\sqrt{\dfrac{(.3436)(.6564)}{1484} + \dfrac{(.3436)(.6564)}{1013}}} = \frac{.04}{.0194} = 2.07$$

e) To find the P value for this test, first find the area in the tail falling to the right of the test statistic z = 2.07. This is .5 - .4808 = .0192. Since this is a two tail test and the normal curve is symmetric, double to area in the right tail to get a P value of .0384. ♦

f) Since the P value is less than the level of significance, fail to reject the null hypothesis. The test statistic falls in the critical region so choose the hypothesis that the proportion of adult U.S. citizens who agree with the statement has changed between 1975 and 1991. ♦

21.   a) $H_0 : p_1 - p_2 = 0 \ H_1 : p_1 - p_2 \neq 0$. Use a two tail test with a .01 level of significance. ♦

$$\underline{\text{Vaccine A}} \qquad\qquad \underline{\text{Vaccine B}}$$

$$n_1 = 350 \qquad\qquad n_2 = 400$$

$$r_1 = 300 \qquad\qquad r_2 = 372$$

$$\hat{p}_1 = .8571 \qquad\qquad \hat{p}_2 = .93$$

TEST STATISTIC = ..8571-..9300= -.0729

b) Since $n_1\hat{p}$, $n_2\hat{p}$, $n_1\hat{q}$ and $n_2\hat{q}$ are all more than 5, we can use a normal curve approximation to the binomial distribution. The critical z_0 values are ± 2.58. ♦

We are assuming that the proportions for the two populations are equal (i.e. that the null hypothesis is true.) To get an estimate for their common value, use

$$\hat{p} = \frac{300 + 372}{350 + 400} = .896 \; .$$

Then $\hat{q} = 1 - .896 = .104$

$$z =$$

$$\frac{.8571 - .9300}{\sqrt{\dfrac{(.896)(.104)}{350} + \dfrac{(.896)(.104)}{400}}} = \frac{-.0729}{.0223} = -3.27$$

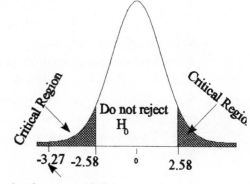

z value for test statistic

e) To find the P value for this test, first find the area in the tail falling to the left of the test statistic
$z = -3.27$. This is $.5 - .4995 = .0005$. Since this is a two tail test and the normal curve is symmetric, double to area in the right tail to get a P value of .0010. ◆

f) Since the P value is less than the level of significance, reject the null hypothesis. The test statistic falls in the critical region so choose the hypothesis that there is a significant difference in the effectiveness of the two vaccines.

25.   a) $H_0 : p_1 - p_2 = 0 \; H_1 : p_1 - p_2 \neq 0$. Use a two tail test with a .01 level of significance.

<u>Bartlett</u>   <u>Le Conte</u>
$n_1 = 850$ $n_2 = 850$
$r_1 = 36$ $r_2 = 54$
$\hat{p}_1 = .0424$ $\hat{p}_2 = .0635$
TEST STATISTIC $= .0424 - .0635 = .0212$

b) Since $n_1\hat{p}$, $n_2\hat{p}$, $n_1\hat{q}$ and $n_2\hat{q}$ are all more than 5, we can use a normal curve approximation to the binomial distribution. The critical z_0 values are ± 2.58.
We are assuming that the proportions for the two populations are equal (i.e. that the null hypothesis is true.) To get an estimate for their common value, use

$$\hat{p} = \frac{36 + 54}{850 + 850} = .0529$$

Then $\hat{q} = 1 - .0529 = .9471$

$z =$

$$\dfrac{.0424 - .0635}{\sqrt{\dfrac{(.0529)(.9471)}{850} + \dfrac{(.0529)(.9471)}{850}}} = \dfrac{-.0212}{.0109} = -1.94$$

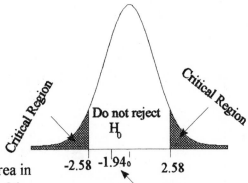

z value for test statistic

e) To find the P value for this test, first find the area in the tail falling to the left of the test statistic z = -1.94. This is .5 - .4838 = .0262. Since this is a two tail test and the normal curve is symmetric, double to area in the right tail to get a P value of .0524.

f) Since the P value is greater than the level of significance, fail to reject the null hypothesis. The test statistic does not fall in the critical region so choose the hypothesis that there is no significant difference in percentages of bad fruit for these two varieties of pears.

Answers to Thinking About Statistics

Male mean $\bar{x}_1$	Female mean $\bar{x}_2$	$\bar{x}_1 - \bar{x}_2$
24	22	2
23	26	-3
19	27	-8
29	24	5
25	21	4
30	27	3
23	26	-3

In some sample pairs the male salaries are higher and the difference is positive. In others, the female salary is higher and the difference is negative. If thousands and thousands of sample pairs were taken and the differences in the means computed, some would be positive and others negative.

When the null hypothesis of $\mu_1 - \mu_2 = 0$ is true, the mean of the distribution of all differences of sample means will be zero. Differences occur because there is variation from sample to sample. When we say a difference is significant at a given level (.01 or .05) we are really saying that we have a difference which is *not* due to variation from sampling, but rather due to the inherent differences between the populations.

Chapter 10

Regression and Correlation

Section 10.1
Introduction to Paired Data and Scatter Diagrams

<u>Review</u>

Up to this point the statistical techniques we studied involved one variable. In this chapter we introduce methods of statistical analysis involving two or more variables.

I. Paired Data
    A. *Correlation of variables*: Relationship between variables.
    B. We use ordered pairs (x,y) and call each pair a *data point.*
        1. x is the **explanatory variable,** the stimulus or the independent variable.
        2. y is the **response** or dependent variable.
    C. Types of correlation
        1. The simplest mathematical graph is a straight line. Therefore we will examine the data to see if there is a straight line (*linear*) relationship or formula between the x and y variables.
        2. There can be other relationships (for example, parabolic or circular), however we will not consider them in this course.
    D. How can we determine if there is a straight line relationship?
        1. Construct a graph of the (x,y) points on a coordinate system as is used in algebra. This is called a *scatter plot*
        2. Try to visualize a straight line describing these points.
            a. If the points fall on a straight line we say there is *perfect correlation.*

      b.   If the points appear to fall close to the straight line, we say there is a *high correlation.*

      c.   If the points are somewhat scattered from the line, we say there is a *moderate correlation.*

      d.   If we can not visualize a line at all we say there is *no linear correlation.*

E.   Direction of the linear relationship

     1.   When the y values increase as the x values increase (while reading the x values left to right, the y values are rising) we say there is a *positive correlation.*

     2.   When the y values decrease as the x values increase (while reading the x values left to right, the y values are falling) we say there is a *negative correlation.*

     3.   If we can not determine a linear pattern, we say there is no linear correlation.

II.   *Linear regression*

A.   The use of a straight line formula to predict y (response) values from specified x (explanatory or stimulus) values.

B.   We will develop methods for writing the equations of these lines in the next section.

Problem Solving Warm-Up

For the problems which follow, variables are listed in (x,y) pairs.

a)   Determine the explanatory variable.

b)   Determine the response variable.

c)   Using intuition, determine whether there is a positive, negative or no correlation between the given variables.

d)   Is this an example or perfect, high, moderate or no correlation between the given variable pairs?

1.   x = temperature in Fahrenheit degrees.

     y = temperature in Centigrade degrees.

     a)   _____

     b)   _____

     c)   _____

     d)   _____

a)   Temp. in ° Fahrenheit.

b)   Temp. in ° Centigrade.

c)   Positive correlation since as the temperature in Fahrenheit increases so does the temperature in Centigrade.

d)   This is a perfect correlation since there is a straight line equation which will precisely predict Centigrade degrees from Fahrenheit. Perfect correlations are very rare when measuring human behaviors or characteristics, but will appear in scientific formulas.

2. x= score on I.Q. test
    y= grade point average for freshman year.

    a) _____

    b) _____

    c) _____

    d) _____

a) Score on I.Q. test
b) G.P.A. for freshman year
c) Positive correlation. People with higher I.Q. values _tend_ to get higher grades.
d) Moderately high. There are many other factors which contribute to getting good grades. A person with a high I.Q. who does not study or attend class will not have a high grade point average. Likewise a person who works hard, even though his I.Q. score is not as high may get high grades. However, in the long run, a person with a high I.Q. will generally have higher grades.

3. x = Supply of a product
    y = Price for that product
    a) _____

    b) _____

    c) _____

    d) _____

a) Supply of the product
b) Price for that product
c) A negative correlation. As the supply of a product increases the price decreases. When the supply of a product is low, the price will usually increase, as in the case of oil prices.
d) The answer to this would depend on the product.

4. x = person's height
    y = person's I.Q. score

    a) _____

    b) _____

    c) _____

    d) _____

a) height
b) I.Q. score
c) No correlation between these variables. Short people can have low I.Q. scores as well as high ones. Likewise tall people can have low or high I.Q. scores.
d) Since there is no correlation, the knowledge of a person's height would not be a factor in predicting his or her I.Q. score.

5. x = person's height

a) height

y = person's shoe size

a) _____

b) _____

c) _____

d) _____

b) shoe size

c) Positive correlation. Taller people *tend* to have larger shoe sizes.

d) moderately high. For the most part a tall person will have a large foot. However, there are likely short people with large feet.

6. x = person's shoe size
   y = person's height

a) shoe size

b) height

c) Positive correlation. People with bigger feet tend to be taller.

d) Moderately high. Notice in this problem the shoe size is the explanatory variable where the height is the response variable.

Thinking About Statistics

Problems 5 and 6 in the Problem Solving Warm-Up involve the same two variables, height and shoe size, however, their roles as explanatory and response variables are reversed. Which of these models would be more suitable for a shoe salesperson who would like to predict a person's shoe size as they walk in the door, and which would be more suitable for a detective who can measure the size of footprints and would like to predict the person's height?

Selected Solutions Section 10.1

1. Moderate positive linear correlation. It is not difficult to visualize a line through the data points, even though they do not fall perfectly on that line. The line we picture rises as we read left to right. This indicates a positive correlation. ♦

2. No linear correlation. There is a curve which would fit this data, but since it is not a straight line, we will not be responsible for determining the formula. ♦

3. High positive linear correlation. ♦

4.   Moderate negative linear correlation. The line we visualize falls as we read from left to right. Furthermore the points are widely scattered from it. ♦

5.   High negative linear correlation. The points fall close to an imagined line. Furthermore, the line falls as we read left to right. ♦

6.   No linear (or any other kind) of correlation. This might be a model of the example of height and I.Q. Knowing x is of no use in predicting y. ♦

7.

c) The correlation is moderate. Draw your own line as you see fit. In later sections you'll learn how to be more precise.

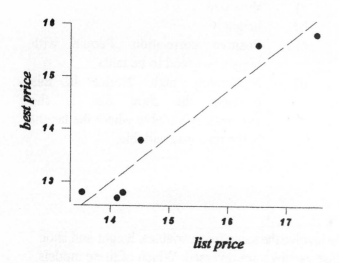

9.

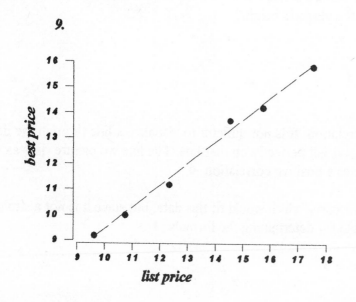

c) The correlation is high

13.

c) The correlation is high.

Answers to Thinking About Statistics

Use "height" as the explanatory variable when you can determine an individual's height and wish to predict their shoe size. In this situation, the response variable is "shoe size". A shoe salesperson would use this model.

On the other hand, (or foot) when the explanatory variable is shoe size (as it would be in the case of a detective who has the measurement of a footprint) the response variable would be the person's height. Thus the detective would predict height (the response variable) from shoe size.

In establishing regression formulas it is important to correctly identify x as the explanatory variable and y as the response variable. The formulas we will use will only be suitable for predicting y from x. This is called the *regression of y on x.*

Section 10.2
Linear Regression and Confidence Bounds for Prediction

Review

I.   Criteria for the "best fit" line:
      A.   Most pairs of variables do not have a perfect correlation so most of the points in a scatter plot will not lie on any one line.
          1.   Let d = the difference between the y value on the data point and y_p, the y value on the line for the same x value.
              a. $d = y - y_p$.
              b.   For data points above the line, this quantity will be positive.
              c.   For data points below the line, this quantity will be negative.
          2.   To eliminate negative values we square each value of d and get d^2.
      B.   The best fit line, *line of regression or line of least squares* is the line in which the *sum of these values of d^2 is minimized.*

II.   The equation of a line
      A.   Any non-vertical line can be written in the form:
$$y = (SLOPE)(x) + Y\text{-}INTERCEPT$$
          1.   In statistics we designate the y-intercept by a.
          2.   The slope is designated by b.
          3.   We write the equation of a line as :

$$y = bx + a$$

      B.   We can write the equation of a line provided we can determine its slope (b) and its y-intercept (a).
          1.   In algebra we could write the equation of a line which would perfectly fit two given points.
          2.   In statistics we will be given 3 or more points and be required to write the equation of the "best fit" line.

III.   Writing the equation of the line
      A.   Determine b, the slope of the line.

$$b = \frac{SS_{xy}}{SS_x}$$

B.   Determine a, the y-intercept

$$a = \bar{y} - b \cdot \bar{x}$$

where $\bar{y}$ = the mean of the y values in the scatter diagram $\bar{x}$ = the mean of the x values in the scatter diagram.

C.   Replace b and a in the equation

$$y = bx + a$$

D.   Necessary definitions

$$SS_{xy} = \sum xy - \frac{(\sum x)(\sum y)}{n}$$

$$SS_x = \sum x^2 - \frac{(\sum x)^2}{n}$$

Later we will need

$$SS_y = \sum y^2 - \frac{(\sum y)^2}{n}$$

IV.   Setting up the computation for a and b
    A.   Write the x values in column I and the corresponding y values in column II.
       1.   Find the sum of the values in column I = Σx.
       2.   Find the sum of the values in column II = Σy.
       3.   Divide each of these sums by n, the number of pairs to compute $\bar{x}$ and $\bar{y}$.

4. Square the sum of column I, to get $(\Sigma x)^2$ and square the sum in column II, to get $(\Sigma y)^2$.

B. In column III compute Σxy.
   1. Multiply each x value by its corresponding y value.
   2. Add the entries in this column.

C. In column IV compute Σx^2.
   1. Square each x value.
   2. Add these squared values.
   3. *Be sure you do not confuse $(\Sigma x)^2$ in which the x values are first added and then that sum is squared, with Σx^2 in which each x value is first squared and then the sum is taken of all the squares.*

D. In column V compute Σy^2.
   1. Square each y value.
   2. Add these squares.
   3. This computation is not necessary for the regression line but will be necessary in future computations.

V. Using the line of regression to predict y values from given x values.
   A. Once the equation of the line of regression is established, substitute a particular value for x into the equation.
   B. Do the indicated computation (multiply by b and add a) to get the value of y_p, the value of y which the line of regression predicts for y for a given value of x.
   C. The point (x,y) is a data point.
   D. The point (x,y_p) is a point on the line of regression.

VI. Measure of dispersion of the data points or "how strong is the correlation?"
    A. One measure of dispersion is called the *Standard Error of Estimate.*

$$s_e = \sqrt{\frac{\Sigma (y - y_p)^2}{n-2}}$$

   1. To calculate, form a column for y_p. In this column. calculate the value of y which is produced by the regression line equation for each of the x values listed.
   2. Subtract each y_p from y (the value in the data point) and square each answer.
   3. Add these squared values.
   4. Divide by n-2.
   5. Take the square root.

B. An alternate formula which is easier to compute is given by:

$$S_e = \sqrt{\frac{SS_y - b \cdot SS_{xy}}{(n-2)}}$$

    1.   Using this formula, the values of SS_y, b and SS_{xy} can be computed while determining the line of regression formula.

  C.   The larger the value for the Standard Error, the more spread out the data points will be from the line.

VII. Confidence intervals

  A.   Since the line of regression is usually established from a *sample* of data points there is probably a slight difference between predictive values from the line and the predictive values which would occur if we had been able to obtain all data points from a *population*.

  B.   For each x value, there is a distribution of y values.

    1.   The mean of these y values is y_p, the value of y on the line.

    2.   The standard deviation is S_e, the standard error of estimate.

  C.   We can form a c confidence interval for y for each value of x by

$$y_p - E \le y \le y_p + E$$

Where y_p is the predicted value of y from a specified x value.

  D.   E is given by:

$$E = t_c \cdot S_e \sqrt{1 + \frac{1}{n} + \frac{(x - \bar{x})^2}{SS_x}}$$

    1. t_c = t-distribution value with n-2 degrees of freedom.

    2. S_e = the standard error of estimate

    3. $x - \bar{x}$ is the deviation of the particular x value given.

    4. $SS_x = \Sigma(x^2) - (\Sigma x)^2 / n$.

  E.   The value of E, and hence the confidence interval will widen as the values of x move away from the mean of x.

Problem Solving Warm-up

The manufacturer of XJJ sports model of the Wego car has collected data on the average speed(x) on a trip and the miles per gallon (y) for a randomly selected sample of 9 car owners. The data is listed in the table that follows.

x (mph)	y (mpg)
20	22
25	21
30	20
35	23
40	19
45	18
50	16
55	14
60	11

a)   Draw a scatter diagram for the data.

b)   Find $\bar{x}$, $\bar{y}$ and b. Then find the equation of the least squares line.

c)   Graph the least squares line on your scatter diagram.

d)   Find the standard error of estimate S_e.

e)   If a person travelled an average of 43 miles per hour, predict the miles per gallon gas consumption he would get.

f)   Find a 95% confidence interval for the miles per gallon when a person is averaging 43 miles per gallon.

Fill in the cells in the chart that follows:

x (mph)	y (mpg)	xy	x^2	y^2
20	22			
25	21			
30	20			
35	23			
40	19			
45	18			
50	16			
55	14			
60	11			

Check your results :

x (mph)	y (mpg)	xy	x^2	y^2
20	22	440	400	484
25	21	525	625	441
30	20	600	900	400
35	23	805	1,225	529
40	19	760	1,600	361
45	18	810	2,025	324
50	16	800	2,500	256
55	14	770	3,025	196
60	11	660	3,600	121
360.00	164.00	6,170	15,900	3,112

Determine each of the following:

Answers:

Σx _____

$\Sigma x = 360$

$\bar{x}$ _____

$\bar{x} = 360/9 = 40$

$(\Sigma x)^2$ _____

$(\Sigma x)^2 = 129600$

Σy _____

$\Sigma y = 164$

$\bar{y}$ _____

$\bar{y} = 18.22$

$(\Sigma y)^2$ _____

$(\Sigma y)^2 = 26896$

Σxy _____

$\Sigma xy = 6170$

Σx^2 _____

$\Sigma x^2 = 15900$

Σy^2 _____

$\Sigma y^2 = 3112$

SS_{xy} _____

$SS_{xy} = 6170 - \dfrac{(360)(164)}{9}$
$= -390$

SS_x _____

$SS_x = 15900 - \dfrac{360^2}{9}$
$= 1500$

SS_y _____

$SS_y = 3112 - \dfrac{(164)^2}{9}$
$= 123.56$

b _____

$b = -390/1500 = -.26$

a _____

$a = 18.22 - (-.26)(40) = 28.62$

Equation for the line of regression

Line of regression
$y = -.26x + 28.62$

_____

$$S_e = \sqrt{\frac{123.56 - (-.26)(-390)}{7}} = 1.78$$

S_e _____

$S_e = 1.78$

predict y when x = 43

predict y when x = 43
$y_p = (-.26)(43) + 28.62 = 17.44$

_____

$$E = 2.365(1.78)\sqrt{1 + \frac{1}{9} + \frac{(43-40)^2}{1500}} = 4.45$$

$E = 4.45$

E = _____

Left boundary = 17.44 - 4.45 = 12.99
Right boundary = 17.44 + 4.45 = 21.89
We are 95% sure that a person travelling at an average of 43 mph will get between 12.93 and 21.95 mpg.

Confidence interval:

_____

Thinking About Statistics

1.   For the Problem Solving Warm-Up example, we obtained the formula for the equation of the line of regression : y = - .26x + 28.62 . This equation establishes a relationship between the x value of any point on the regression line and its corresponding y value.
Use the equation to predict y_p the value of y when x = 63 mph, x = 93 mph, x = 23 mph and x= 3 mph. Although we can substitute any value for x in the formula and obtain a y value, do you think there should be a restriction on which values give meaningful results?

2.   While doing your calculations, you should be aware that SS_x and SS_y are both *always positive.* The value of SS_{xy} can be positive or negative. Since the slope is obtained by dividing SS_{xy} by SS_x what is the connection between the sign of b (the slope) and the sign of SS_{xy}?

Selected Solutions Section 10.2

Since different calculators and computers will get slightly different results (due to rounding off), do not be concerned if some of the answers vary slightly from the ones you obtain.

Although these formulas look intimidating, they only involve adding, subtracting, multiplying, dividing and finding a square root, all of which are done on a calculator. Keep your work neatly organized in charts and you should have no difficulty.

1 a and c)

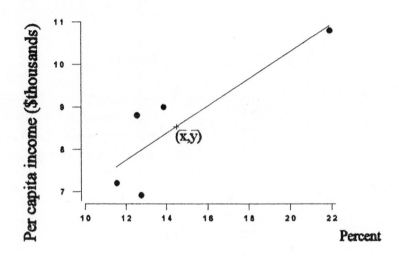

Construct a table with columns of x, y, xy, x² and y².

x	y	xy	x²	y²
13.8	9.0	124.2	190.44	81
21.9	10.8	236.52	479.61	116.64
12.5	8.8	110	156.25	77.44
12.7	6.9	87.63	161.29	47.61
11.5	7.2	82.8	132.25	51.84
72.4	42.70	641.15	1119.8	374.53

$\Sigma x = 72.4$ $\bar{x} = 14.48$ $(\Sigma x)^2 = 5241.76$

$\Sigma y = 42.70$ $\bar{y} = 8.54$ $(\Sigma y)^2 = 1823.29$

$\Sigma xy = 641.15$ $\Sigma x^2 = 1119.84$ $\Sigma y^2 = 374.53$

$$SS_{xy} = 641.15 - \frac{(72.4)(42.7)}{5} = 22.854$$

$$SS_x = 1119.84 - \frac{5241.76}{5} = 71.488$$

$$SS_y = 374.53 - \frac{1823.29}{5} = 9.872$$

$$\bar{x} = 14.48 \qquad \bar{y} = 8.54 \qquad b = \frac{22.854}{71.488} = .3197 \qquad a = 8.54 - (.3197)(14.48) = 3.91$$

Line of regression: **y** = 3.91 + 0.320x.

d)

e)

$$S_e = \sqrt{\frac{9.872 - (.3197)(22.854)}{3}} = \sqrt{.855} = .9248 \ \blacklozenge$$

when x = 20 percent the line of regression predicts :
$$y_p = 3.92 + 0.3197\,(\mathbf{20}) = 10.314 \text{ thousand dollars } \blacklozenge$$

$$E = 1.638\,(.9248)\sqrt{1 + \frac{1}{5} + \frac{(20 - 14.44)^2}{71.488}} = 1.638\,(.9248)\sqrt{1.632} = 1.9354$$

f)   Left boundary = 10.314 - 1.9354 = 8.378
Right boundary = 10.314 + 1.9354 = 12.249
We are 80% sure that when x =20 percent, y is between $8,378 and $12,249 $\blacklozenge$

5a) and c)

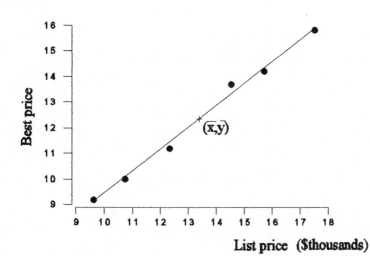

x	y	xy	x^2	y^2
9.6	9.2	88.32	92.16	84.64
10.7	10	107.00	114.49	100.00
12.3	11.2	137.76	151.29	125.44
14.5	13.7	198.65	210.25	187.69
15.7	14.2	222.94	246.49	201.64
17.5	15.8	276.50	306.25	249.64
80.3	74.1	1,031.17	1,120.93	949.05

$\Sigma x = 80.3$ $\bar{x} = 13.3833$ $(\Sigma x)^2 = 6448.09$

$\Sigma y = 74.1$ $\bar{y} = 12.35$ $(\Sigma y)^2 = 5490.81$

$\Sigma xy = 1031.17$ $\Sigma x^2 = 1120.93$ $\Sigma y^2 = 949.05$

$$SS_{xy} = 1031.17 - \frac{(80.3)(74.1)}{6} = 39.465$$

$$SS_x = 1120.93 - \frac{(80.3)^2}{6} = 43.24833$$

$$SS_y = 949.05 - \frac{(74.1)^2}{6} = 33.915$$

b) $\bar{x} = 13.3833$ $\bar{y} = 12.35$ $b = \dfrac{39.465}{46.24833} = .853$

    $a = 12.35 - (.85333)(13.3833) = .930$

Line of regression: **y = .930 + .853x** ♦

d)

$$S_e = \sqrt{\frac{33.915 - (.85333)(39.465)}{4}} = \sqrt{.05958} = .2441$$

e)   when x = 16.5 the line of regression predicts y_p = .930 + .853(16.5) = 15.0045 ♦

$$E = 2.776(.2441)\sqrt{1 + \frac{1}{6} + \frac{(16.5 - 13.383)^2}{43.2483}} = 2.776(.2441)\sqrt{1.39132} = .799$$

f)   Left boundary = 15.0045 - .799 = 14.2055

    Right boundary = 15.0045 + .799 = 15.8035

We are 95% sure that when x =16.5, y is between 14.183and 15.827 ♦

9.a) and c)

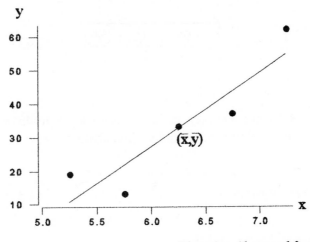

Elevation (thousand feet)

x	y	xy	x^2	y^2
5.25	19	99.75	27.5625	361
5.75	13	74.75	33.0625	169
6.25	33	206.25	39.0625	1,089
6.75	37	249.75	45.5625	1,369
7.25	62	449.50	52.5625	3,844
31.25	164	1080.00	197.8125	6,832

$\Sigma x = 31.25$ $\bar{x} = 6.25$ $(\Sigma x)^2 = 976.5625$

$\Sigma y = 164$ $\bar{y} = 32.8$ $(\Sigma y)^2 = 26896$

$\Sigma xy = 1080$ $\Sigma x^2 = 197.8125$ $\Sigma y^2 = 6832$

$$SS_{xy} = 1080 - \frac{(31.25)(164)}{5} = 55$$

$$SS_x = 197.8125 - \frac{(31.25)^2}{5} = 2.5$$

$$SS_y = 6832 - \frac{(164)^2}{5} = 1452.8$$

$$b = \frac{55}{2.5} = 22 \qquad a = 32.8 - 22(6.25) = -104.7$$

Line of regression: **y = -104.7 + 22.0x**♦

d)

$$S_e = \sqrt{\frac{1452.8 - (22)(55)}{3}} = \sqrt{80.933} = 8.996♦$$

e)   when x = 6.5 thousand feet the line of regression predicts y_p = -104.7 + 22(6.5) = 38.3 as the percentage of culturally unidentified artifacts. ♦

$$E = 1.423(8.996)\sqrt{1 + \frac{1}{5} + \frac{(6.5 - 6.25)^2}{2.5}} = 1.423(8.996)\sqrt{1.225} = 14.168$$

f)   Left boundary = 38.3 - 14.168 = 24.132
Right boundary = 38.3 + 14.168 = 52.468
We are 75% sure that when x = 6.5 thousand feet, y = the percentage of culturally unidentified artifacts is between 24.132 and 52.468 ♦

13.a) and c)

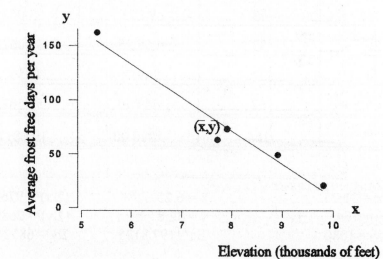

x	y	xy	x^2	y^2
5.3	162	858.60	28.0900	26,244
7.7	63	485.10	59.2900	3,969
7.9	73	576.70	62.4100	5,329
8.9	49	436.10	79.2100	2,401
9.8	21	205.80	96.0400	441
39.6	368	2562.30	325.0400	38,384

$\Sigma x = 39.6$ $\bar{x} = 7.92$ $(\Sigma x)^2 = 1568.16$

$\Sigma y = 368$ $\bar{y} = 73.6$ $(\Sigma y)^2 = 135424$

$\Sigma xy = 2562.3$ $\Sigma x^2 = 325.04$ $\Sigma y^2 = 38384$

$$SS_{xy} = 2562.3 - \frac{(39.6)(368)}{5} = -352.26$$

$$SS_x = 325.04 - \frac{(39.6)^2}{5} = 11.408$$

$$SS_y = 38384 - \frac{(368)^2}{5} = 11299.2$$

$$b = \frac{-352.26}{11.408} = -30.87833 \qquad a = 73.6 - (-30.878)(7.92) = 318.15376$$

Line of regression: **$y = 318.15376 - 30.87833x$** ◆

d)

$$s_e = \sqrt{\frac{11299.2 - (-30.87833)(-352.26)}{3}} = \sqrt{140.666} = 11.86029 ◆$$

e)   when x = 6 thousand feet the line of regression predicts y_p = 318.15376 - 30.87833(6) = 132.88 as the average number of frost free days per year in Colorado Springs. ◆

$$E = 1.924(11.86029)\sqrt{1 + \frac{1}{5} + \frac{(6 - 7.92)^2}{11.408}} = 1.924(11.86029)\sqrt{1.52314} = 28.159$$

f)   Left boundary = 132.88 - 28.159 = 104.72

Right boundary =132.88 + 28.159 = 161.039
We are 85% sure that when x =6 thousand feet, y = the average number of frost free days
in Colorado Springs is between 104.72 and 161.04

Answers to Thinking About Statistics

1.   The regression formula gives the following results:

x	-.26x + 28.62 y$_p$	
63	-.26(63)+28.62	12.24
93	-.26(93)+28.62	4.44
23	-.26(23)+28.62	27.08
3	-.26(3) +28.62	49.72

Predictions obtained by the regression formula are only meaningful when the values of x are
within (or close to) the range of values of x in the study. In the problem, the values of x
went from 20 to 60. When substituting 63 or 23 for x the predictions for y are meaningful.
However, the values of x = 93 and x = 3 give misleading results. It is not reasonable to
expect to travel at either of these averages, anyway. Note that if you substitute a value for
x such as 123, you would get a negative value for y. This would be mathematically correct,
but would have no meaning in the physical world.

2.   The sign of SS_{xy} and the sign of b are always the same. Thus if your scatter drawing
indicates a line that is falling from left to right (negative slope) the value of SS_{xy} will also be
negative. When your scatter diagram shows a positive slope the value of SS_{xy} will be
positive as well.

Section 10.3
The Linear Correlation Coefficient

Review

In this section we will answer the question "how well do the data points fit the line of regression?"

I.   The Standard Error of Estimate
- A.   As discussed in the last section S_e is a way of measuring how the data is "spread out" from the regression line.
  1.   Larger values of S_e indicate more scatter in the points.
  2.   It is measured in the same units as the y value.
  3.   It is not always possible to compare values of S_e from different studies.

II.   The *Correlation Coefficient, r*
- A.   Always a number between -1 and +1.
  1.   A value of r = 1 indicates a perfect positive correlation as in x= degrees Fahrenheit and y = degrees Centigrade.
  2.   A value of r = -1 indicates a perfect negative correlation as in x = distance you have already travelled on a trip and y = the remaining distance.
  3.   A value of r =0 indicated no linear correlation as in x = height and y = I.Q.
  4.   Values close to 1 or close to -1 indicate a good fit.
  5.   Values close to 0 indicate a poor fit.
- B.   The correlation coefficient, r, has no units so the values of r from different studies can be compared.
- C.   Formula for r:

$$r = \frac{SS_{xy}}{\sqrt{SS_x \cdot SS_y}}$$

  1.   Note that the values of SS_x, SS_{xy}, and SS_y can be obtained when calculating the formula for the line of regression.
  2.   The sign of r will be the same as the sign of SS_{xy} which is the same as the sign of the slope of the regression line.

III.   *Coefficient of Determination, r^2*
- A.   When the value of x is unknown, the mean of y is the best predictor of a value of y.
  1.   Let $\bar{y}$ be a base line for the y values.
- B.   The regression line predicts y_p = bx +a for y when x is known.
- C.   The value of y on the data point is usually different from either of these.
- D.   Deviations
  1. $y - \bar{y}$ is the TOTAL DEVIATION. (Difference between y value on data point and the mean of y.)
  2. $y_p - \bar{y}$ is the EXPLAINED DEVIATION. (Difference between the y value on the line and the mean of y. This difference can be attributed to the properties of x, the explanatory variable.)
  3. $y - y_p$ is the UNEXPLAINED DEVIATION. (Changes in the value of y which are due to factors other than those attributed to x.)

$$r^2 = \frac{\text{Explained Variation}}{\text{Total Variation}}$$

E. r^2 is the coefficient of determination.
   1.   It gives the ratio of explained variation to total variation, the proportion of change in the y value from $\bar{y}$ which can be attributed to the properties of x.
   2.   It computed by :
       a.   Finding r the correlation coefficient.
       b.   Squaring the value of r.

Problem Solving Warm-Up

The manufacturer of XJJ sports model of the Wego car has collected data on the average speed (x) on a trip and the miles per gallon (y) for a randomly selected sample of 9 car owners. Compute the correlation coefficient r and the coefficient of determination r^2. What percent of the variation in y can be <u>explained by the corresponding variation in x</u>? What percent of the variation in y is <u>unexplained</u>?

x (mph)	y (mpg)
20	22
25	21
30	20
35	23
40	19
45	18
50	16
55	14
60	11

x (mph)	y (mpg)	xy	x^2	y^2
20	22	440	400	484
25	21	525	625	441
30	20	600	900	400
35	23	805	1,225	529
40	19	760	1,600	361
45	18	810	2,025	324
50	16	800	2,500	256
55	14	770	3,025	196
60	11	660	3,600	121
360.00	164.00	6,170	15,900	3,112

$$SS_{xy} = 6170 - \frac{(360)(164)}{9} = -390$$

$$SS_x = 15900 - (360)^2/9 = 1500$$

$$SS_y = 3112 - (164)^2/9 = 123.56$$

$$r = \frac{-390}{\sqrt{(1500)(123.56)}} = -.91$$

The coefficient of determination is $(-.91)^2 = .82$.

82% of the variation in gas consumption can be explained by the average speed of the car.

18% of the variation in gas consumption is unexplained by speed. Some other factors might be whether driving is done on a highway or in a city, or the type of driver.

Thinking About Statistics

It has been found that there is an extremely high correlation between the amount of ice cream consumed in a given week with the number of people who drown during that week at the New Jersey shore. Therefore we can conclude that buying ice cream is a cause of drowning.

Discuss what is wrong with the reasoning behind the previous statement.

Selected Solutions Section 10.3

1.   a)   No, not unless they are so large that they block the view of the driver.
      b)   An increase in the population of South Dakota would result in more accidents as well as more safety stickers being issued.

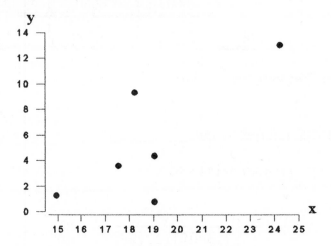

5. The correlation coefficient appears to be closer to 1. The line that would best approximate the data would have a positive slope.

x	y	xy	x^2	y^2
24.2	13.0	314.60	585.64	169.00
19	4.4	83.60	361.00	19.36
18.2	9.3	169.26	331.24	86.49
14.9	1.3	19.37	222.01	1.69
19	0.8	15.20	361.00	0.64
17.5	3.6	63.00	306.25	12.96
112.80	32.40	665.03	2167.14	290.14

$$SS_{xy} = 665.03 - \frac{(112.80)(32.40)}{6} = 55.91$$

$$SS_x = 2167.14 - \frac{(112.80)^2}{6} = 46.5$$

$$SS_y = 290.14 - \frac{(32.40)^2}{6} = 115.18$$

$$r = \frac{55.91}{\sqrt{(46.5)(115.18)}} = .764$$

The coefficient of determination is $(.764)^2 = .584$.

58.4% of the variation in violent crimes can be explained by the variation in the percentage of 16 to 19 year olds not in school and not high school graduates.

The remaining 42.6% of the variation in violent crimes is unexplained by the percent of 16 to 19 year olds not in school and not high school graduates.

9 . The correlation coefficient appears to be closer to -1. The line that would best approximate the data would have a negative slope.

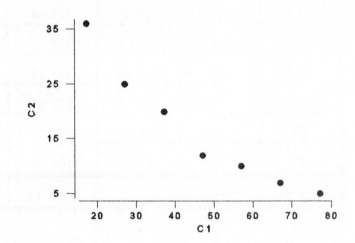

x	y	xy	x^2	y^2
17	36	612	289	1,296
27	25	675	729	625
37	20	740	1,369	400
47	12	564	2,209	144
57	10	570	3,249	100
67	7	469	4,489	49
77	5	385	5,929	25
329	115	4,015	18,263	2,639

$$SS_{xy} = 4015 - \frac{(329)(115)}{7} = -1390$$

$$SS_x = 18263 - \frac{(329)^2}{7} = 2800$$

$$SS_y = 2639 - \frac{(115)^2}{7} = 749.714$$

$$r = \frac{-1390}{\sqrt{(2800)(749.714)}} = -.959$$

The coefficient of determination is $(-.959)^2 = .92$.

92% of the variation in the percentage of all fatal accidents for a given age can be explained by the variation in the age of a licensed automobile driver.

8% of the variation is unexplained. ♦

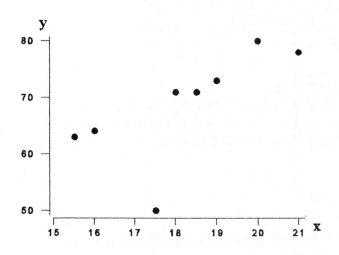

13. The correlation coefficient appears to be closer to 1. The line that would best approximate the data would have a positive slope.

x	y	xy	x^2	y^2
17.5	50	875.0	306.25	2,500
20	80	1600.0	400.00	6,400
21	78	1638.0	441.00	6,084
19	73	1387.0	361.00	5,329
15.5	63	976.5	240.25	3,969
18.5	71	1313.5	342.25	5,041
16	64	1024.0	256.00	4,096
18	71	1278.0	324.00	5,041
145.50	550	10092.0	2670.75	38,460

$$SS_{xy} = 10092 - \frac{(145.50)(550)}{8} = 88.875$$

$$SS_x = 2670.75 - \frac{(145.50)^2}{8} = 24.469$$

$$SS_y = 38460 - \frac{(550)^2}{8} = 647.5$$

$$r = \frac{88.875}{\sqrt{(24.469)(647.5)}} = .706$$

The coefficient of determination is $(.706)^2 = .499$.

49.9% of the variation in body height can be explained by the length of the femur.

50.1% of the variation in body height is unexplained by the length of the femur. Some other factors might be that of a person's eating habits or length of torso etc. ♦

Answers to Thinking About Statistics

The correlation coefficient tells us how well a set of data points fit a line. Thus if we knew how much ice cream was consumed for the week, we probably would be able to predict fairly accurately, the number of people who drown. However, this does not imply that ice cream consumption causes drowning. Always be on the alert for variables which might be a common cause for both. In this case, when the weather is hot, more people will buy ice cream and more people will go swimming.

Section 10.4
Testing the Correlation Coefficient

Review

In the last section we saw how r was computed from a sample of data points.

I.   The meaning of ρ, the population correlation coefficient.

     A.   When we compute the sample statistic r, we are really interested in the population parameter, ρ (Greek letter rho).

     B. ρ is the correlation coefficient which would be obtained if all the data points in the population could be obtained.

II.   How do we know if the value of r we computed from our sample, is close enough to -1 or to 1 to indicated a significant correlation?

    A.   Run a hypothesis test about the parameter ρ, using r as your test statistic.

        1.   Set up a pair of hypotheses.

            a. H_0: $\rho = 0$ NO SIGNIFICANT CORRELATION

            b.   Choose an alternate hypothesis H_1

                (1) $\rho > 0$ Use a right tail test if you claim a positive correlation.

                (2) $\rho < 0$ Use a left tail test if you claim a negative correlation.

                (3) $\rho \neq 0$ Use a two tail test if you believe there is a correlation but are not sure of the direction.

        2.   Assume H_0 is true. That is there is no significant correlation.

        3.   Based on this assumption, there will be a distribution of values of r. This distribution is symmetric and mound shaped with a mean at $r = 0$.

        4.   The critical values r_0 for r are found in a table in Appendix I of your text.

            a.   Critical value depends on the level of significance.

            b.   Critical value depends on the number of data pairs in your sample.

    B.   Making the decision

        1.   If your sample statistic r falls in the critical region, reject H_0. This will indicate *there is a significant correlation.*

        2.   If your sample statistic r falls in the acceptance region, accept H_0. This will indicate that *there is NO significant correlation.*

Problem Solving Warm-Up

In the last section we obtained a value of r = -.91 from the sample of 9 cars of the XJJ model of the Wego car. Is this a significant negative correlation at the .01 level?

Set up a pair of hypotheses:

H_0 : _____

H_1 : _____

H_0: $\rho = 0$ (no correlation)

H_1: $\rho < 0$ (a negative correlation)

The level of significance is:

_____

$\alpha = .01$

Assume H_0 is true and determine the critical value from the table:

_____

Look under one tail, n = 9 and find .75. We use $r_0 = -.75$ since this is a left tail test.

Sketch the r distribution, placing the mean, the critical value and finally, the statistic in appropriate order.

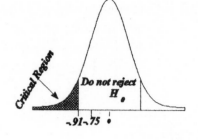

Your decision: _____

Since the test statistic of r = -.91 is in t h e critica l region, it is correct to reject H_0. Our conclusion is that there IS a significant correlation.

Thinking About Statistics

Analyze what happens to the critical value of r as n, the number of pairs increases.

Selected Solutions Section 10.4

1. H_0: $\rho = 0$ H_1: $\rho > 0$ Use a right tail test ♦
      $\alpha = .05$ $n = 10$
      $r_0 = .54$ ♦
The test statistic r= .384 does not fall in the critical region. There is not enough evidence to reject the null hypothesis and we conclude there is no significant positive correlation. ♦

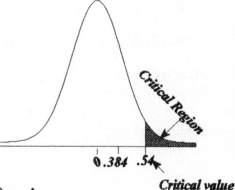

Critical value

5. H_0: $\rho = 0$ H_1: $\rho < 0$ ♦
      $\alpha = .05$ $n = 10$

$r_0 = -.54$ ♦
The test statistic r= -.766 falls in the critical region. Therefore we reject H_0 and choose the hypothesis that there is a significant negative correlation. ♦

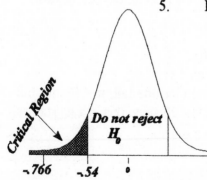

9. $H_0: \rho = 0$ $H_1: \rho > 0$ ♦
       $\alpha = .01$ $n = 30$

       $r_0 = .42$ ♦
       The test statistic $r = .982$ falls in the critical region. Therefore we reject H_0 and conclude there is a significant positive correlation. ♦

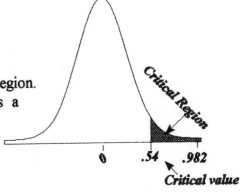

Answers to Thinking About Statistics

As the number of pairs *increases,* the critical value *decreases.* The more ordered pairs there are the less evidence we need to be able to reject H_0: $\rho = 0$. When there are only 3 pairs, we need a statistic of $r = 1$ (or $r = -1$) before we can reject H_0. In other words, with three pairs, unless all three points are on a line we will accept H_0 that there is no correlation. With 20 pairs we only need a statistic of .52 or more in a right tail .01 level test in order to reject H_0 and conclude that the correlation is significant. If we have 30 or more pairs there is an even lower critical value of .42 for the same type of test. This means if we get a value of $r = .42$ or more as our statistic with 30 pairs, we can reject H_0 and conclude that there is a significant correlation.

Section 10.5
Multiple Regression

Review

In the last section we saw how one variable, x, might be used to predict another variable, y. Since it is often more accurate to use several variables to predict a response variable, we will look at techniques by which this can be done.

I.   **Multiple Regression**
       A.   Uses several explanatory variables to predict a response variable.
       B.   Formulas are complicated so we will focus on the outputs a computer would produce using a multiple regression program. In this discussion, we will use the Minitab software program, but others such as SPSS, SAS or Systat (Mystat) would do as well. ComputerStat is another program that can be used.
       C.   To use multiple regression for predicting a response variable

1. Identify one of the variables in your study as the response variable. We will call it x_1 as ComputerStat does. (Minitab will label it as y.)
2. The remaining variables will be called explanatory variables and will be labeled x_2, x_3, x_4, and so on.
3. Enter your data as instructed by the program.
4. Examine the output of the program.
    a. b_0 is called the constant. It is the value of the response variable when all the other variables are valued at 0.
    b. b_2 is the coefficient for the explanatory variable x_2. It can be thought of as a slope. If we hold all other explanatory variables constant and change the value of x_2 by one unit, the value of x_1, the response variable will change by the amount b_2.
    c. b_3 is the coefficient of the explanatory variable x_3, b_4 is the coefficient of x_4 and so on. There is no limit to the number of explanatory variables you could have.
5. Multiple Regression equation

$$x_1 = b_0 + b_2 x_2 + b_3 x_3 + b_4 x_4 + \ldots b_n x_n$$

6. To use the equation to predict a value for x_1 when you are given specific values for each of the explanatory variables, multiply the value of each explanatory variable by its coefficient. Add the constant b_0 to the sum of all the products of the explanatory variables times their coefficients.

II. Confidence Interval for the coefficient of a specific explanatory variable, say x_3.
   A.   The point estimate is given by the value b_3 in the computer printout.
   B.   Compute E, the error from $E = t \cdot S_3$.
       1.   t is in the t-distribution table. d.f. = number of data points - number of explanatory variables - 1.
       2. S_3, the standard error for x_3, will be listed in the printout.
   C.   The left endpoint for the confidence interval will be b_3-E and the right endpoint will be $b_3 + E$.

III. Does a particular variable actually provide useful information which "explains" x_1, the response variable?
   A.   Use a hypothesis test.
       1. H_0: $\beta_3 = 0$ (the population coefficient is zero and the variable x_3 is of no value in predicting x_1)
       2. H_1: $\beta_3 \neq 0$ (the population coefficient is not zero and hence can be used to predict x_1.)

324

3. Use a t distribution with d.f. = (number of data points) -(number of explanatory variables) - 1.
4. The critical values for the statistic b_3 are given by $\pm t S_3$.
5. Make your decision.
    a. Accept H_0 if the sample coefficient b_3 is in the acceptance area. This means the variable x_3 is not influencing the response variable x_1 and should probably be omitted from the study.
    b. Reject H_0 if the sample coefficient b_3 is in the critical area. This means the variable x_3 has a significant effect on x_1.

Problem Solving Warm-Up

Several years ago a study was conducted at a large company in order to determine if the salary structure at the company was a fair one. (A fair salary would be one that it influenced by factors of experience and educational background and not by factors such as who hired the person, when they were hired or their gender.)

An individual's current salary was identified as the response variable, x_1.

Explanatory variables were:
  x_2 = The number of years with the company.
  x_3 = The number of years of experience prior to working at the company.
  x_4 = The years of education after high school.

A random sample of 10 individuals produced the following data:

No.	x_1	x_2	x_3	x_4
1	38,985	18	7	9
2	28,938	12	35	4
3	32,920	15	3	9
4	34,708	16	6	6
5	31,138	11	11	6
6	26,184	6	30.5	6
7	41,889	22	16	6
8	36,073	16	11	6
9	38,791	21	4	6
10	39,828	18	6	6

The following output was obtained from Minitab

```
The regression equation is
x1 = 19396 + 966 x2 - 27.5 x3 + 146 x4

Predictor        Coef        Stdev       t-ratio         p
Constant        19396         5750          3.37     0.015
x2              965.9         166.2          5.81     0.001
x3             -27.49         88.33         -0.31     0.766
x4              145.9         528.5          0.28     0.792

s = 1825       R-sq = 91.5%     R-sq(adj) = 87.3%
```

1.   Identify the constant b_0.

    _____

2.   Identify the coefficient for x_2.

    _____

1.   19395 This would be the predicated salary for a person with no education after high school and no job experience.

2.   966 If all other factors were held constant and the person had one more year of experience with the company, this would be the increase in his salary.

3.   Identify the coefficient for x_3.

_____

3.   -27.49. Evidently, more years of prior experience tends to decrease a salary.

4.   Identify the coefficient for x_4.

_____

4.   145.90.

5.   Write the regression equation

_____

5. $x_1 = 19395.84 + 965.94x_2 - 27.49x_3 + 145.90x_4$

6.   Use the regression equation to predict a person's salary with 9 years at the company, 6 years of prior experience and 6 years of post high school education.

_____

6. $x1 = 19396 + 966 (9) - 27.5 (6) + 146 (6)_1 27.49(6) + 145(6) = \$28,800$.

7.   Use the regression equation to predict a person's salary with 14 years at the company, 17 years prior experience and 6 years of post high school education.

_____

7. $x1 = 19396 + 966 (14) 27.5(17) + 146 (6) = \$33,372$

Thinking About Statistics

The difference between the actual value of x_1 and the value predicted by the regression equation x_{1p} or $x_1 - x_{1p}$ is called the residual.

1.   The individual from problem 6 of the problem solving warm-up has a salary of 27235. Compute the residual.

2.   The individual from problem 7 has a salary of 36007. Compute the residual.

Selected Solutions Section 10.5

1.   a)   The response variable is x_1. The explanatory variables are x_2, x_3, and x_4. ◆
      b)   The constant term is 1.6. Note that if 0 were substituted for each of the three explanatory variables, the value of x_1 would be 1.6. ◆

variable	coefficient
x_2	3.5
x_3	-7.9
x_4	2.0

      c)   Substituting the given values of the explanatory variables into the linear regression equation we get: $x_1 = 1.6 + (3.5)(2) + (-7.9)(1) + (2)(5) = 10.7$ ◆

      d)   If x_3 and x_4 were held at fixed values and x_2 increased by one unit, x_1 would increase by 3.5 units. ◆
             If x_2 were increased by two units x_1 would increase by 2(3.5)=7 units. ◆
             If x_2 were decreased by four units, x_1 would *decrease* by 14 units. ◆
      e)   The point estimate for the coefficient of x_2 is 3.5. $E = tS_2$.
             12 data points - 3 explanatory variables -1 → 8 degrees of freedom.
             t = 1.860 for c = .90, so E = (1.860)(.419) = .78.
             The left boundary of the confidence interval is 3.5 - .78 = 2.72. ◆
             The right boundary of the confidence interval is 3.5 + .78 = 4.28. ◆
      f) H_0: $\beta_2 = 0$ (Population coefficient for x_2 is zero.)
             H_1: $\beta_2 \neq 0$ (Population coefficient is not zero.)
             The t distribution for this test has 8 d.f.. The t value for the test statistic is

$$\frac{b_2}{s_2} = \frac{3.5}{.419} = 8.35 \text{ and the critical values for the statistic } \pm 2.306$$

             The test statistic t = 8.35 falls in the right tail critical region, therefore we reject H_0 The conclusion is that the variable x_2 is significant in explaining the response variable x_1. ◆

5.   We get the following information with Minitab.

	MEAN	STDEV	CV
x1	85.2	33.8	39.67
x2	8.74	3.89	44.51
x3	4.900	2.480	50.61
x4	9.92	5.17	52.11

328

Minitab will output the mean and standard deviation. To compute the coefficient of variation for each variable, divide the standard deviation by the mean and multiply by 100.

Using Minitab the following is part of the output of the regression command.

The regression equation is
x1 = 7.68 + 3.66 x2 + 7.62 x3 + 0.828 x4

```
Predictor          Coef        Stdev        t-ratio          p
Constant          7.676        6.760          1.14      0.299
x2                3.662        1.118          3.28      0.017
x3                7.621        1.657          4.60      0.004
x4               0.8285       0.5394          1.54      0.175

s = 7.541        R-sq = 96.7%        R-sq(adj) = 95.0%
```

The following table gives the correlation coefficient for each pair of variables
MTB > Correlation 'x1'-'x4'.

```
              x1          x2          x3
x2         0.917
x3         0.930       0.790
x4         0.475       0.429       0.299
```

To get the coefficient of determination, square each entry.

The following answers have been obtained using ComputerStat. If you use Minitab the answers will be slightly different due to rounding off.

b)   Relative to its mean, x_4 has the largest spread of data values since its coefficient of variation is 52.15. The coefficient of variation is computed by dividing the standard deviation by the mean and multiplying by 100. Thus a large mean such as 85.24 for x_2 relative to the standard deviation, would produce a smaller CV. ♦

c) x_4 has the least influence on receipts since the coefficient of determination of this variable is .2253. 84% of the variation in box office receipts can be attributed to the corresponding variation in production costs. ♦

d)   The coefficient of multiple determination is .9668. this means 96.68% of the variation in box office receipts can be explained by the combination of the other three variables.♦

e)   The regression equation is: $x_1 = 7.67 + 3.66x_2 + 7.62x_3 + .83x_4$. When all other costs are held fixed and x_3, promotional costs is increased by 1 million dollars, box office receipts, x_1 should increase by 7.62 million dollars. ♦

f)   Test the null hypotheses: $_H0$: $\beta_2 = 0$, $\beta_3 = 0$ and $\beta_4 = 0$.

Use a t distribution with 6 d.f. t= ±2.447. Critical values for t = ±2.447. The t value for the test statistic b_2 is $t = \dfrac{3.6616}{1.1178} = 3.275$ is in the critical region so we reject $H_0 : \beta_2 = 0$ and

conclude x_2 contributes information to x_1.

The t test statistic for b_3 is 7.6210/1.6573 = 4.599 which is in the critical region, so we conclude x_3 contributes information about x_1.

The t test statistic for b_4 is .8285/.5394 = 1.536 is in the acceptance region. We conclude that x_4 is probably not contributing much information about x_1. ♦

g)   The 85% confidence interval for β_2 is between 1.49 to 5.83. For β_3 4.40 to 10.84 and for β_4, 0 to 1.88. (We wouldn't allow for negative values here.

h) x_1 = 7.67 + 3.66(11.4) + 7.62(4.7) + .83(8.1) = 91.93 million dollars. The confidence interval is 77.56 to 106.33♦

h)   The forecast value for x_3 = 5.63 million dollars. The interval is 4.21 to 7.04 ♦

Answers to Thinking About Statistics

1.   The individual with a salary of 27235 had a residual: 27235-28799.74 = -1564.

2.   The individual with a salary of 36007 had a residual: 36007-33326.99 = 2680.

When the value of x_1 is greater than the value of x_{1p}, we say there is a positive residual and their actual salary is higher than what is predicted by the regression equation. When the value of x_1 (the actual value) is less than the predicted value, we say there is a negative residual. Individuals with negative residuals ar earning less than the regression formula predicts is fair.

In the company that did the study on salary fairness, a salary adjustment was given to all those individuals who had negative residuals. Since computations are done with a computer, the actual number of data points in a study can be as large as necessary.

Chapter 11

CHI-SQUARE AND F DISTRIBUTIONS

Section 11.1
Chi Square: Tests of Independence

<u>*Review*</u>

I.   Independence of Variables
   A.   In Chapter 4 we learned that if two variables A and B are **independent**, the occurrence (or non-occurrence of A) does *not* affect the probability of the occurrence of B.
       1.   If we flip a coin and roll a die, we know intuitively that whether or not the coin lands on "tails" the probability of the die landing on a 4 is 1/6 therefore "coin is tails" and "die is a four" are independent events.
       2.   Conversely, if we draw two cards from a deck of 52 without replacing the first, the probability of getting a king on the second card is dependent on whether or not the first card was a king. "King on first card" and "king on second card" are *not* independent events.
       3.   In the real world, independence of variables is not obvious.
           a.   Does sugar have an effect on the behavior or delinquent boys.
           b.   Should you hire a male or a female for a managerial position? (Are job performance and gender independent?)
           c.   Would you rather buy a car which is assembled on a Tuesday than on a Friday? (Is the day of the week independent of the quality of the product manufactured that day?)
           d.   Does drinking coffee place a person at a greater risk of a heart attack? (Is having a heart attack independent of drinking coffee?)

II.   Several important statistical tests, including a test for independence of variables, use a probability distribution known as **chi square**, denoted χ^2.

A. χ^2 is a family of distributions. The graph of the χ^2 distribution depends on the number of degrees of freedom (number of free choices) in a statistical experiment.

B.   The χ^2 distributions are not symmetric.

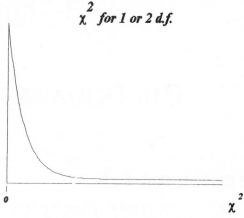

1.   With 1 or 2 d.f. the shape is:

2.   With 3 or more d.f. the shape is shown at the right.

3.   The peak of the curve occurs at n-2 d.f.

4.   As the number of d.f. increases the χ^2 curves look more like a normal distribution.

C.   Critical χ^2 values are found in the χ^2 table in the Appendix.

1.   Entries under $\alpha = .050$ (fourth column from the right) represent the χ^2 value such that 5% of the area under the curve falls to the right of that value. For example: In a distribution with 5 d.f., 5% of the area will fall to the right of $\chi^2 = 11.07$.

2.   Entries under $\alpha = .010$ (second column from the right) represent the χ^2 value such that 1% of the curve falls to its right.

III.   Test for independence of variables

A.   Categorize each member of the sample for the first variable and then for the second.

B.   Construct a **contingency table** entering the number of members from the sample which correspond to each cell. The number in each cell obtained from the sample is called the **observed value** of that cell.

C. We will use a hypothesis test:
1. H_0 : The variables are independent
2. H_1 : The variables are dependent

D. Assume that H_0 is true (variables are independent) and compute the **expected frequency E** for each cell by the following:

$$E = sample\ total \cdot P(A) \cdot P(B)$$

1. A is the trait in the row containing the cell.
2. B is the trait in the column containing the cell.

$$E = sample\ total \cdot \frac{(total\ of\ row\ A)}{sample\ total} \cdot \frac{(total\ of\ column\ B)}{sample\ total}$$

Which can be simplified to:

$$E = \frac{(total\ of\ row) \cdot (total\ of\ column)}{sample\ total}$$

3. Compute the value of E for each cell. Note that since the totals for E must equal the totals for the **observed frequency, 0,** it is not necessary to use the above formula to determine the last entry for each row or the last entry for in each column. These values should be obtained by adding the E values obtained for that row (or column) and subtracting from the total value of O in that row (or column).
4. The χ^2 square test for independence is valid only when each value of E is 5 or more. If you determine a value of E to be less than 5, you may have to get a larger sample.

E. Compute the χ^2 statistic:

$$\chi^2 = \sum \frac{(O-E)^2}{E}$$

1. Find the difference between the O and the E values of each cell.
2. Square each difference to eliminate negative values.

3.   Divide by E to have a measure relative to the size of the expected value. A difference of 2 is a large difference when E = 7, however when E = 1000, a difference of 2 is relatively small.

4.   Take the sum of these quotients.

F.   Find the critical value for χ^2, denoted χ^2_α.

1.   Use the χ^2 distribution with
d.f. = (number of rows -1)(number of columns -1).

2.   Appropriate value will be found under $\alpha = .010$ or $.050$.

G.   Sketch the appropriate χ^2 distribution.

1.   Locate χ^2_α and shade the critical region which, for tests of independence, will be the region to the right of the critical value.

2.   Place your χ^2 statistic in the appropriate region.

H.   Make your decision.

1.   If the χ^2 statistic falls in the critical region, reject H_0 and conclude that the variables are dependent.

2.   If the χ^2 statistic falls in the acceptance region, fail to reject H_0 and conclude that the variables are independent. Any differences between the observed values and the expected values are due to sampling differences.

Problem Solving Warm-Up

1.   Determine the number of degrees of freedom for a test of independence of variables using a contingency table of:

a)   4 rows and 5 columns   a) $(4-1)(5-1) = 3(4) = 12$ d.f.

_____

b)   3 rows and 8 columns   b) $(3-1)(8-1) = 2(7) = 14$ d.f.

_____

2.   The following table reflects the job performance evaluation of 150 newly hired business majors by Ameritech Corporation according to the gender of the employee. Test the claim that job performance is independent of gender at $\alpha = .01$ level of significance.

Job Performance

	Low	Average	Superior	Total
Male	15	60	25	100
Female	10	35	5	50
Total	25	95	30	150

The values in the table above represent the observed or O values from the sample.

Formulate the hypotheses.

H_0 : _____ H_0 : Gender and Job Performance are
_____   independent

H_1 : _____ H_1 : Gender and job performance are
_____   dependent.

Assume that H_0 is true and calculate the expected values for each cell.

For cell 1 (low and male) $(100)(25) \div 150$ =   16.67
For cell 2 (average and male) $(100)(95) \div 150$ =   66.33

The remaining expected values for each cell can be calculated by subtracting the computed values from the given totals. The expected values for each cell are shown in the table below.

Job Performance

	Low	Average	Superior	Total
Male	16.67	63.33	20	100
Female	8.33	31.67	10.00	50
Total	25	95	30	150

Construct a table to compute the χ^2 statistic: Fill in the missing entries.

O	E	O-E	(O-E)²	(O-E)²/E
15	16.67	-1.67	2.79	.17
60	63.33			
25	20			
10	8.33			
35	31.67			
5	10			
150.00	150.00			

Check your answers:

O	E	O-E	(O-E)²	(O-E)²/E
15	16.67	-1.67	2.79	0.17
60	63.33	-3.33	11.09	0.18
25	20	5.00	25.00	1.25
10	8.33	1.67	2.79	0.33
35	31.67	3.33	11.09	0.35
5	10	-5.00	25.00	2.50
150.00	150.00			4.78

The χ^2 statistic is _____ $\chi^2 = 4.78$ (computation in last column)

d.f. = _____   d.f.$=(2-1)(3-1)= 1(2) =2$

The critical χ^2 value is: _____ $\chi^2_{.01} = 9.21$ (from Appendix table)

Sketch the χ^2 distribution and locate
the critical region. Place the
computed value of χ^2 on the graph
and make your decision.

decision: _____

conclusion: _____

Since χ^2 is in the acceptance region, fail to reject H_0 and conclude that job performance and gender are independent variables.

4.78   9.21 χ^2

Thinking About Statistics

What would the value of χ^2 be if the value of O was equal to the expected value for every cell?

Selected Solutions

The values given are the O (observed values). Compute the expected values for each cell.
1.

O	E	O-E	(O-E)²	(O-E)²/E
20	25.81	-5.81	33.76	1.31
20	16.13	3.87	14.98	0.93
10	8.06	1.94	3.76	0.47
100	103.23	-3.23	10.43	0.10
65	64.52	0.48	0.23	0.00
35	32.25	2.75	7.56	0.23
40	30.96	9.04	81.72	2.64
15	19.35	-4.35	18.92	0.98
5	9.69	-4.69	22.00	2.27
310.00	310.00			8.93

The χ^2 distribution has $(3-1)(3-1)=2\cdot2=4$ d.f.

The χ^2 statistic is 8.93

The critical value is $\chi^2_{.05} = 9.49$

337

Since the chi-square statistic of 8.93 is less than the critical value, and is in the acceptance region, we fail to reject H_0 and conclude that salary and job satisfaction are independent. ♦

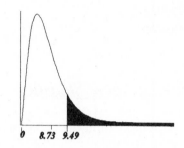

5. Since the **expected** value in the cell for "without music" and "more than 20,000" is less than 5, we do not have a large enough sample to come to a valid conclusion. When this happens we could increase the sample size. An alternate solution to this problem would be to combine categories of "10,000-20,000" and more than "20,000" to produce a single category of "more than 10,000". This would produce an expected value of 14 which would be large enough to continue with the study. ♦

9.

O	E	O-E	(O-E)²	(O-E)²/E
8	9.78	-1.78	3.17	0.32
15	16.63	-1.63	2.66	0.16
22	18.59	3.41	11.63	0.63
12	10.22	1.78	3.17	0.31
19	17.37	1.63	2.66	0.15
16	19.41	-3.41	11.63	0.60
92.00	92.00			2.17

The χ^2 distribution has $(3-1)(2-1)=2 \cdot 1 = 2$ d.f.

The critical value is $\chi^2_{.01} = 9.21$.

The χ^2 statistic is 2.17

Since the chi-square statistic of 2.17 is less than the critical value, and is in the acceptance region, we fail to reject H_0 and conclude that party affiliation and dollars spent in home districts are independent. ♦

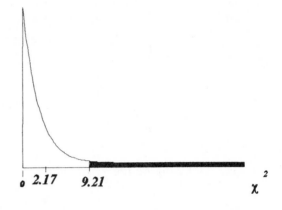

Answer to Thinking About Statistics

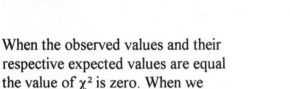

When the observed values and their respective expected values are equal the value of χ^2 is zero. When we assume the null hypothesis is true, we assume there is no difference between the observed and the expected values and that the value of χ^2 is 0. Small values of χ^2 usually can be attributed to sampling and lead to the conclusion that the variables are independent. Large values of χ^2 indicate there is a large difference between the observed values and the expected values for independent variables. A large difference will usually lead to the conclusion that the variables are dependent.

Section 11.2
Chi Square: Goodness of Fit

Review

I.   We use a χ^2 **Goodness of Fit** to test whether or not a population follows a specified probability distribution.

   A.   It can be used to determine whether changes have occurred in circumstances such as in marketing situations.

   B.   It can be used to verify or to disprove theories for genetics and medicine.

II.   Steps to follow in conducting a Goodness of Fit test.

   A.   Formulate the hypotheses:

1. H_0:   The distribution fits. (There is no change or difference).
2. H_1:   The distribution does not fit. (There has been a change.)

B.   Classify each member of the sample into one of n mutually exclusive categories and count the frequency in each category. This count represents the O or observed value for each category.

C.   Assume H_0 is true and that the distribution fits. Calculate the expected value for each category by:

$$E = \% \times total \ in \ sample$$

D.   Compute the χ^2 statistic from:

$$\chi^2 = \sum \frac{(O-E)^2}{E}$$

E.   Use a χ^2 distribution with n-1 degrees of freedom to determine the critical χ^2 value.

F.   Sketch the χ^2 distribution, shading the critical region which will be to the right of the critical value. Place your χ^2 statistic on the graph.

G.   Make your decision.
1.   Reject H_0 if your χ^2 statistic is in the critical region and conclude that the distribution does not fit the one that is proposed.
2.   Accept H_0 if your χ^2 statistic is in the acceptance region and conclude that the distribution fits.

Problem Solving Warm Up

1.   Blood types can be classified into one of four categories: A, B, O and AB.
It is believed that 40% of the population has type A, 20% of the population has type B, 30% of the population has type O and 10% has type AB. A random sample was tested for blood type and it was found that 74 had type A, 48 had type B, 53 had type O and 25 had type AB. Test at the .01 level of significance to see if the distribution fits the one proposed using a χ^2 Goodness of Fit test.

Organize the information in table form:

Type	O	%	E = %·total	O -E	(O - E)²	(O-E)²/E
A	74	.40	80.00	-6.00	36.00	0.45
B	48	.20	40.00	8.00	64.00	1.60
O	53	.30	60.00	-7.00	49.00	0.82
AB	25	.10	20.00	5.00	25.00	1.25
	200	1.00	200.00			4.12

The χ^2 statistic is:_____ $\chi^2 = 4.12$

d.f.= _____   There are 4-1 =3 d.f.

Critical Value is _____ $\chi^2_{.01} = 11.34$

Sketch the distribution, locating the critical value and the critical region. Locate the χ^2 statistic.

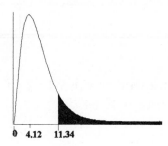

0   4.12   11.34

Decision _____   Accept H_0
The distribution fits the proposed
Conclusion_____   distribution.

Thinking About Statistics

In a Goodness of Fit test with n categories, we use the χ^2 distribution with n-1 degrees of freedom. Explain why this is a logical choice.

Selected Solutions

1.   Fill in the table as indicated. Be sure that the total in the expected column is equal to the total in the observed column.

years	O	%	E = %·total	O -E	(O - E)²	(O-E)²/E
more than 5	48	.20	40	8	64	1.60
2-5	75	.30	60	15	225	3.75
less than 2	77	.50	100	-23	529	5.29
	200	1.00	200			10.64

Use a χ^2 distribution with 3-1 =2 d.f.
The χ^2 statistic is 10.64
The critical value is 9.21.

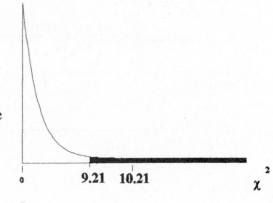

Since the χ^2 statistic falls in the critical region, we reject H_0 and conclude that there is a change in the distribution. ♦.

5.

size	O	%	E = %·total	O -E	(O - E)²	(O-E)²/E
1	15	.07	7.00	8.00	64.00	9.14
2	19	.13	13.00	6.00	36.00	2.77
3	22	.15	15.00	7.00	49.00	3.27
4	20	.25	25.00	-5.00	25.00	1.00
5	12	.28	28.00	-16.00	256.00	9.14
more than 5	12	.12	12.00	0.00	0.00	0.00
	100	1.00	100.00			25.32

The χ^2 statistic is 25.32

Use a χ^2 distribution with
6-1 =5 d.f..
The critical value is 15.09.

Since the χ^2 statistic falls in
the critical region, we
reject H_0 and conclude that
there is a change in the
distribution when the noise
level is increased by 30
decibels. ♦

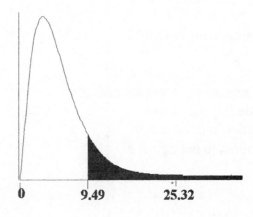

9.

Ethnic Origin	O (sample)	%	E = %·total	O -E	(O - E)²	(O-E)²/E
Black	127	.10	121.50	5.50	30.25	0.25
Asian	40	.03	36.45	3.55	12.60	0.35
Anglo	480	.38	461.70	18.30	334.89	0.73
Spanish American	502	.41	498.15	3.85	14.82	0.03
American Indian	56	.06	72.90	-16.90	285.61	3.92
others	10	.02	24.30	-14.30	204.49	8.42
	1,215.00	1.00	1,215.00			13.70

The χ^2 statistic is 13.70

Use a χ^2 distribution with 6-1 =5 d.f..
The critical value is 15.09.

Since the χ^2 statistic falls in the critical region, we reject H_0 and conclude that the census distribution and the sample distribution do not agree. ♦

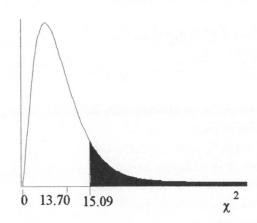

0   13.70   15.09 χ^2

Answer to Thinking About Statistics

The degrees of freedom represents the number of free choices available. The total of the expected values must be equal to the total of the observed values. After we compute n-1 of the expected values, the last one must be found by subtracting it from the total. Thus there are n-1 free choices.

Section 11.3

Testing and Estimating Variances and Standard Deviations

Review

I.   Many problems concern the variability of a specified measure.
   A.   Variability of time that a medication is effective.
   B.   Variability in waiting time on a line.
   C.   Variability in the diameter of a machine gear.

II.   We use a hypothesis test about the variance of a measure. Note that conclusions reached about the variance can be easily translated into conclusions about its square root, the standard deviation.
   A.   Formulate the pair of hypotheses:

      1.   The null hypothesis, H_0: $\sigma^2 =$ a value.   (The population variance equals some number)

      2.   Choose an alternate hypotheses
         a. H_1: $\sigma^2 \neq$ a value OR
         b. H_1: $\sigma >$ a value OR
         c. H_1: $\sigma <$ a value
   B.   Assume that values of s^2 (the sample standard deviation) are normally distributed and compute the χ^2 statistic:

$$\chi^2 = \frac{(n-1) \cdot s^2}{\sigma^2}$$

      1.   n is the number in the sample.
      2. s^2 is the variance of the sample.
      3. σ^2 is the variance of the population which is proposed in H_0.
   C.   Using the χ^2 table to compute the critical value(s).

345

1. Recall that the entries in the χ^2 table are determined by the percent of the area which falls to the *right*. To determine critical values in a right tail test use the entries as listed under the appropriate α.

2. To determine the critical value in a left tail, use the entry under the value of 1-α. Thus for a left tail test with α = .05, the critical value for χ^2 will be found under the column headed by 1-.05 = .95. (It makes sense that if we need a value such that 5% of the area falls to the left of it, we can determine this value from the fact that it is the same as the one such that 95% falls to its *right*.)

3. For two tail tests compute $\frac{\alpha}{2}$ to determine the area in each tail. Read directly under the number $\frac{\alpha}{2}$ determined for the right tail value and read under the column headed by $1 - \frac{\alpha}{2}$ for the left tail value.

D. Sketch the appropriate χ^2 distribution, shading the critical region(s). Place the χ^2 statistic on the graph.

E. Make your decision.

　　1. Reject H_0 if the χ^2 statistic falls in the critical region.
　　2. Accept H_0 if the χ^2 statistic falls in the acceptance region.

III. Estimating values of σ^2 (and consequently σ)

A. We can form a confidence interval for σ^2 in a similar manner to the confidence intervals formed for the population parameters of μ and p in chapter 8.

B. The left boundary of the interval is given by:

$$Left\ boundary\ =\ \frac{(n-1) \cdot s^2}{\chi^2_U}$$

C. The right boundary of the interval is given by:

$$Right\ boundary\ =\ \frac{(n-1) \cdot s^2}{\chi^2_L}$$

　　1. n is the number in the sample.
　　2. s^2 is the sample variance.
　　3. χ^2_U can be found using d.f.= n-1 and $\alpha = \frac{1 - c}{2}$
　　4. χ^2_L can be found using d.f.= n-1 and $\alpha = \frac{1 + c}{2}$

D.   The c% confidence interval consists of the values between the left and the right boundaries.

Problem Solving Warm Up

At peak hours a bank finds that with individual lines at each teller's window, the waiting time in line is normally distributed with a standard deviation of 6.2 minutes. The bank experiments with a single waiting line and finds that for a random sample of 25 customers the waiting times have a standard deviation of 3.8 minutes.

1.   Test the claim that there has been a significant drop in the variation at the $\alpha = .05$ level.

Form the hypotheses:

H_0 : _____ H_0 : $\sigma^2 = (6.2)^2 = 38.44$

H_1 : _____ H_1 : $\sigma^2 < 38.44$

Compute the test statistic: $\chi^2 = \dfrac{(n-1)s^2}{\sigma^2}$

$\chi^2 = $ _____ $\chi^2 = \dfrac{(24)(14.44)}{38.44}$

                                           $\chi^2 = 9.02$

Find the critical value of χ^2 Using 25-1 = 24 d.f. and $\alpha = 1-.05=.95$
$\chi^2_{.05} = $ _____ $\chi^2_{.05} = 13.85$

Sketch the distribution and shade the critical region. Place the χ^2 statistic on the graph.

Make your decision:

_____

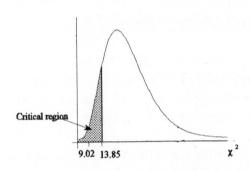

Since our statistic falls in the critical region we reject H_0 and conclude that the variation in waiting times is decreased when using a single waiting line.

2.   Form a 95% confidence interval for s, the population standard deviation based on the sample data.

n = _____   n = 25

s²= _____   s²= (3.8)² =14.44

χ^2_U= _____ χ^2_U= 39.36 ($\alpha = \dfrac{1 - .95}{2}$ =.025)

χ^2_L= _____ χ^2_L = 12.40 (α = .975)

Left boundary=   Left boundary for variance = 24·144/39.36 = 87.80. The left boundary for s = $\sqrt{87.80}$ =9.37

_____

Right boundary=   Right boundary for variance = 3456/12.40 = 278.71. The right boundary for s = $\sqrt{278.71}$ = 16.69.

_____

Confidence interval for s   We are 95% sure that the standard deviation is between 9.37 and 16.69

Selected Solutions Section 11.3

1.   a) $H_0 : \sigma^2 = 9$ months
         $H_1 : \sigma^2 < 9$ months
      $\alpha = .05$

      $\chi^2_{.95} = 13.09$
      (23 d.f., $\alpha = .95$)

      $\chi^2 = \dfrac{(24-1)(1.9)^2}{9} =$
      9.23

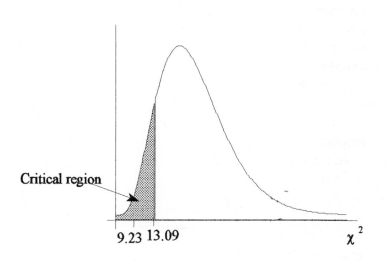

Critical region

9.23 13.09 χ^2

Since the χ^2 statistic is in the critical region, we reject H_0 and conclude that the new shot has a smaller variance. ♦

b) For χ^2_U use $\alpha = \dfrac{(1-.99)}{2} = .005$ and for χ^2_L use $\alpha = \dfrac{(1+.99)}{2} = .995$

$\chi^2_U = 44.18$ and $\chi^2_L = 9.26$

23(1.9)²/44.18 = 1.88   23(1.9)²/9.26 = 8.97
$\sqrt{1.88} = 1.37$ $\sqrt{8.97} = 2.99$

We are 99% sure that σ is between 1.37 and 2.99 ♦

5.   a) $H_0 : \sigma^2 = .15$ mm. $H_1 : \sigma^2 > .15$ mm. $\alpha = .01$

$$\chi^2 = \frac{(61-1)(.27)}{.15} = 108 \qquad\qquad \chi^2_{.01} = 88.38 \ (60 \text{ d.f., } \alpha=.01)$$

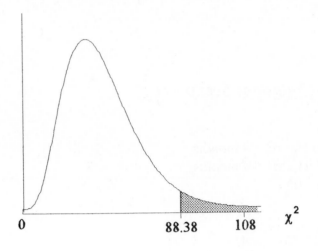

The χ^2 statistic is in the critical region so we reject H_0 and conclude that the variance is too large and the fan belts must be replaced. ♦

9. a) $H_0 : \sigma^2 = 15$ months
    $H_1 : \sigma^2 \neq 15$ months
    $\alpha=.05$

$\chi^2_{.025} = 35.48 \ (21 \text{ d.f.,}$ $\alpha=.025)$

$\chi^2_{.975} = 10.28 \ (21 \text{ d.f.,}$ $\alpha=.975)$

$\chi^2 = \frac{(22-1)(14.3)^2}{15} = 20.02$

χ^2 is not in the critical region so we fail to reject H_0 and conclude that there is no significant difference in variance. ♦

b) For $\chi^2_U \ \alpha = (1-.90)/2$
   $=.050$
   $\chi^2_U = 32.67$

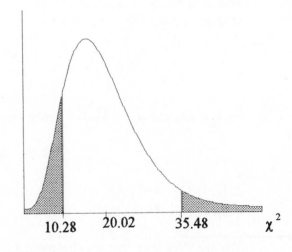

For χ^2_L use $\alpha = (1+.90)/2 = .950$ $\chi^2_L = 11.59$

$21(14.3)^2/32.67 = 9.19$ $21(14.3)^2/11.59 = 25.91$

We are 99% sure that σ^2 is between 9.19 and 25.91 ♦

c)   Finding the square roots of the variance boundaries,
        we are 99% sure that σ is between 3.03 and 5.09 ♦

Section 11.4
ANOVA: Comparing Several Sample Means

Review

I.   **Analysis of Variance (ANOVA)**
        A.   In chapter 9 we studied methods by which we could compare the means of two
                population. Analysis of Variance is a statistical tool which enables us to compare
                the means of several populations.
        B.   Types of variation used in ANOVA
                1.   Variation **between groups**- differences which occur because of different
                        treatment given to different populations. For example: the mean in group
                        A and the mean of group B are not equal because individuals of group A
                        received different treatment from those in group B.
                        a.   This variation is called the **Mean Square Between** .
                        b.   It is denoted $MS_{Bet.}$
                2.   Variation **within groups**- differences which occur between individuals
                        within the same group. For example: two individuals in group A will have
                        different values because of natural variation in sampling.
                        a.   This variation is called the **Mean Square Within**.
                        b.   It is denoted MS_W.
                3.   If all populations have equal means (indicating the different treatments
                        had no significant effect on the means) then the variation between groups
                        will equal the variation within groups and the ratio of :

$$\frac{variation \quad between \quad groups}{variation \quad within \quad groups} = 1$$

4.   In analysis of variance we use an F ratio test of:

$$F = \frac{MS_{Bet}}{MS_{w}}$$

II.   Computing Variances
A.   The formulas used for ANOVA involve the following computations. For ease in illustration, we have selected the case of three groups. All formulas can be naturally extended for more than three groups.
   1. Σx_1, Σx_2 and Σx_3 represent the sums of the values in each of the three groups.
   2. $\Sigma x_1 + \Sigma x_2 + \Sigma x_3 = \Sigma x_{TOT}$.
   3. n_1, n_2 and n_3 represent the sample sizes for the three groups.
   4. $n_1 + n_2 + n_3 = N$
   5. Σx_1^2, Σx_2^2 and Σx_3^2 represent the sum of the squares of each value for each of the groups.
   6. $\Sigma x_1^2 + \Sigma x_2^2 + \Sigma x_3^2 = \Sigma x_{TOT}^2$.
B.   When we computed the variance of a sample we used the formula

$$s^2 = \frac{SS}{(n-1)}$$

   1. $SS = \Sigma x^2 - \dfrac{(\Sigma x)^2}{n}$
   2.   n-1 = d.f.
C.   We will use similar formulas to calculate different types of variances.
   1.   Total variance for all samples is given by

$$\frac{SS_{TOT}}{d.f.}$$

$$\text{where } SS_{TOT} = \sum x^2{}_{TOT} - \frac{\left(\sum x_{TOT}\right)^2}{N}$$

gives us the numerator for the total variance.

D.   Numerator for variance between groups:

$$SS_{Bet} = \frac{(\sum x_1)^2}{n_1} + \frac{(\sum x_2)^2}{n_2} + \frac{(\sum x_3)^2}{n_3} - \frac{(\sum x_{TOT})^2}{N}$$

E.   Numerator for variance within groups= $SS_1 + SS_2 + SS_3$.

$$SS_W = [\sum x_1^2 - \frac{(\sum x_1)^2}{n_1}] + [\sum x_2^2 - \frac{(\sum x_2)^2}{n_2}] + [\sum x_3^2 - \frac{(\sum x_3)^2}{n_3}]$$

F.   After these are computed, check that $SS_{TOT} = SS_{Bet} + SS_W$.

III.   Other necessary computations
- A. $d.f._{TOT}$ = N-1
- B. $d.f._{Bet}$ = k-1   where k is the number of groups (in this case, k=3)
- C. $d.f._W$ = (N-1) -(k-1) = N - k

IV.   Steps to perform in Analysis of Variance
- A.   Formulate the hypotheses.
  1. H_0 : The population means are all equal.
  2. H_1 : At least two of the population means are not equal.
- B.   Compute each of the following SS for the numerators of the variances.
  1. SS_{Tot}
  2. SS_{Bet}
  3. SS_W
- C.   Determine the degrees of freedom for the total variance, the variance between and the variance within.
- D.   Compute the variances (mean squares) between and within by dividing SS by the degrees of freedom for each.
- E.   Set up the F ratio MS_{Bet} /MS_W.
- F.   Determine the critical value for F, using the table in the Appendix.
  1.   d.f. numerator   = k-1
  2.   d.f. denominator   = N-k
- G.   Sketch the F distribution and shade the critical region which will be to the right of the critical value.
- H.   Make the decision
  1.   Reject H_0 if the F ratio is in the critical region. This will indicate that there is a difference among the means.
  2.   Accept H_0 if the F ratio is in the acceptance region. The conclusion here is that there is no significant difference in the means of the groups.

Problem Solving Warm Up

Three different machines are use to produce an airplane part and the number of defects are recorded for batches randomly selected on different days. Use a .05 significance level to test the claim that the machines produce the same mean number of defects per batch.

For Machine A: 10, 8, 5, 12, 14, 11
For Machine B: 6, 9, 8, 13
For Machine C: 14, 13, 10, 17, 16

Formulate the hypotheses.

H_0 : _____

H_1 : _____

H_0 :   All machines have the same mean number of defects.

H_1 :   There are at least two machines in which the mean number of defects are not equal.

Organize the information into table form.

Machine A x	Machine A x^2	Machine B x	Machine B x^2	Machine C x	Machine C x^2
10	100.00	6	36.00	14	196.00
8	64.00	9	81.00	13	169.00
5	25.00	8	64.00	10	100.00
12	144.00	13	169.00	17	289.00
14	196.00			16	256.00
11	121.00				
60.00	650.00	36.00	350.00	70.00	1,010.00
$n_1 = 6$		$n_2 = 4$		$n_3 = 5$	

$\Sigma x_{Tot} = 60 + 36 + 70 = 166$ $\Sigma x^2_{Tot} = 650 + 350 + 1010 = 2010$

$N = 6 + 4 + 5 = 15$

$SS_{TOT} = 2010 - (166)^2/15 = 2010 - 1837.07 = 172.93$

$SS_{Bet} = (60)^2/6 + (36)^2/4 + (70)^2/5 - (166)^2/15 = 600 + 324 + 980 - 1837.07 = 66.93$

$SS_W = 650 - (60)^2/6 + 350 - (36)^2/4 + 1010 - (70)^2/5 = 106$

Check: $172.93 = 66.93 + 106$

d.f. between = 3-1 = 2   d.f. within = N-k = 15 -3 = 12

Complete the following table to perform the F test

Source of Variation	Sum of Squares	Degrees of freedom	Mean Square (Variation)	F Ratio	F Critical Value	Test decision
Between groups						
Within groups						
Total						

Check your results

Source of Variation	Sum of Squares	Degrees of freedom	Mean Square (Variation)	F Ratio	F Critical Value	Test decision
Between groups	66.93	2	33.47	3.79	3.88	Accept H_0
Within groups	106	12	8.83			
Total	172.93	14				

Selected Solutions Section 11.4

1. H_0 : All three population means are equal.
        H_1 : There are at least two population means that are not equal.

        Organize the information into table form.

Mound I x	0.00	Mound II x	0.00	Mound III x	0.00
22.3	497.29	20.5	420.25	25.6	655.36
19.1	364.81	22.1	488.41	25.9	670.81
22.5	506.25	24.7	610.09	26.8	718.24
20.7	428.49	24.9	620.01	22.5	506.25
84.60	1,796.84	92.20	2,138.76	100.80	2,550.66
$n_1 = 4$		$n_2 = 4$		$n_3 = 4$	

$\Sigma x_{Tot} = 84.60 + 92.2 + 100.8 = 277.6$

$\Sigma x^2_{Tot} = 1796.84 + 2138.76 + 2550.66 = 6486.26$

$N = 4 + 4 + 4 = 12$

$SS_{TOT} = 6486.26 - (277.6)^2/12 = 64.4467$

$SS_{Bet} = (84.60)^2/4 + (92.20)^2/4 + (100.80)^2/4 - (277.6)^2/12 = 32.8467$

$SS_W = 1796.84 - (84.60)^2/4 + 2138.76 - (92.20)^2/4 + 2550.66 - (100.80)^2/4 = 31.60$

Check: $64.4467 = 32.8467 + 31.60$

d.f. between = 3-1 = 2   d.f. within = N-k = 12 - 3 = 9

Source of Variation	Sum of Squares	Degrees of freedom	Mean Square (Variation)	F Ratio	F Critical Value	Test decision
Between groups	32.8467	2	16.424	4.678	4.26	Reject H_0
Within groups	31.60	9	3.511			
Total	64.4467	11				

Conclusion: There are at least two means which are significantly different. This indicates that all three mounds were not made by the same tribe. ♦

5. H_0 : All three population means are equal.
        H_1 : There are at least two population means which are not equal.

        Organize the information into table form.

I x	0.00	II x	0.00	III x	0.00	0.00	0.00
12.7	161.29	8.3	68.89	20.3	412.09	??	ERR
9.2	84.64	17.2	295.84	16.6	275.56	??	ERR
10.9	118.81	19.1	364.81	22.7	515.29	??	ERR
8.9	79.21	10.3	106.09	25.2	635.04	??	ERR
16.4	268.96		0.00	19.9	396.01	??	ERR
58.10	712.91	54.90	835.63	104.70	2,233.99	0.00	0.00
n_1 =5		n_2 =4		n_3 =5		n_4 =5	

$\Sigma x_{Tot} = 58.10 + 54.90 + 104.70 + 81.80 = 299.5$
$\Sigma x^2_{Tot} = 712.91 + 835.63 + 2233.99 + 1435.10 = 5717.63$
$N = 5 + 4 + 5 + 5 = 19$

$SS_{TOT} = 5717.63 - (299.5)^2/19 = 496.565$

$SS_{Bet} = (58.10)^2/5 + (54.90)^2/4 + (104.70)^2/5 + (81.8)^2/5 - (299.5)^2/19 = 238.225$

$SS_W = \{712.91 - (58.10)^2/5\} + \{835.63 - (54.90)^2/4\} + \{2233.99 - (104.70)^2/5\} + \{1435.1 - (81.80)^2/5\} = 258.34$

d.f. between = 4-1 = 3   d.f. within = N-k = 19 -4 = 15

Source of Variation	Sum of Squares	Degrees of freedom	Mean Square (Variation)	F Ratio	F Critical Value	Test decision
Between groups	238.225	3	79.408	4.611	3.29	Reject H_0
Within groups	258.340	15	17.223			
Total	496.565	18				

Conclusion: There are at least two means which are significantly different. This indicates that there is a difference in the earnings of immigrants from the four different countries. ♦

9. H_0 : All three population means are equal.
       H_1 : There are at least two population means which are not equal.

Rural X	0.00	Suburban X	0.00	Urban X	0.00
15	225.00	19	361.00	40	1,600.00
14	196.00	27	729.00	36	1,296.00
21	441.00	20	400.00	22	484.00
17	289.00	33	1,089.00	27	729.00
67.00	1,151.00	99.00	2,579.00	125.00	4,109.00
$n_1 = 4$		$n_2 = 4$		$n_3 = 4$	

$\Sigma x_{Tot} = 67 + 99 + 125 = 291$ N = 4+4+4 = 12
$\Sigma x^2_{Tot} = 1151 + 2579 + 4109 = 7839$

$SS_{TOT} = 7839 - (291)^2/12 = 782.25$

$SS_{Bet} = (67)^2/4 + (99)^2/4 + (125)^2/4 - (291)^2/12 = 422$

$$SS_W = 1151 - \frac{(67)^2}{4} + 2579 - \frac{(99)^2}{4} + 4109 - \frac{(125)^2}{4} = 360.25$$

Check: $782.25 = 422 + 360.25$

d.f. between = 3-1 =2   d.f. within = N-k = 12 -3 = 9

Source of Variation	Sum of Squares	Degrees of freedom	Mean Square (Variation)	F Ratio	F Critical Value	Test decision
Between groups	422	2	211	5.271	4.26	Reject H_0
Within groups	360.25	9	40.028			
Total	782.25	11				

Conclusion: There are at least two means that are significantly different. This indicates that all three rates of arrest are not all the same. ♦

Chapter 12

NONPARAMETRIC STATISTICS

Section 12.1
The Sign Test

Review

In Chapter 9 we studied techniques that can be used test the difference between means of two populations. Recall that in order to perform these tests, however, it was necessary to have a sample of 30 or more for each of the populations OR to make assumptions about the populations being normally distributed having equal standard deviations. We'll now look at several types of tests for which no assumptions about the population are required.

I.   **Nonparametric tests**
    A.   Require no assumptions about the population(s) in the test.
    B.   Are quick and easy to apply.
    C.   Are generally less accurate than tests where information about the population is known.

II.   **Sign Test**
    A.   Tests the difference between two population means using paired samples.
    B.   Used to test dependent populations.
    C.   For example: before and after tests or identical twin studies or tests with matched pairs.

III.   Steps in a Sign Test

    A.   List the paired values from group I and group II in parallel columns and record the *sign* of the difference between them.

        1.   If group I value is larger than that of group II, record a + sign.
        2.   If group II value is larger than that of group I, record a - sign.
        3.   If the two values are equal, record N.D. for "no difference."

    B.   Formulate the hypotheses:
        1. $H_0 : \mu_1 - \mu_2 = 0$ (no difference)
        2.   Select an alternate hypothesis
            a. $H_1 : \mu_1 - \mu_2 > 0$ OR
            b. $H_1 : \mu_1 - \mu_2 < 0$ OR
            c. $H_1 : \mu_1 - \mu_2 \neq 0$

    C.   Form the following proportion:

$$r = \frac{number\ of\ +\ signs}{total\ number\ of\ +\ and\text{-}\ signs}$$

    D.   If the null hypothesis is true there will be an equal number of + signs and - signs and the proportion r will = .5.

    E.   When the total number of plus and minus signs is 12 or more the sampling distribution will be:
        1.   Approximately Normal
        2.   Mean equal to p.
        3.   Standard deviation of $\sqrt{\dfrac{pq}{n}}$

    F.   To find the critical value(s) for this test use

	right tail test	left tail test	two tail test
$\alpha = .01$	z = 2.33	z = -2.33	z = 2.58 and z = -2.58
$\alpha = .05$	z = 1.645	z = -1.645	z = 1.96 and z = - 1.96

    G.   Calculate r, the ratio of + sign to total + and - signs.(omit any cases where the difference is 0.) (r is the sample statistic.)

H.   Compute the z value for the r statistic with: $\quad z = \dfrac{r - p}{\sqrt{\dfrac{pq}{n}}} = \dfrac{r - .5}{\sqrt{\dfrac{(.05)(.05)}{n}}} = \dfrac{r - .05}{\dfrac{.5}{\sqrt{n}}}$

I.   Sketch a normal distribution curve, locate your critical z_0 value(s) and shade the critical region(s).

J.   Place the z value for your statistic r on your graph and make your decision:
1.   Reject H_0 if the z value for r is in the critical region.
2.   Fail to reject H_0 if the z value for r is in not the critical region.

Problem Solving Warm Up

Muscle strength is measured by the score on a special machine. 26 people are matched (forming 13 pairs) on relevant attributes. One person in each pair is randomly selected and given a diet supplemented with Vitamin V. The other person from the pair is given the same diet without the Vitamin V supplements. Both are given the test on muscle strength and their scores are recorded below. Use the Sign Test on the difference of muscle strength scores to test the hypothesis at the 5% level that Vitamin V has a positive effect on people's muscle strength.

Scores for each pair are given in the chart that follows. Calculate the sign of the difference to complete the entries for the diff. column. Check your results.

Pair	With V	With-out V	Sign of diff.
1	58	63	
2	73	73	
3	58	51	
4	76	80	
5	69	42	
6	43	37	
7	56	43	
8	62	59	
9	58	56	
10	58	61	
11	71	63	
12	75	68	
13	85	82	

Pair	With V	With-out V	Sign of diff.
1	58	63	-
2	73	73	N.D.
3	58	51	+
4	76	80	-
5	69	42	+
6	43	37	+
7	56	43	+
8	62	59	+
9	58	56	+
10	58	61	-
11	61	63	-
12	75	68	+
13	85	58	+

Formulate the hypotheses:

H_0 :_____

H_1 :_____

H_0 :$\mu_1 - \mu_2 = 0$ (or $\mu_1 = \mu_2$)

H_1 :$\mu_1 - \mu_2 > 0$

The number of + signs = _____

The number of - signs = _____

r = _____

There are 8 + signs.

There are 4 - signs.

r = 8/12 = .67

The critical value is:

_____

Calculate the z value for the r statistic

Sketch the distribution and make your decision:

_____

z = 1.645 since this is a right tail test with α = .05

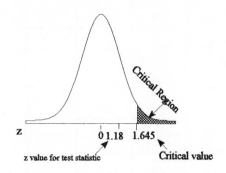

$$z = \frac{.67 - .5}{\frac{.5}{\sqrt{12}}} = 1.18$$

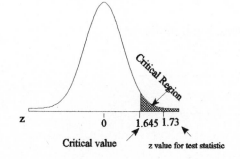

z value for test statistic   Critical value

Fail to reject H_0. It appears that there is no difference in the means since the test statistic is not in the critical region.

Selected Solutions Section 12.1

1.   a) $H_0 : \mu_1 - \mu_2 = 0$
         $H_1 : \mu_1 - \mu_2 > 0$.
      Use a right tail test with α = .05.♦

      b) Use a normal sampling distribution.

      The critical value is .z = 1.645. ♦

Critical value   z value for test statistic

d) There are 9 + signs and 3 - signs.
   $r = 9/12 = .75$.

The z value for the test statistic is $z = \dfrac{.75 - .5}{\dfrac{.5}{\sqrt{12}}} = 1.73$

The test statistic is in the critical
region. Reject H_0 and conclude that the mean writing life of the new tip is longer than
that of the old tip. ♦

5.   a) $H_0 : \mu_1 - \mu_2 = 0$ $H_1 : \mu_1 - \mu_2 \neq 0$.
      Use a two tail test with $\alpha = .05$

      There are 7 + signs and 5 - signs.
      $r = 7/12 = .58$

      b) Since there are 12 or more signs, the
      sampling distribution is normal. The
      critical values are $z_0 =. \pm 1.96$.

      d) The z value for the r test statistic is

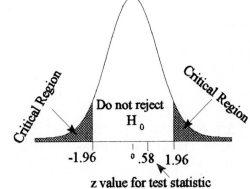

♦

$$z = \dfrac{.58 - .5}{\dfrac{.5}{\sqrt{12}}} = .55$$

e) Since $z = .55$ is not in the critical region, fail to reject H_0. There is not enough
evidence to conclude that the schools are not equally effective. ♦

9.   a) $H_0 : \mu_1 - \mu_2 = 0$ $H_1 : \mu_1 - \mu_2 \neq 0$. Use a two tail
      test with $\alpha = .01$

      There are 9 + signs and 5 - signs.
      $r = 9/14 = .64$

      b) The sampling distribution of r is
      normal since there are at least 12
      signs. The critical values are $z_0 = \pm$
      2.58♦

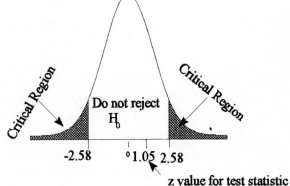

      d) The z value for the test statistic is:
      $$z = \dfrac{.64 - .5}{\dfrac{.5}{\sqrt{14}}} = 1.05$$

e) The z value for the test statistic is not in the critical region. Fail to reject H_0 and conclude that the mean pulse rates are the same. ♦

Section 12.2
The Rank Sum Test

Review

I.   The **Rank Sum Test** for equal means
    A.   Used with independent samples (data is not paired).
    B.   Can be used when you can not assume that the population is normal or that the populations have equal standard deviations.

II.   Steps to perform the Rank Sum Test
    A.   Formulate the hypotheses.
        1. $H_0 : \mu_1 - \mu_2 = 0$
        2.   Select an alternative hypothesis:
            a. $H_1 : \mu_1 - \mu_2 > 0$ OR
            b. $H_1 : \mu_1 - \mu_2 < 0$ OR
            c. $H_1 : \mu_1 - \mu_2 \neq 0$
    B.   Data from each of two samples, A and B is given.
        1.   Let n_1 = the sample size for group A.
        2.   Let n_2 = the sample size for group B.
        3.   There will be a total of $n_1 + n_2$ values from both samples.
    C.   Using all the data from both groups as if they were in one sample, rank the data and record which sample each piece of data came from.
    D.   Compute R, the sum of the ranks of the smaller sample.
        1.   If the sample size for group A is less than or equal to that of for group B then R is the sum of the ranks for group A.
        2.   If the sample size for group B is smaller then let R = the sum of the ranks for group B.
    E.   The sampling distribution of R

1.   Is normal when each group is size 8 or more.

2.   The mean and standard deviation are:

$$\mu_R = \frac{n_1(n_1 + n_2 + 1)}{2}$$

$$\sigma_R = \sqrt{\frac{n_1 n_2(n_1 + n_2 + 1)}{12}}$$

F.   The critical values are:
1.   For $\alpha = .05$, $z_0 = \pm 1.96$
2.   For $\alpha = .01$, $z_0 = \pm 2.58$

G.   The z value for the R statistic is : $z = \dfrac{R - \mu_R}{\sigma_R}$

H.   Sketch a normal distribution locating the critical values and the critical regions. Place the z value for the sample statistic R on this graph.

I.   Make your decision.
1.   Reject H_0 if R is in the critical region.
2.   Fail to reject H_0 if R is not in the critical region.

Problem Solving Warm Up

There are two groups of employees working on a computer project for a managerial consulting company. Group A had been given 20 hours of intensive training and Group B was given none. Each individual's number of "billable hours" needed to complete a specified computer program is recorded below. Use a Rank Sum test to test the difference between the means of the two groups.

Group A	40	27	4	10	22	32	35	6		
Group B	6	24	8	28	3	23	15	1	30	41

$n_1 = 8$ $n_2 = 10$. Rank the 18 values and record which group they came from. Note that there is a "tie" since two values are equal to 6. *When there are equal scores, both scores must be assigned to the same rank. This rank is computed as the mean of the ranks they would fall in as different scores. In this case the score of 6 would occupy ranks 4 and 5. We assign a rank of 4.5 to make the ranks equal.*

Rank	Time	Group
1	1	B
2	3	B
3	4	A
4.5	6	B
4.5	6	A
6	8	B
7	10	A
8	15	B
9	22	A

Rank	Time	Group
10	23	B
11	24	B
12	27	A
13	28	B
14	30	B
15	32	A
16	35	A
17	40	A
18	41	B

Formulate the hypotheses:

H_0 : _____

H_1 : _____

H_0: $\mu_1 - \mu_2 = 0$ There is no difference between the groups.

H_1: $\mu_1 - \mu_2 \neq 0$ There is a difference between the groups.

Find R

_____

The ranks of the scores from Group A are: 3, 4.5, 7, 9, 12, 15, 16 and 17.
R = 83.5 the sum of these ranks.

Calculate μ_R

_____

$\mu_R = 8(19)/2$

$\mu_R = 76$

Calculate σ_R

_____

$\sigma_R = 11.25$

Find the critical values

_____

The critical values are -1.96 and 1.96

Compute the z value for the R
statistic.

_____

$$z = \frac{83.5 - 76}{11.25} = .67$$

Make a sketch of a normal
distribution and place the critical
values on it. Shade the critical
region. Place the z value for the R
statistic on the graph.

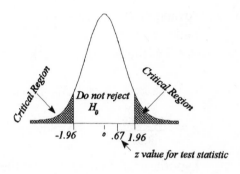

Decision:

_____

Since z = .67 is not in the critical region, fail
to reject H_0 . The conclusion is that there is
no difference in the number of billable hours
between the two groups.

Selected Solutions Section 12.2

1. $n_1 = 9$ $n_2 = 10$.
    Arranging the 19 score in rank order, we find Group A scores are in ranks:
    1, 3, 5, 7, 10, 11, 12, 15 and 18.
    R = the sum of the ranks for Group A = 82.
    $\mu_R = 9(20)/2 = 90$ and $\sigma_R = 9(10)(20)/12 = 12.25$

    The critical values are ± 1.96. The z value for the R statistic is z = $\frac{82 - 90}{12.25}$ = - .65.

    The z value of -.65 does not fall in the critical region. Therefore we conclude that there
    is no significant difference between the mean scores of the two schools. ◆

5. Arranging the 21 scores in order, we find that the ranks of the scores in Group A are:
    1, 2, 4, 6, 7, 9, 11, 12 and 14.

R = 66 (The sum of the ranks from Group A.)

$\mu_R = 99$ and $\sigma_R = 14.07$

Since $\alpha = .05$, the critical values are ± 1.96. The z value for the R test statistic is z = $\dfrac{66 - 99}{14.07}$ = - 2.34.

The z value for the test statistic R falls in the left critical region, so we reject H_0 and choose the hypothesis that there is a difference in values. ♦

9.   Arranging the 16 scores in order, we find the scores in Group A are in the following ranks: 1, 4, 8, 9, 12, 13, 15 and 16.
R = 78 (the sum of the ranks from Group A)

$\mu_R = 68$ and $\sigma_R = 9.52$. The critical values are ± 2.58.. The z value for the R statistic is:

z = $\dfrac{78 - 68}{9.52}$ = 1.05. Since this value is not in the critical region fail to reject the null

hypothesis and conclude that there was no difference in the scores of the children taught by each of the two methods. ♦

Section 12.3
Spearman Rank Correlation

Review

In chapter 10 we studied the correlation of data that was at the interval or ratio level. In this section we will see how correlation of data can be determined if the data is at the ordinal level (ranked data).

I.   **Correlation of Ranked data**
     A.   Data is organized in ordered pairs.
          1.   x = *rank* from one source.
          2.   y = *rank* from a second source.
     B.   Types of relationships

1.   x and y are said to have a **monotone increasing** relation if when the rank of x increases, the rank of y also increases. A high rank from source I is paired with a high mark from source II.

2.   x and y are said to have a **monotone decreasing** relationship if when the rank of x increases, the rank of y decreases. A high rank from source I is paired with a low rank from source II.

3.   x and y have **no monotone relationship** if as x increases, y both increases and decreases. There is no consistent pattern of ranking.

II.   The **Spearman Rank Correlation** Coefficient, denoted r_s

    A.   Values are always between -1 and 1, inclusive.

        1.   Values close to -1 indicate a monotone decreasing relationship.

        2.   Values close to 1 indicate a monotone increasing relationship.

        3.   Values close to 0 indicate no monotone relationship.

    B.   Formula for r_s.

$$r_s = 1 - \frac{6\sum d^2}{n(n^2 - 1)}$$

        1. n = the number of pairs.

        2. $d = x - y$ (the difference between ranks).

III.   Steps necessary to test the Spearman Rank Correlation Coefficient

    A.   Formulate the hypotheses about ρ_s the population correlation coefficient.

        1. H_0: $\rho_s = 0$ (There is no monotone relation.)

        2.   Choose an alternate hypothesis:

            a. H_1: $\rho_s > 0$ (monotone increasing relation)

            b. H_1: $\rho_s < 0$ (monotone decreasing relation)

            c. H_1: $\rho_s \neq 0$ (monotone relation which might be either)

        3.   Construct a table to compute the value of the statistic r_s.

        4.   Determine the critical value(s) for your statistic from the table of critical values for the Spearman Rank Correlation in the Appendix.

        5.   Sketch the distribution and determine the critical region(s).

        6.   Make your decision to fail to reject or reject H_0 based on the location of your statistic, r_s.

Problem Solving Warm Up

Seven candidates applied for a position at Xavier and Young Advertising Company, Inc. The seven candidates were placed in rank order first by Xavier and then by Young. The results of the rankings are listed below. Using a .05 level of significance, test the claim that the relation between the rankings of Xavier and the rankings of Young is monotone positive.

Candidate	Xavier rank = x	Young rank = y
A	1	2
B	7	7
C	2	6
D	5	3
E	4	5
F	3	1
G	6	4

Formulate the hypotheses.

H_0 : _____ H_0: $\rho_s = 0$

H_1 : _____ H_1: $\rho_s > 0$

Complete the following table.

Candidate	x	y	d=x-y	d²
A	2	1		
B	4	4		
C	1	3		
D	5	2		
E	7	6		
F	3	1		
G	6	7		

Check your answers below.

Candidate	x	y	d=x-y	d²
A	2	1	1.00	1.00
B	4	4	0.00	0.00
C	1	3	-2.00	4.00
D	5	2	3.00	9.00
E	7	6	1.00	1.00
F	3	1	2.00	4.00
G	6	7	-1.00	1.00
			0.00	20.00

Calculate r_s

$$r_s = 1 - \frac{6\sum d^2}{n(n^2-1)}$$

$$r_s = 1 - \frac{6(20)}{7(7^2-1)} = 1 - .357$$

$$r_s = .643$$

The critical value is: Critical Value = .715

_____

Decision: Since the statistic .643 does not fall in the
                                          critical region, fail to reject H_0 and conclude
_____   that there was no positive monotone
                                          relationship between the rankings of Xavier
                                          and Young.

Selected Solutions Section 12.3

1. H_0: $\rho_s = 0$ H_1: $\rho_s \neq 0$

Person	x	y	d=x-y	d²
1	6	4	2.00	4.00
2	8	9	-1.00	1.00
3	11	10	1.00	1.00
4	2	1	1.00	1.00
5	5	6	-1.00	1.00
6	7	7	0.00	0.00
7	3	8	-5.00	25.00
8	9	11	-2.00	4.00
9	1	3	-2.00	4.00
10	10	5	5.00	25.00
11	4	2	2.00	4.00
			0.00	70.00

$r_s = 1 - \dfrac{6(70)}{11(120)} = .682$ Critical values are $\pm .619$.

Since the statistic .682 falls in the critical region, reject H_0 and conclude that there is a monotone relation between the rankings. ♦

5. H_0: $\rho_s = 0$ H_1: $\rho_s \neq 0$

Soldier	x	y	d=x-y	d²
1	5	1	4.00	16.00
2	3	7	-4.00	16.00
3	4	3	1.00	1.00
4	2	5	-3.00	9.00
5	1	4	-3.00	9.00
6	7	6	1.00	1.00
7	6	2	4.00	16.00
			0.00	68.00

$$r_s = 1 - \frac{6(68)}{7(48)} = -.214$$ Critical value is - .715

Since the statistic -.214 does not fall in the critical region, fail to reject H_0 and conclude that there is no monotone relation between the rankings. ♦

9. $H_0 : \rho_s = 0$ $H_1 : \rho_s \neq 0$

City	x	y	d=x-y	d²
1	6	5	1.00	1.00
2	7	4	3.00	9.00
3	1	2.5	-1.50	2.25
4	8	8	0.00	0.00
5	3	6	-3.00	9.00
6	2	1	1.00	1.00
7	5	7	-2.00	4.00
8	4	2.5	1.50	2.25
			0.00	28.50

$$r_s = 1 - \frac{6(28.50)}{8(63)} = .661$$

Critical value is .881. Since the statistic .661 does not fall in the critical region, fail to reject H_0 and conclude that there is no monotone relation between the rankings. ♦